Mediating Fictions

Mediating Fictions

Literature, Women Healers,
and the Go-Between in Medieval
and Early Modern Iberia

Jean Dangler

Lewisburg
Bucknell University Press
London: Associated University Presses

© 2001 by Associated University Presses, Inc.

All rights reserved. Authorization to photocopy items for internal or personal use, or the internal or personal use of specific clients, is granted by the copyright owner, provided that a base fee of $10.00, plus eight cents per page, per copy is paid directly to the Copyright Clearance Center, 222 Rosewood Drive, Danvers, Massachusetts 01923. [0-8387-5452-X/01 $10.00 + 8¢ pp, pc.]

Associated University Presses
440 Forsgate Drive
Cranbury, NJ 08512

Associated University Presses
16 Barter Street
London, WC1A 2AH, England

Associated University Presses
P.O. Box 338, Port Credit
Mississauga, Ontario
Canada L5G 4L8

The paper used in this publication meets the requirements of the American National Standard for the Permanence of Paper for Printed Library Materials Z39.48-1984.

Library of Congress Cataloging-in-Publication Data

Dangler, Jean.
    Mediating fictions : literature, women healers, and the go-between in medieval and early modern Iberia / Jean Dangler.
      p. cm.
    Includes bibliographical references and index.
    ISBN 0-8387-5452-X (alk. paper)
    1. Spanish literature—To 1500—History and criticism. 2. Spanish literature—Classical period, 1500–1700—History and criticism. 3. Women healers in literature. 4. Go-betweens in literature. 5. Roig, Jaume, d. 1478. Spill. 6. Rojas, Fernando de, d. 1541. Celestina. 7. Delicado, Francisco, 16th cent. Retrato de la Loçana andaluza. I. Title

PQ6060 .D36 2001
863'.209352042—dc21

00-040383

PRINTED IN THE UNITED STATES OF AMERICA

Contents

Acknowledgments	7
Introduction	9
1. Medieval Women Healers, Popular Literature, and the Professionalization of Medicine	19
2. Eva/Ave: *Ramería,* Reproduction, and the Song of Roig in Jaume Roig's *Spill o Llibre de les dones*	51
3. Eva and Not Ave: Marginalization and the Palimpsest Principle in Fernando de Rojas's *La Celestina*	84
4. Eva and Not Eva: The Irony of Well-Being in Francisco Delicado's *La Lozana andaluza*	128
Conclusion	174
Notes	181
Works Cited	209
Index	221

Acknowledgments

This book is in a way the product of my desire over twenty years ago to learn Spanish in order to communicate with a broad range of people in San Diego, California. Little did I know then that this wish for a connection with others nowadays would develop further into a deep attachment to Iberia's medieval past. I am indebted to many mentors, colleagues, and friends for motivating the intellectual and personal relations in the present that made possible the completion of this book about the past.

My doctoral advisor and friend at Emory University, Michael Solomon, has most significantly encouraged my research and my dialogue with history, and this book could not have been written without his guidance and critical comments. I am profoundly grateful to many of the faculty at Emory for their encouragement in my career and in this book's writing, namely Hazel Gold, Emilia Navarro, and Karen Stolley. But I especially want to thank Carlos Alonso, whose support of my work has been limitless and invaluable.

I wish to thank the other mentors and colleagues who have inspired my work and professional development. Joe Snow at Michigan State University welcomed me to medieval studies from the start, and has continued to serve as a role model in the profession. Nina Gerassi–Navarro at Mount Holyoke College was a most significant mentor during the year I taught in South Hadley. In my MA studies at the University of Minnesota, Connie Sullivan, Hernán Vidal, and Tony Zahareas encouraged me to explore what were at the time fairly exotic issues related to Hispanic bodies. As an undergraduate studying English and American literature, communications, and women's studies I am fortunate to have participated in a most challenging intellectual environment at the University of California, San Diego, where many professors encouraged my critical thinking.

My friends in Spain have welcomed me with open arms over the years, and to them I am deeply grateful: Pedro Briega, Lisa Dillman Whitelegg, Teresa Izquierdo González, Kristin Naupert Briega, Alejandro Rupert Moreno, and especially María José Serrano Cejalvo.

Their interest in my work and their affection have facilitated numerous research trips to the peninsula.

I extend warm thanks to my colleagues in Spanish at Florida State University, whose collegiality has aided in this book's completion: Santa Arias, Brenda Cappuccio, David Darst, Roberto Fernández, Juan Carlos Galeano, Delia Poey, Ernie Rehder, Jo Stepp-Greany, and Jim Wyatt. Jean Graham-Jones's mentoring has been matchless, and Shonna Trinch's friendship and intellectual contributions have been inspiring. Many colleagues in other areas of my department have demonstrated immeasurable support of my research, especially Bill Cloonan, Leona LeBlanc, Mark Pietralunga, and Lori Walters, and Aimée Boutin has been a dear friend and colleague.

The University of Wisconsin Press, Scripta Humanistica, and Cátedra graciously agreed to reproduce citations from works in this book. Unless otherwise noted, all translations into English are my own.

This book is dedicated to my partner Ainslee Beery, whom I cherish without fail.

Introduction

Women intercessors (*medianeras*) pervade a variety of medieval Iberian texts that depict them as healers. Medical treatises, hagiography about holy women, and Marian literature about the Virgin contain favorable representations of *medianeras* who are linked by their commonality as healers. The word *medianera* should not be confused with modern psychological or legal connotations implied by English terms such as *mediation* or *mediator*. It shall be used in this book as it concretely relates to medieval and early modern women intermediaries who negotiated a gamut of realms for their clients, including sickness and health, and contentment and misery. These women provided physical and affective relief to individuals, they aided the sick in the restoration of well-being, and they satiated desire. Both sacred and secular texts demonstrated the efficacious mediations of women intercessors. Certain medieval medical treatises and faith-promoting literature such as Marian and hagiographic works were compelling in their time because they insisted on the protection and restoration of the well-being of medieval readers and listeners through the interventions of women.

The depiction of these women was significant in the medieval period because it supported women's participation in the healing arts. Professional medicine was not dominant in the Middle Ages, and the medieval sick had at their disposal a wide variety of women healers from whom to choose. They relied on educated doctors and surgeons, semieducated bloodletters, apothecaries, midwives, and illiterate healers. Medical treatises, hagiographic literature, and Marian works favorably depicted women's participation in medieval healing in such a way that medieval readers and listeners would have recognized the similarities between them and women in medieval society. This literature provided readers with valuable information about whom to rely on for effective healing in times of illness. It also presented models to these readers about the ways in which women were to participate in medieval society.

The favorable representation of women healers changed dramatically in the fifteenth century. Instead of promoting the work of women healers, late medieval and early modern writers began to depict them pejoratively as incompetently augmenting disease. This change was motivated by the incipient professionalization of medicine, which from the late fourteenth century on, tried to elevate medicine and the male physician. In order to achieve its goals, the professionalization of medicine relied on strategies that included the marginalization of traditional women healers from licit medical practice. Women healers were increasingly debased and their licit participation in healing practice was progressively restricted. This strategy of exclusion was carried out through institutionalized legal and educational means that included laws prohibiting the practice of women healers, and new requirements of university study for the licensing of physicians. Since women were barred from entering medieval universities, they could not complete studies at medical faculties.

But the professionalization of medicine was often ineffective in curbing the popularity of women healers. For this reason, late medieval and early modern authors, complicit with the ideology of the newly elevated male physician, sought to transform the older medieval textual models that had previously supported the practice of women healers. Writers of popular works such as Jaume Roig's *Spill o Llibre de les dones*, Fernando de Rojas's *La Celestina*, and Francisco Delicado's *La Lozana andaluza* colluded with the broader professionalization of medicine in striving to elevate and legislate the mediations of educated men physicians by maligning traditional women healers.

These authors used various strategies to transform medieval models of women healers, and to realize their discrediting goals. They relied on the same analogies that medieval readers and listeners had made in linking the beneficent mediations of textual women healers with the efficacious interventions of women healers in their own cities or neighborhoods. But the later writers subverted the older paradigms by creating mundane women characters who augmented rather than healed disease.

The resemblance between the interventions of the Virgin and holy women, and those of ordinary women was dissolved. The Virgin either became the only woman capable of healing, in contrast to the dangerous healing attempts of all other women, or she was increasingly stylized and removed from palpable contact with sinners and the sick. The later authors presented vilified models of mundane women healers in order to dissuade readers from seeking the services of traditional women healers in their own society. The late medieval and early modern reader was encouraged to avoid earthly women altogether, and to rely on the healing capabilities of the Virgin or the male physician.

Roig, Rojas, and Delicado provided readers with the "valuable" salutary information that the interventions of earthly women healers were prejudicial to individual well-being and the general social order. These three authors produced works that were not merely entertaining and otherwise innocuous in their time. What was at stake for these writers was the authority to determine those people who constituted efficacious healers and workers in late medieval and early modern Iberian society. These efforts through literary or textual means were widely compelling and influential, and carried with them powerful social consequences.

The contrast that these authors established between the male physician and earthly women healers constituted a forceful method of social control, since questions of healing, sickness, and well-being in any society are ultimately founded upon issues of power, domination, and social order.[1] A community's trust in authorized healers simultaneously reinforces the society that grants them effectiveness in healing. The fact that Roig, Rojas, and Delicado fashioned themselves arbiters of authorized, efficacious healers also rendered them arbiters of the social order.

These writers were motivated by the knowledge that healing is not simply a beneficent activity for the sole purpose of ameliorating illness and affliction. It also confirms important information about social relations and organization. Illness is chaotic and disruptive of routine biological and social bodily functions.[2] The healer restores bodily and communal order, harmony, and function, and is a potentially dominant formulator of all classes of individual and social meaning.

The healer is not merely a trusted person who ideally rectifies the dysfunction of sickness, thereby restoring an individual's sense of health. Rather, she or he has tremendous influence over notions so banal as the ways in which people think about their bodies and those of others, to how people may "best" behave on any given day to generate the most salutary effects. Moreover, healers dictate social organization because they determine who is sick and who is not. Embedded in this authority to delimit and define sickness and well-being is the ability to prescribe social order. Healers are charged with the ability to generate, stabilize, confirm, and potentially change the ways in which people regard individual and social relations.

Late medieval and early modern authors were not ignorant of the consequences of the professionalization of medicine, nor were they uninformed about the compelling mediations of healers. These concerns constituted the nature of what was at issue in the later representation of women healers. As I will show in this book, Roig, Rojas, and Delicado were eminently influenced by the fact that healers both generated and reinforced a series of cultural values connected to ethnicity, gender, morality, sexuality, social class, marriage, inheritance, and lineage. Their project to disparage traditional women healers was undeniably misogynist, as vilified ordinary women characters were implicitly and explicitly contrasted to skillful men physicians and to a beneficent and stylized Virgin.

The following chapters will further demonstrate that Roig, Rojas, and Delicado were informed to varying degrees about the professionalization of medicine and about the social measures enacted and carried out at the time to exclude traditional women healers from the licit practice of medicine. The works that these three authors created played out that process of exclusion while simultaneously encouraging it.

The *Spill*, *La Celestina*, and *La Lozana andaluza* were powerful instruments for societal marginalization, since they characterized traditional healers by their alterity or otherness, in contrast to the normative mediations of authorized healers. Furthermore, because the professionalization of Iberian society extended beyond that of the medical field into, for instance, prostitution and textile industries, social governors and legislators required the designation of contrastive "others" against whom exalted figures could be opposed. The literature of Roig, Rojas, and Delicado served as an accessible, popular means of dissemination of these women others because it sought to undermine well-known, popular models of women healers. Thus, these authors distinguished between the effectiveness of holy and profane intercessors, and they treated mundane women healers and women in general as repulsive and dangerous.

The designating of women as malicious and therefore worthy of marginalization from traditional healing duties was a misogynist process that was inherently connected to the well-being of men. Michael Solomon has demonstrated that the intimate relation between "medieval medical theory and the rhetorical conventions of misogynist discourse" was a product of increased anxiety about men's health, and especially about their sexual well-being.[3] Men were encouraged to avoid women because the latter were believed to seriously threaten men's health. Solomon indicates that women's disparagement in the *Spill* and in Alfonso Martínez de Toledo's fifteenth-century *Arcipreste de Talavera* was due to medical and cultural distress about female and male sexuality, and that their vilification provided men with valuable salutary information for the maintenance of their own well-being.[4] I will demonstrate that Roig, Rojas, and Delicado are complicit with these misogynist attacks on women because they seek to malign women's interventions as healers. They attempt to provide men with hygienic information about whom to seek out and whom to avoid in times of illness.

The antifeminist accusations toward women and women healers in these works were highly dependent upon both the rise of the professionalization of medicine, and the growing interest in men's health as the gauge and constituting element of the social order. Men became evermore entrenched in Iberian society as the purveyors of the social organization and as the recipients of its beneficial effects. As Solomon shows throughout *The Literature of Misogyny in Medieval Spain*, medicine was a most compelling domain for the constitution of society's normative model of being, the male body, which was contrasted to the deficient female body.

Yet the cultural value of the male body was also being redefined in the later Middle Ages, to the extent that by the sixteenth century the only male body worthy of elevation was the old Christian one. The worthiness of this refined male, Christian body is evident in the increasing degradation of Jewish and Muslim men throughout the fifteenth and sixteenth centuries. Medical circles were not immune to this homogenizing process, as the professionalization of medicine initiated restrictions against traditional Jewish and Arabic male healers that went hand in hand with sanctions against women.[5] The exclusion of Jewish and Muslim men from licit medical practice indicates that gender alone was insufficient in limiting the healing duties of unwanted healers.

Their ostracizing also demonstrates a connection between the exclusionary tactics of the professionalization of medicine and the rise of newly formed homosocial groups of Christian men in medieval and early modern Iberia.[6] Attacks by the professionalization of medicine on Jewish and Muslim males, and on all women healers may be explained not only by gender, ethnic, and religious biases, but also by the homosocial alliances among Christian men in societal realms such as business, religion, and government. Limitations on all these healers underscore the efforts by the professionalization of medicine to impose both gender differences among healers, and more detailed ethnic or religious distinctions among men. The rejection of non-Christian men from the licit practice of medicine occurred more or less simultaneously with their general exclusion from the homosocial alliances of late medieval and early modern Iberian society, culminating in the sixteenth-century *limpieza de sangre* (purity of blood) statutes. Despite the fact that some converted Christian doctors have been shown to maintain and justify their practice in early modern Iberia, the Christian, male paradigm cannot be overstated.[7]

These homosocial alliances are crucial not only to the tangible marginalizing of women, Jews, and Muslims from traditional healing practice, but are also significant in the misogynist portrayals of women healers in literary works. The following chapters will illustrate the close relationship between Roig, Rojas, and Delicado, and the male medical profession. Roig, Rojas, and Delicado may have appropriated misogynist conventions to provide male readers with warnings about women healers, but the forging of the homosocial in the male medical profession was as potent a cause of women's maligning in literature as misogyny. The limitations on women healers were not due to a transhistorical, ineffable, and deeply rooted cultural hatred of women, but rather, to concrete cultural conditions whereby homosocial groups of male medical professionals benefited from antifeminist assaults and prejudices.

It is undeniable that many of the strategies that Roig, Rojas, and Delicado used to participate in the ostracizing of women healers from traditional healing practice originated in a long line of antifeminist literary conventions, including women's verbosity, their similarity to Eve, and their excess.[8] In fact, Michael Solomon has demonstrated that a tradition of popular medieval Iberian stories and fables provided readers and listeners with pejorative images or models of women as the source of disease, disorder, and contagion. He indicates that Roig and Martínez employed these paradigms in their works in order to establish women as agents of contagion.[9] These misogynist portrayals are evident in Roig's, Rojas's, and Delicado's books, but are intended for a new purpose, which is to transform the compelling, favorable models that had previously supported the work of women healers. These authors relied on conventional, misogynist strategies to malign women healers, but inconstant social conditions further prompted them to employ differing antifeminist tactics and to invent new ones in order to alter the textual models that bolstered women's work.

Despite the assessment of these three books as antifeminist, they also continue to be entertaining, pleasurable, and sometimes funny. But their entertainment value is always double-edged, and often at the expense of women characters. The entertaining, comical, yet denigrating ways in which these characters were understood by late medieval and early modern readers were not confined to the texts themselves, but extended to the profound social changes taking place in healing practice. Roig, Rojas, and Delicado maligned earthly *medianeras* to provide men with salutary information about their well-being. The value of these books was remarkable in an early modern Iberian society that increasingly relied on medicine and the male medical professional to partially determine its own organization and composition.

Mediating Fictions

1
Medieval Women Healers, Popular Literature, and the Professionalization of Medicine

In thirteenth-century Castile, when King Alfonso X, el Sabio, was sick, he called on the healing mediations of the Virgin in order to restore his health. In one of the songs, or *cantigas*, told about the Virgin's beneficent intercessions, the Pope and several physicians thought that the Castilian king was sure to die.[1] But on an Easter day in Valladolid, the Virgin intervened on Alfonso's behalf and restored him to health. Around one hundred years later, when the Castilian nobleman and author don Juan Manuel sometimes found himself so burdened by the worries of his office that he could not sleep, he enlisted the aid of a servant to read him stories in order to alleviate his insomnia.[2]

Juan Manuel relied on the intervention of a confabulator, an intercessor who orally facilitated the amelioration of an uncomfortable or painful affliction. By way of the confabulations of the intercessor / reader, Manuel's worries were diminished and his insomnia alleviated.[3] Manuel relied so strongly on the hygienic worth of this oral narrative method that he recommended it to his brother-in-law don Juan of Aragon.[4]

Medieval Iberian accounts such as those retold by Alfonso and Juan Manuel attest to the reliance of royalty, nobility, and the general populace alike on earthly and holy intercessor-healers. Medieval Iberians sought out intercessors such as the Virgin, confabulators, saints, apothecaries, midwives, and physicians to intervene on behalf of their health, correcting and amending the disruptions of everyday life that threatened bodily integrity and social order. Since medical practice was only one of the many ways in which the medieval sick could get well, medieval Iberians relied on healers who would not be considered approved healers today such as the Virgin, saints, and confabulators.

In the Middle Ages, women constituted legitimate practitioners of the healing arts, and medieval Iberians relied on a variety of women healers such as the literate and educated physician (*física*) and doctor (*médica*), the semieducated midwife (*partera*), the illiterate medicine woman (*curandera*), and preternatural intercessors such as the Virgin and saints. Women were sought to heal illnesses as diverse as eye ailments, skin diseases, and lovesickness, and were typically expected to exercise surgical procedures and child delivery, prescribe drug and herbal remedies, and employ logotherapies such as conjurations and incantations.

The *exarmadora*, for instance, typified the kind of woman healer to whom medieval Iberians could turn. She was a mobile practitioner who healed throat problems: "Su especialidad consiste en 'guarir de mal de guola alguns que'n tenien'" [Her specialty consists of healing throat problems, any that patients might have].[5] Much in demand by the inhabitants of small towns who wanted her to stay for an extended period mostly during April and May, the *exarmadora* was also paid well for her services.

The *ensalmadora* was another popular woman healer who invoked the incantation known as the *ensalmo*, a logotherapeutic, secular prayer to influence preternatural powers and persuade them to relieve a patient's affliction ("oraciones que pretendían tener la virtud de influir en los poderes sobrenaturales, invocándolos para dominar el mal") [prayers that tried to be so forceful as to influence supernatural powers, invoking them in order to do away with an illness].[6] Conjurers (*coniuratrices*) who used the conjuration, another type of non-Christian prayer, were also popular healers who treated children, adults, and animals alike. In the early fourteenth century, for instance, women conjurers in Catalonia such as Na Orpina and Na Benvinguda de Mallnovell treated *gotornons del coll*, swelling of the throat that usually affected children. Mallnovell healed other ailments as well, such as a heart irregularity or palpitation (*panteix de cor*), a headache (*mal de cap*), and St. Anthony's fire (*foc salvatge*), ergotism that could produce swelling, blisters, and gangrene.[7]

Historians have identified many other medieval women healers in Iberia, such as doctors (*metgesses*) and medicine women (*comadronas*) who practiced in the Crown of Aragon.[8] Iberian women healers include medical practitioners such as a doctor (*metgessa*) described in 1379 as the individual responsible for healing the hand and foot of Francesc Monyoç, an important figure in the city of Valencia.[9] Educated Iberian women healers worked as surgeons and physicians until the fifteenth and sixteenth centuries, as evidenced by the medical practice of Peregrina of Morella, authorized by the king in 1436 to treat both men and women; Na Guillamona who practiced as a doctor in Valencia in 1405; Margarida Tornerons, a doctor from Vic; Antonia, authorized by the medical examiner (*protomédico*) Joan de Vesach in 1460 to treat certain illnesses;[10] and a Byzantine physician, Na Anthònia de Sancta Soffia, who treated and prescribed medicines for the royal court in 1420.[11] In 1332, a woman named Çahud was found practicing surgery in the royal household of the kingdom of Valencia.[12] In a case that took place in 1384, a woman from Valencia named Juana was given a license by the king to practice surgery and medicine.[13]

These documented cases are by no means exhaustive accounts of the Iberian presence of medieval women practitioners of the healing arts. According to Monica Green, the number of practicing medieval women healers greatly exceeded modern estimates.[14] As historians have begun to point out, documenting the work of medieval women healers has been hampered by the fact that women's participation in medieval healing often has been distorted in modern accounts.

Some difficulties in documenting women healers have occurred due to the biases and presumptions that inform historians' approaches to documents. For instance, the variety of women healers who actively practiced in the medieval period has been obscured by historians' assumption that they were uneducated charlatans and hence unworthy of scholarly attention.[15] Because of this bias, historians have traditionally discounted and disregarded the vast majority of empirical or nonmedical women healers such as the conjurers described above.

Furthermore, many scholars also have categorically assumed that all women healers were midwives. But as recent historians have confirmed, the midwife constituted only one practitioner within a diverse range of women healers. The stringent notion that all women practitioners were midwives who served only women clients has also been proven narrow and erroneous. Evidence now reveals that many women healers served women, men, and children alike.[16]

Despite the emphasis on midwifery as the paradigm for the work of women healers, the results of archival study in medieval European domains including Iberia indicate the scarce presence of midwives, even in the heavily researched Crown of Aragon. This seems to indicate a methodological problem in documenting women healers since it is widely believed that women were routinely present in birthing chambers during labor. While Teresa Ortiz shows that midwives clearly practiced in Iberia, it is possible that they were often simply left out of documentation as Michael McVaugh suggests. Jaume II's (1292–1327) household accounts indicate the employment of wet nurses but not midwives (*obstetrices*) to care for his ten children. It can generally be assumed, however, that midwives assisted at deliveries without assuming an occupational title.[17] This evidence suggests that at least one of the difficulties in identifying midwives and other kinds of women healers is an inaccurate or inconsistent nomenclature used to describe them.

Midwives' absence from official written records indicates another general difficulty in documenting medieval women healers. Their apparent lack of vocational title renders them invisible to the modern day scholar. Moreover, their absence from documentation suggests the possibility that women healers did not work contractually but were employed based on verbal terms. It appears that midwives practiced more or less autonomously until the late fifteenth century, when the birthing chamber and especially Caesarean births increasingly became the domain of men physicians.[18] Women do not seem to have been employed as assistants to men physicians nor do they appear to have been regularly salaried employees of courts and noble families. Their independence could have rendered their status not illegitimate, but rather informal and temporary.

Another assumption that has obscured the documentation of women healers is the belief that midwives exercised only obstetrical duties. As I have already explained, midwives were far from mere assistants to physicians and were expected to perform Caesarean and other surgical duties when needed. Historians have further challenged the belief that midwives' tasks were exclusively obstetrical. Myriam Greilsammer claims that midwives in the Low Countries fulfilled many kinds of duties; they examined women and girls who were raped, they determined whether women prisoners were pregnant, and they gave opinions in cases of infanticide and abortion.[19]

Documenting women healers has also been affected by modern assumptions about the sites in which healing took place. The conditions and places within which the majority of medieval women healers practiced did not exist separately from the rest of society. Unlike our modern-day containment of healing practice in hospitals and clinics, medieval healers often visited the sick at home, or the sick visited the healer at her home, shop, or marketplace.

Modern scholars' vocational assumptions about women workers

have also impeded the identification of women healers. Because women often exercised more than one occupation in a lifetime, healing functions typically constituted one of several jobs that they practiced. The traditional male paradigm of a life-long occupation is misleading with regard to medieval women, and produces inaccurate conclusions about who was considered a healer in the Middle Ages.[20] Identification by occupation may have been highly irregular for medieval women, so that the modern model linking individuals and their occupations did not have the degree of importance it does now.[21]

Women healers not only changed occupations but were often multivocational, simultaneously working in healing and other fields such as dress or shoemaking. Since general healing practice was "frequently combined with one or more of a variety of other petty trades and crafts," it is likely that sick people sought out therapies and remedies from multivocational healers in a variety of public areas, including shops and brothels.[22] Some women healers were often mobile as they practiced their skills throughout a town, or traveled from one town to another. Others frequently worked from a domestic setting or from a place of employment that was not necessarily related to their healing practice.

It is likely that women healers learned their skills through a combination of three ways; they acquired them from family members, in guilds, and by means of first-hand experience. Even medical training was acquired through these means, since women were prohibited from studying at university medical faculties. Women's education in the healing arts was probably learned from husbands, fathers, and even mothers, as documents illustrate occupational alliances in medicine and healing between husbands and wives, fathers and daughters, and perhaps between mothers and daughters.[23] Women probably worked as apprentices to family members or other women healers since medieval healing was largely considered a skill and a craft.[24]

In one case a woman named Elicsenda took over her husband's business as an herbalist (*especier*) when he died in Valencia in 1312. She became known as an apothecary (*apothecaria*) upon his death.[25] Their son Berenguer assumed responsibility of the business when Elicsenda died. In another case, Luis García Ballester has noted that Juan de Luna taught his daughter "medical things," and she later taught them to her son Román Ramírez who asserted that the transmission of information between them was purely oral.[26]

Married women frequently became their husbands' partners in

their trades, or took over their practices if the husbands died.²⁷ As late as 1566, in a petition to the courts of Madrid, Isabel Pérez de Peromato claimed that she and her dead husband had invented a controversial oil for the curing of wounds.²⁸ Because of its therapeutic benefits, she entreated the courts to accept the oil's recipe instead of prohibiting its use. The case attests to a wife-husband partnership in healing practice, and indicates that Pérez de Peromato continued the practice after her husband's death.

Women also learned their skills through their participation in medieval healing and artisan guilds.²⁹ Historians have shown that some women were granted entry into guilds only upon the death of a husband or father, while others seem to have participated on their own. Women definitely participated in medieval guilds related to healing, although the documentation is scarce. Some evidence suggests that the medieval surgical guild of Paris recognized the expertise of women surgeons and included them as members.³⁰ Also, it appears that several women apprentices were admitted to British barber-surgeons' guilds after they were organized in the thirteenth century.³¹ Katharine Park has demonstrated the participation of women doctors in late-fourteenth- and early-fifteenth-century Florence's Guild of Doctors, Apothecaries, and Grocers, although their gender largely excluded them from responsibility within the guild. At least two of the women practitioners were daughters of Florentine men doctors.³² Women's presence in medieval guilds corroborates the theory that women learned their skills and trades from family members. The familial link explains in part how women medical practitioners circumvented requirements of university study from which they were barred. Women's affiliations with men family members also explain how some women had access to increasingly gender-exclusive guilds even as late as the fifteenth century.

The final way in which women healers acquired their skills and knowledge was by means of practical experience. Before the late medieval emphasis on book learning, both women and men healers relied on practical instruction in order to learn their trades. At the early and famed center of medical practice and learning in Salerno, men and women practitioners before the twelfth century were lauded for their practical healing rather than their bookish learning.³³ The tenth-century Arabic medical encyclopedist and writer al-Razi (Rhazes, d. 925) even wrote a treatise that evidently spelled out women's efficaciousness, which he called "The Reason Why the Ignorant Physicians, the Common People, and the Women in the

Cities Are More Successful than Men of Science in Treating Certain Diseases."[34] Al-Razi's treatise attests to the desirability of women healers especially in medieval urban society.

One of the reasons why the sick sought these women healers was their ubiquitous public presence in cities and towns. Their availability in markets, on streets, and in homes fortified the public's reliance on them. Some women healers such as the throat-healing *exarmadora* described earlier had mobile practices that took them from town to town and made them highly accessible healers. The sick also turned to women healers because men physicians were small in number in the Middle Ages. When they were available, their fees were often prohibitive, causing the sick to seek the services of nonmedically trained healers.[35]

The medieval sick also sought the services of women healers because their interventions were efficacious. Women's healing practice was not largely considered inferior to that of men, and juxtapositions that were created between traditional women healers and learned men physicians were not extensively forged until the end of the Middle Ages. Through at least the first half of the fourteenth century, medical and nonmedical women healers competed for clients with a variety of men healers, and they vied for this client base among themselves.

Popular Literature and Women Healers

Women healers were favorably depicted in medieval literature in a way that fortified their legitimate status in medieval society. These texts not only supported women's work; they also encouraged the medieval sick to seek out and trust the mediations of women healers. Medieval literature provided readers and listeners with valuable information about whom to seek in times of illness, and it offered models to these readers about the tasks that women performed in medieval society. Women's favorable representation as *medianeras* and restorers of well-being sent a powerful message to readers and listeners about whom to rely on for relief from illness and pain.

Medical treatises are one kind of literature that depicted women in medical contexts. A corpus of medical manuscripts known as the Trotula texts were believed to have been written by the eleventh-century Salernitan woman physician Trotula. They provided extensive information on a variety of topics including gynecological and cosmetic advice, remedies and medical advice on the care of children, and information on a variety of topics concerning both men and women, such as emetics, insanity, and snake bites.[36] They circulated among healers throughout Europe in the thirteenth, fourteenth, and fifteenth centuries, and came to represent "the most widely circulated medical work on gynecology and women's problems of their time."[37] According to John F. Benton, the Trotula manuscripts were largely intended for a readership of men physicians ignorant about women's bodies and sexuality.[38]

The Trotula manuscripts represent an important source of hygienic information for many ailments, but especially for those associated with women's health. Benton has shown that probably none of the three early manuscripts was authored by a twelfth-century woman, nor was reference made to "Trotula" before the thirteenth century. It appears that these manuscripts were linked to the *mulieres Salernitane*, the more anonymous "Salernitan women healers."[39] Nonetheless, it is likely that the association of Salernitan women healers (and, starting in the thirteenth century, of the name "Trotula") with an authoritative body of medical manuscripts helped to establish the widespread social confidence in the efficacy of women healers. According to Benton's account, men physicians throughout Europe relied on "Trotula's" knowledge and expertise in order to effectively treat women clients.

Another kind of medical treatise that depicted women healers in medical contexts were practical guides on coitus and sexual hygiene. One such manual is the Catalan *Speculum al foderi* (*Mirror of Coitus*), written anonymously in the fifteenth century. It instructs readers about how to benefit from the salutary effects of moderate coitus, as it discusses the appropriate times for coitus, the most beneficial coital positions, and the damage brought on by excessive coitus. It also describes medicinal aphrodisiacs that augment desire.

The eighth chapter discusses the manners and customs of women ("Lo vuitè capítol que parla en les maneras e les custumes de les fembres") [Chapter Eight: Which Treats of the Manners and Customs of Women], and instructs the reader on how to seduce women and win their love. When a man is unable to seduce a woman on his own, the *Speculum* directs him to employ the services of a woman messenger (*missatger*) who shall seduce the woman for him.

This messenger-healer should have eight characteristics, including the qualities of discretion, ingeniousness, and deception:

> E sie fembra que haja en ella set coses: la primera, que sia fembra celada; la segona, que sie enginyosa e sabent de engan; la tersa, que sie d'aquelles que han occasió de ésser ab les fembres; la quarta, que no

sia maridada; la quinta, que sea plasent en ses maneras, e que les fembre[s] troben plaser en ella; la sisena, que sie d'aquelles que entren en les cases per so que no la sirquen; la setena, que non sie de les pobres que mendigen; la vuitena, que us de sis coses: que sia traccadora de matrimonis, o levadora, o corradora de joyes de fembres, o corradora de draps, o matrona, o baguines.

[This messenger should be a woman with seven characteristics: first, she should be discreet; second, she should be ingenious and know how to deceive; third, she should be the type that has opportunities to be with other women; fourth, she should not be married; fifth, she should be pleasant in her ways so that other women find her pleasing; sixth, she should be the type of woman who can make her way into a household even when she has not been summoned; and seventh, she should be neither poor nor a beggar. As an additional characteristic, she should have one of the following professions: matchmaker, midwife, vendor of women's jewelry, vendor of cloth, matron, or Beguine].[40]

She must have ample opportunities to be with other women, and must possess the ability to enter other people's houses even when not invited. Any one of the vocations mentioned (matchmaker, midwife, etc.) authorizes this multivocational healer to practice her skill in satiating a man's desire and restoring his well-being. Through a series of verbal strategies in which she tells the desired woman that a certain man is "crazy" for her, the woman healer attempts to seduce the woman lover for the man. She acts as a confabulator who uses verbal expertise in order to seduce the woman and thereby satiate the man's desire.

The *Speculum*'s advice of employing the woman healer has many important connotations for understanding the relationship between traditional women healers and medieval health. Sexuality and sexual hygiene were medical concerns through at least the sixteenth century, and women were traditional health practitioners for sexual well-being. Ancient and medieval medical writers recognized and verified the hygienic effects of moderate coitus through the emission of bodily fluids called seed.[41] The *Speculum* illustrates the close medieval connection between illness, health, medicine, sexuality, and desire.

Furthermore, the *Speculum* was not anomalous in its efforts to disseminate practical information about sexual practice and health, since the connection was widely recognized by medical healers and writers at this time.[42] It renders the woman healer's skills in this medical capacity as desirable, encouraging readers to seek these women when they were needed. The messenger-healer is a multivocational, active, mobile worker who is implored to facilitate the good health of her client. Not only does she assist in the medically desirable emission of seed but one of her main tasks entails satiating the man's desire.

The connection that the *Speculum* makes between illness, health, medicine, sexuality, desire, and the role of the woman healer makes manifest the diverse functions that women healers had in Iberian society. Restituting well-being and satiating desire were closely linked because healing, medicine, coitus, and desire were interrelated medical concerns in the medieval period. Women were depicted as healers who both restored health and satiated desire because, as evidenced by the *Speculum*, these were traditional tasks of women healers. Through its favorable rendering of the woman healer's skills in this medical context, the *Speculum* encouraged readers to seek these women when they were needed. It also verified and authorized the participation of women healers in medical practice, thereby encouraging them to practice medicine.

Another source of models of women healers was the variety of medical treatises that dealt with general salutary issues, which frequently mentioned the roles or tasks of the midwife or other woman healer. For instance, the anonymous *Tratado de patología general* begins an extensive discussion of women's health beginnning on folio 99r, and Bernard of Gordon covers women's health starting on folio 172r, where he mentions the midwife's crucial role in treating suffocation of the womb on folio 173r.[43] In his translation of the medieval Jewish gynecological treatise, "A Record of the Diseases Occurring in the Genital Members," Ron Barkai demonstrates that the midwife was called on in cases of fetus retention and suffocation of the womb.[44]

The last kinds of medical literature to depict women in healing contexts were treatises that discussed the postnatal care of infants. Twelfth- and thirteenth-century medical writers throughout Europe devoted portions of treatises to concerns with women's bodily fluids, and specifically to the healthful care of mothers, nurses, fetuses, and infants. Medical writers believed that nutritious bodily milk was transformed from blood, but were skeptical of the mother's ability to create it just after birth. Drawing on information from Arabic encyclopedists such as Haly Abbas, al-Razi (Rhazes), and Avicenna, medical writers deemed the employment of a wet nurse necessary for the health of the newborn.[45]

The nurse was responsible for neonatal duties including lactation. She should try to simulate the mother's "good health and qualities" as best she could. Her desirable attributes could be deduced from her physical appearance, as she should bear a moderate weight and be from twenty-five to thirty years of age. Other signs of an appropriate wet nurse included the woman's habits, "the shape of her breasts, the quality of her milk, and the time since her last parturition (one or two months)." Medical writers stressed the regimen that the wet nurse was required to follow in order to effectively carry out her duties and assure the transformation of blood into milk. They focused on the selection of foods, exercise, and the maintenance of a temperate emotional state. They suggested that if such a regimen were rigorously followed, either mother or wet nurse could capably nurse the infant.[46]

Iberian medical treatises that surveyed the conditions of healthful nursing included Francisco López de Villalobos's *Sumario de medicina*, and the *Tratado de patología general*.[47] In the latter treatise, the author delineates the wet nurse's qualities:

> E como deue ser el ama para mamantar el ninno deue ser jouen e non vieja branca avisada de cuerpo e de bonas carnes e de bonos braços e de bonas piernas e fermosa de rrostro e de bonas maneras e que non se ensane de lligero e que sea dolençia non tenplada en grosura e que sean sus tetas de bonas maneras nin pequenas nin grandes[48]
>
> [The Qualities a Wet Nurse Must Have to Nurse a Child. She should be young, not old, white, with a well-formed body, good flesh, good arms and legs, and well-mannered with a pleasant face; she should be healthy, not too corpulent, and should not anger easily; her breasts should be well-formed, not too large or too small][49]

Iberian medical information about neonatal care and the effective participation of women extended into the sixteenth century in Damián Carbón's *Libro del arte de las comadres o madrinas y del regimiento de las preñadas y paridas y de los niños* (Mallorca 1541), where he claimed that women were much needed in matters of childbirth and nursing: "fue necessario por honestidad de dexar estas cosas en poder de muger" [for reasons of modesty, it was necessary to leave these things to the care of women].[50] Carbón describes the midwife's occupational status as belonging to the *artes mechanicas*. But, before she can successfully carry out her duties, she must be well informed and well instructed, which is the objective of Carbón's treatise.[51]

Despite the favorable accounts by Carbón and others of women's role in birthing and childcare, one scholar, William F. MacLehose, has indicated that women's roles as mothers and wet nurses were often regarded as ambivalent.[52] For instance, the twelfth- and thirteenth-century concern with women's fluids was motivated by an increasing distress with their potential to cause harm. Medical writers expressed apprehension at women's abilities to nurse children ably, and they linked the possible ill health of the infant to women's potentially contaminated fluids. Nonetheless, medical writers agreed that a healthful regimen on the part of mothers and nurses enabled them to effectively care for infants. These carefully crafted instructions on neonatal supervision supported women's roles in the sanitary care of newborn children, even if they encouraged readers to take responsible precautions.

Hagiography was the second kind of mediating text that fomented women's participation in medicine and encouraged the sick to rely on their capabilities. Iconography and written texts alike showed how women saints healed the sick. Stories about saints compiled in works such as Jacobus de Voragine's renowned *Legenda aurea* (*The Golden Legend*) not only inspired a vast production of painting and art in the medieval and early modern periods, but also promoted the erection of healing shrines and popular cults of healing.

Saints in the medieval period were more often honored for their ability *to do things* than for their piety. The cult of the Fourteen Holy Helpers is connected to this medieval, practical appeal. It is constituted by fourteen men and women saints who were sought for the healing of maladies and for protection in difficult situations. For instance, Barbara was appealed to against lightning, fire, explosion, and sudden death, and Margaret was sought by pregnant women and invoked during childbirth.[53]

Besides the Fourteen Holy Helpers, women saints such as Lucy and Agatha were famous as holy healers. Lucy became the patron saint of the eyes, and Agatha was sought out to heal afflictions of the breast, colic, and dysentery.[54] Saints were sought out to heal the same kinds of maladies or tortures that they themselves had endured. Earthly women who were afflicted with breast illness could readily esteem the pain and torment endured by Agatha: "The torments which a saint who had normal breasts is shown to have endured could readily be appreciated by women afflicted with diseases, who were themselves subjected to the same agonies."[55] It is alleged that Lucy was once found praying at Agatha's shrine to cure her mother's dysentery.[56]

Two women saints were legendary for their assistance to pilgrims along the Jacobean route to Santiago de Compostela. Bona de Pisa was entreated to aid travelers with difficulties on the route, since she herself had made the trip many times accompanied by Italian pilgrims.[57] Felicia was another traveler to Santiago who was beheaded en route by her brother. In a clear allusion to her death by beheading, she was implored to heal headaches.[58]

Along with these holy women, the Virgin was widely sought for her healing mediations. Marian works were the last kind of medieval literature that encouraged women's healing practice by depicting a woman in a healing context. The two most popular collections of Marian miracles in Iberia were Alfonso X's *Cantigas de Santa María* and Gonzalo de Berceo's *Milagros de Nuestra Señora*. In them, the Virgin healed individuals afflicted with a variety of ailments such as blindness, deafness, paralysis, and mutilation. The Virgin acted as a midwife who aided pregnant women in childbirth. She was able to intervene in the most adverse of situations, such as when a pregnant woman was about to be swept away by a river in miracle nineteen.

The Virgin was omnipresent yet her healing mediations were discrete and practical. She was so powerful that she possessed not only the ability to restore health, but also to subvert it. *Cantiga* sixty-one recounts the story of a man from Soissons who did not believe that a shoe truly belonged to the Virgin. When the Virgin found out about his disbelief, she distorted his mouth in such a way that everyone who saw him was horrified. To make matters worse, the physical mutilation was very painful:

> e torceu-xe-ll' a boca en tal maneira
> que quen quer que o visse espantar-s-ia.
> ....
> E tal door avia que ben cuidava
> que ll' os ollos fora da testa deitava[59]
>
> [and his mouth was turned in such a way
> that whoever saw him would become afraid of him.
> ....
> and he was in so much pain that he thought
> his eyes would jump out of his head]

The Virgin completely dominated the condition of this man's well-being as she ably restored the integrity of his mouth once he had repented.

The powerful and ubiquitous Virgin used a variety of techniques to heal medieval sinners. Often she healed by way of her benevolent breast milk, as in *cantiga* fifty-four when she brought a monk back to life. The consistency of the Virgin's healing mediations were analogous to the wholeness and goodness of her bodily fluids. The tangibility of her interventions made her an accessible healer to be relied upon in times of illness.

The Virgin and holy women were important models for emulation by women in the medieval period. From as early as the exhortations of the Council of Nicaea in 325, the Virgin Mother was the supreme paradigm of emulation, since all women were entreated to follow her example. Depending on the historical period, women were encouraged to resemble the Virgin's many desirable attributes such as her humility, poverty, and obedience.[60]

This appeal to emulate the Virgin was one of the evident objectives of Isabel de Villena's late-fifteenth-century *Vita Christi* (1497). Despite its title, Villena's work contains a great deal of information about the life of Mary and holy women, and goes to great lengths to establish Mary's human qualities and the worthy attributes of both holy and mundane women. The link that Villena forges between the goodness of Mary and holy women, and the beneficence of earthly women, makes manifest the expectation that women were to emulate the Virgin and saints.

Marian literature and hagiography had compelling implications for the establishment of ethical and behavioral norms for women. Yet they also had significant ramifications for the establishment of conventions related to gender identity and women's work.[61] The Virgin constituted the principal model for the making of the female gender in medieval Iberian society. Some scholars have negatively interpreted her medieval influence, criticizing what they see as the elevation of her chastity, and of her obedience to male figures. In her captivating study of women in the *Cantigas*, *Women in Thirteenth-Century Spain as Portrayed in Alfonso X's* Cantigas de Santa María, Connie L. Scarborough suggests that medieval women could never live up to the Virgin's superiority as a virginal mother, claiming that Mary failed to ameliorate women's place in society: "The idea that the Virgin helped glorify the role of women and vice versa is one that upon further analysis proves to be quite the opposite . . . [Alfonso's] adulation of Mary will be to the exclusion of all other women, whom he finds wanting in comparison."[62] Scarborough regards Alfonso's troubadour rhetoric as an attempt to isolate the Virgin's singularity and power from common people, while at the same time establishing her servitude to the dominant male poet.[63]

However, scholars have demonstrated that Scarborough's assessment is wanting.[64] Although the Virgin's superiority to other women was mentioned throughout Marian literature, her tangible accessibility was crucial to her popular appeal. The visual force of the *Cantigas*, for instance, lies in the lesson imparted to the viewer of the Virgin's close approximation to other human beings, as the supreme intermediary of the individual's relationship to God. The Virgin's obedience to God as his handmaid indicated not her passivity as a follower, but the constant activity of a doer.[65] The possible offensive consequences of the centuries-long pairing of Mary with different qualities such as Mother or Virgin only tell one side of Mary's story throughout history.

The vast quantity of visual and textual Marian material produced in the twelfth and thirteenth centuries throughout Europe probably had favorable repercussions on those who viewed or heard them. As they instructed women on how to be women, the miracles retold in the *Cantigas* and in Berceo's *Milagros* recounted the ways in which Mary mediated the relationship between humankind and God, an intercession dependent upon good acts, not upon passivity or fragility.[66] Christian women were expected to emulate Mary because Marian literature and hagiography taught them that they could secure redemption through the imitation of "the metamorphosis of fallen Eve to the blessed Mary."[67] Marian literature served as a palpable resource to assist individuals with valuable information about healing, protection, and the fulfillment of desire, and it also established the Virgin as a model of the female gender through her works.

In writings as late as Damián Carbón's sixteenth-century treatise on obstetrics, *Libro del arte de las comadres o madrinas*, the Virgin as intercessor, her birth of Christ, and her work were invoked as forceful aids in the dissemination and understanding of the text: "Inuocando el diuino auxilio: con la intercession dela Virgen Maria señora nuestra. La qual concibio por obra del obra del Spiritu sancto / y pario virgen / y crio su bendito hijo" [Invoking divine aid, with the intercession of Our Lady the Virgin Mary, who conceived by way of the Holy Spirit, and gave birth as a virgin, and raised her blessed son].[68] It is likewise not coincidental that the Virgin's beneficent acts and good works should be summoned in a treatise directed toward the instruction of women healers. Her position as mother is as an intercessor between gestation and life, just as the woman healer should, according to Carbón, assure the delivery of human life in her role as midwife. In this treatise, the Virgin acts as a textual model of women's gender and behavior.

The plethora of Marian literature and hagiography that dealt with healing served as an important support for women's legitimate role in the healing arts, and for encouraging the sick to seek relief with women. It created models of healers for women to imitate and it fomented the sick to seek relief with both holy and mundane women. For instance, women who worked as wet nurses in medieval Iberian society (such as those described in medical treatises) were supported in their vocations by Marian literature that described the goodness of the Virgin's milk.

Medieval literature supported women's participation in the healing arts. Medical, hagiographic, and Marian literature all served as sources of information for medieval readers and listeners about how to heal illness, and about whom to seek as healers. Medieval readers and listeners would have linked the beneficent, holy interventions of the Virgin and women saints to the mundane mediations of women healers in their own society. They would have recognized the efficacy of earthly women healers as extensions of the interventions of holy women.

THE PROFESSIONALIZATION OF MEDICINE

The encouragement that medieval women healers received from medical, hagiographic, and Marian literature began to change dramatically in the fifteenth century. This change was motivated by transformations in medieval healing that were brought on by the professionalization of medicine. The professionalization of medicine took place throughout much of Western Europe at this time and can be defined broadly as a systematic attempt to elevate medicine and men physicians. To this end, it employed several strategies to exclude traditional women healers from the licit practice of medicine. Women were increasingly restricted from healing practice and their work was progressively described as standing in opposition to the work of the learned male physician.

The Iberian efforts to professionalize medicine were most intense from the fourteenth through sixteenth centuries, and were part of progressively concerted monarchical, municipal, ecclesiastical, and educational attempts to gain control of healing in the peninsular territory. What had previously constituted only one of many ways in which medieval Iberians could mediate illness—that is, by enlisting the services of the learned physician—became finally institutionalized and preferred.

The professionalization of medicine in Western Europe at this time had four general developments: (1) the requirement of university study in a medical faculty, a requirement with which women could not comply since they were prohibited from university entrance;[69] (2) the enactment of laws that regulated medical practice and barred traditional healers from licit medical practice, including women, Jews, and Muslims; (3) the establishment of licensing boards responsible for the examination and licensing of physicians, and sometimes surgeons, apothecaries, and others; and, (4) the rise of hospitals and clinics.[70] These general developments range in importance from region to region, but all played significant roles in the promotion of medical practice and of medical healers as professionals who composed an exclusive group possessing skills and knowledge presumably superior to those of nonprofessionals. Yet, these developments were not entirely new, since sanctions regarding Western medicine and medical practice can be traced as far back as ancient Rome.[71]

Medical regulations before the fourteenth century also exist in medieval Iberia, and include the royal decrees about Castilian medical healers in the legal codes or *Fuero juzgo* of the Visigoths (years 642–49) and Alfonso X's thirteenth-century legal writings in the *Siete Partidas*.[72] Moreover, medieval regulatory measures outside Iberia had been in effect in Sicily since about 1140, in Paris since 1220, and in Montpellier since 1239.[73] Thus, laws, decrees, and directives related to the management of medical practice and healing had been extant for generations prior to the fourteenth century. However, what distinguishes the professionalization of medicine in the fourteenth through sixteenth centuries from the earlier attempts is mainly the systematic intensification and confluence of all these developments at more or less the same time.[74]

These efforts are significant because medicine gained a great deal of institutional ground in this period through royal, legal, municipal, and educational means. Perhaps more importantly for Western European social history, the professionalizing process created a hierarchy of healing that privileged the expertise and worth of learned medicine and its practitioners over that of traditional nonmedical healers and mediating techniques. In the case of Iberia, most of the documentation and scholarship currently available about this process applies to the Crown of Aragon. This is due to several factors including Aragon's wealth of extant archival documentation, the region's relatively close proximity and relationship to medical faculties at Montpellier and Paris, Valencia's stellar medieval reputation as a center for healing, and the evident interest of modern historians in the Levant region of the peninsula. Much of the documentation and analysis that would relate to medieval Castile is lacking otherwise.[75]

Several events and conditions spawned the intensified professionalizing process in Iberia at this time, many of which were endemic to widespread conditions across Western Europe. Starting in the eleventh and twelfth centuries, Western European medical practice began to change along with societal vicissitudes such as increased urbanization, population increase, economic growth, and "the development of more sophisticated forms of secular and ecclesiastical government administration."[76] The need for more advanced occupational literacy and an emphasis on philosophical, scientific, and technical learning influenced the sanction of "theoretical" over "practical" medicine. Because healers largely learned their trades by practice, that is, through their experiences working with clients, and by way of an oral transmission of information, the emphasis on medical theory "produced a gap between theory and practice."[77]

Although medical historians such as John M. Riddle believe that the traditional medieval healer largely ignored the theory, it is misleading to assume that traditional healers never referred to textual theory and instruction. Healers were not always illiterate.[78] They were often obligated to read recipes of remedies located in learned medical works but more commonly found in portable handbooks such as the *vademecum* or single-page charts designed for the itinerant healer.[79] Handbooks of this sort facilitated the rapid access to information about a number of health-related topics including anatomy and medical astrology. It is commonly assumed that nonmedical medieval healers had no recourse to medical literature, although recent scholarship suggests that many kinds of healers were exposed to medical treatises and other writings whose teachings were applied in practice.[80]

In conjunction with changes in medieval society, medical historians generally posit three interrelated causes for the change in healing emphasis from practice to theory: (1) the authority rendered to book and manuscript learning; (2) the rise of universities and their concomitant founding of medical faculties; and (3) the translation of Arabic medical texts into Latin. University training, especially the completion of the four-year *studium generale*, became a common requirement for the licensing of physicians. The twelfth-century medical faculty at Salerno was the first to differentiate medical activity from philosophy. When Salerno was attacked in 1193 by Henry VI, some of its doctors moved to the school at Montpellier, which developed into a bastion of medical learning and was strongly associated with the Crown of Aragon.[81] The medical faculty in Paris was established during the first half of the thirteenth century, as was the medical *studium* at Lerida. About one hundred years later in 1301, Jaume II established the Leridan medical faculty in order to provide his realm with trained physicians and to serve the faculty at Montpellier in an adjunct capacity.[82]

Furthermore, the translations of Arabic manuscripts into Latin from the end of the eleventh century onwards brought about a renewed interest in Galenic, Hippocratic, and Arabic medical theory. Translations of Islamic medical writers such as Haly Abbas, al-Razi, Avicenna, Averroës, and Albucasis profoundly affected the course of medieval healing and medicine. Many of their writings constituted primary materials of study at European medical faculties such as the University of Bologna's in 1405.[83] One of the earliest examples of this new dissemination is that of Constantine the African, who brought Arabic texts to Montecassino at the end of the twelfth century. He translated these texts into Latin and also supplied his own, the *Viaticum*, a medical handbook for travelers.[84] Not only did the written nature of the appearance and dissemination of Arabic medical texts correspond to an increasing societal approval of book knowledge, technical learning, and science, but Arabic authors had access to a larger number of Galenic works and Greek philosophical tracts than Christian medical theorists. Arabic medical literature was highly valued in Islam and the West for its sophisticated and systematic treatment of disease, symptoms, and remedies.[85]

In Iberia, Arabic continued to serve as a language of communication between Arabs, Christians, and Jews, even after the Christian conquest of Muslim-ruled areas.[86] In regions where physicians of all three population groups were capable of reading Arabic, medical manuscripts and treatises were read by them all in the original Arabic. In Valencia, for example, the majority of the population spoke Arabic in the last half of the twelfth century and the beginning of the thirteenth. Some fifty years later, the renowned Valencian Christian physician Arnau de Vilanova (1240–1311) translated three works of medicine from Arabic into Latin.

Arabic works continued to be of interest to physicians in Valencia through the end of the fifteenth century. In Toledo, the Jewish community was responsible for composing, copying, and transmitting a large number of manuscripts in Arabic. The strong medieval tradition of translation and manuscript dissemination in Toledo (approximately 1150–1300) played a crucial role in the transmission of Arabic medical texts.[87] Hence, the development of universities and the wider dissemination of medical writings facilitated the influence of medical learning in Iberia, and were manifestations of the more expansive process of the professionalization of medicine at this time.

The second development of the professionalization of medicine consists of the legislation enacted to regulate medical healers by controlling the length and type of university study required, and by mandating the license requirement. Some of the earliest legal attempts in Iberia were dictated during the late-thirteenth-century reign of Alfons III (1285–91), and then throughout the terms of successive rulers in the kingdoms of the Crown of Aragon.

Two pieces of legislation were most significant. The first consisted of the laws enacted by the courts of Monzón in 1289 under the aegis of Alfons III. They regulated the practice of lawyers and were applied to physicians and surgeons:

> Capítol XVII. Item ordonam e statuïm qu algun savi en dret no ús en alguna cort de inquisicions, ne de advocacions, ne de jutjaments entrò serà examinat per los prohòmens de cascum loch ensemps ab los altres savis en dret; e aquels que seran elets, juren que se hauran feelment en advocacions e en les altres coses en poder del veguer o del batle e dels dits prohòmens d'aquell loch.
> Idem capítol XVIII. Item ordonam e statuïm que allò mateix se fasa en los metges e cirurgians.
>
> [17. Likewise we ordain and decree that no lawyer (*savi en dret*) shall take part in *inquisicions* or *advocacions* or judgments in any court unless he has been examined by the councilors (*prohòmens*) of the town together with other lawyers; and those who are examined shall swear that they will act faithfully in *advocacions* and in the other cases heard by the *veguer* or by the bailiff and the said councilors of the town.
> 18. Likewise we ordain and decree that the same thing be done with physicians and surgeons.][88]

The second piece of legislation consisted of the statutes (provisions 1–7) from the kingdom of Valencia enacted by Alfons IV in the courts of 1329, which were more comprehensive than the edict of 1289. According to García-Ballester, McVaugh, and Rubio Vela, the most important part was the beginning:[89]

> <1> Manam e establim que.l justícia e els//jurats cascun any lo terçer jorn ans de Nadal eligen .II. físichs de actoritat, los quals sien exami-

nadors de tots los metges de físicha que novellament vinguen per praticar en la ciutat e en les viles del regne, e aquell que trabaran suffitient, e que almenys haja oÿda art de físicha o medicina per .IIII. anys en estudi general, sia reebut a praticar la dita art, e en altra manera no ysia reebut.

[1. We command and ordain that the justiciar and the *jurats* elect, every year, three days before Christmas, two leading physicians who shall be the examiners of all the practitioners of physic who have recently come to practice in the city or in the towns of the kingdom; and those whom they find competent, and who have followed the art of medicine for at least four years in a *studium generale*, shall be admitted to practice the said art, and if not they shall not be admitted.][90]

The introductory section established the creation of a medical examination board to oversee individuals seeking to attain the titles of physicians or surgeons, and included the requirement that the university training of a *studium generale* constitute the deciding factor for licensing. University training became "the standard for qualification" in the Crown of Aragon. These regulatory standards were applied to the entire Crown in the legislation declared at the courts of Cervera in 1359.[91]

In 1336, the council of the city of Valencia organized a municipal board to oversee the licensing and examination of physicians and surgeons. It consisted of two to three examiners who served one-year terms.[92] However, the regulations that the examiners were supposed to enforce were routinely ignored. The low physician-surgeon / inhabitant ratio (six to seven physicians and surgeons to every ten thousand inhabitants), due in part to the refusal by the city's council to establish a *studium generale* in the city, helps to explain the continued pervasive practice of nonlicensed empirics and other healers. The council decided to support the "freedom to teach" statute, "allowing every master . . . that he may hold a school with or without another master in association," and thus effectively facilitated a number of different practitioners to call themselves *physicians* (*medici*), even though legally they were not. In other words, by the year 1400, the system of medical examination in the city was not at all systematic, and what was evidenced instead was a vacillation or "a balance" between a need for medical standards and the urgency that the kingdom's health demands be met.[93]

Measures were taken as well in fourteenth- and fifteenth-century Castile to regulate local medical practice. Juan I of Castile (1379–90) declared that all potential medical practitioners had to be subjected to some kind of examination. He formed the regulating body with examiners whom he appointed and called *alcaldes mayores examinadores*, learned judges charged with overseeing the examination process. The royal doctor or *médico primero* of his court was also assigned to the board. In 1422, Juan II sanctioned the same type of board to examine and license possible candidates for medical practice: "This same king also authorized his physician to assume jurisdiction over medical crimes without allowing any appeal to the king."[94] Enrique IV (1454–74) also confirmed the existence of this royal Castilian board during his reign.

At the end of the fifteenth century, the Catholic kings (*Reyes Católicos*) sought to regulate practitioners on a wider scale, especially in the pragmatics of 1477, 1491, and 1498. They were concerned with two aspects of fifteenth-century healing: the fact that unlearned or uninitiated men practiced in great numbers, and the lack of uniformity in medical legislation within the Iberian kingdoms. They instituted the third key development of the professionalization of Iberian medicine, the regulating board of the *Real Protomedicato*. In 1477, they decreed that the examiners, including both medical examiners called *protomédicos* and judges known as *alcaldes examinadores*, had to examine anyone wanting to practice as physician, surgeon, bonesetter, apothecary, dealer in aromatic drugs, herbalist, "and any other persons who 'in whole or in part' practice these professions—women as well as men."[95] They also granted the power to the *alcaldes examinadores* of fining physicians and surgeons if they should refuse to appear before them for examination, which suggests that their interests may have been more directed toward those two groups.

The Catholic kings sought to submit healers to rigorous examinations and to make such regulation and licensing uniform and systematic throughout the peninsula. Nonetheless, their harsher measures at the end of the fifteenth century betray less than complete control over peninsular medical practice. Uniform *Spanish* medicine did not exist until around the late eighteenth century, after the publication in 1751 of Miguel Eugenio Muñoz's *Recopilación de las leyes, pragmáticas, reales decretos y acuerdos del Real Proto-Medicato*, a collection of the medical laws, decrees, orders, and accords in existence on the peninsula. Published immediately following the annexation of the Protomedicato of Valencia to the Real Protomedicato, the *Recopilación* was intended to be distributed to "medical men" so that they could present it to the Protomedicato "to determine on the spot what the law was when a question arose."[96]

About one hundred years after the Real Protomedicato's inception, Felipe II (1556–98) was forced to renew his active support of it because the medical environment was still in disarray.[97] He was distressed by some of the questionable procedures carried out by the licensing board, such as the fact that it regularly ignored the practice of medicine or surgery by unlicensed practitioners. Felipe II enticed the Protomedicato officials to execute their duties with promises of monetary compensation, and he conceded to paying them one third of the fine meted out to unlicensed practitioners. There was also a great deal of difficulty during Felipe's reign with the forgery of documents verifying the completion of study at a university medical faculty.[98] A further complication was the lack of clarity about the legislation involving the Real Protomedicato prior to Felipe's reign. For instance, it was unclear as to whether or not there should be one or two medical examiners, nor was it clear whether medicine and surgery were concomitant or separate fields.

Late-sixteenth-century laws clarified many of these issues and gave further control to the king, who would name not one, but three medical examiners at will. According to Lanning, by the end of the sixteenth century, Felipe stabilized the Real Protomedicato to such a degree that it became the model for the regulation of medicine in America.[99] Hence, the establishment of the Real Protomedicato had increasingly detrimental effects on traditional medieval healers through its ostracizing, elitist requirements.

The fourth development of the professionalization of medicine was the late medieval and early modern rise of hospitals. Hospitals as they are known today did not exist during the medieval period. In Aragon they seem to have taken on many of their modern attributes from around the late fourteenth century on.[100] Early medieval hospitals were established for the poor, and while their duties entailed caring for the sick, they largely functioned as places of charity and not as medical institutions for the control of disease. Their main role was that of hospitality, not medicine.[101] They often served as inns or hostels for travelers to spend the night, and were especially needed along the pilgrim routes.[102] Located away from monasteries on these routes, they were nonetheless mostly staffed and managed by friars, canons, or nuns who often possessed medical training and knowledge.[103] Medieval hospitals occasionally retained a physician to work regular hours.[104] Thirteenth-century urban hospitals in Valencia and Barcelona were managed by ecclesiastics who provided shelter and aid to the poor.[105]

During the late Middle Ages, hospitals began to focus more steadily on the relationship between physician and patient. They created administrative and physical mechanisms to enable more extensive control over the conditions of medical practice. For instance, attempts to quarantine patients were intensified with the continued and novel establishment of places for specialized healing such as *leprosaria* or hospitals that treated only one affliction such as Valencia's Sant Antoni, dedicated to the disease of ergotism called St. Anthony's fire.[106] Furthermore, pharmacies became fixtures in hospitals in around 1500 to facilitate physicians' and other healers' rapid access to medicines.[107] Changes such as these aided in the edification of buildings within which healing conditions could be readily sanctioned and controlled.

In contrast to the containment of healing in hospitals, and before the professionalization of medicine established itself in the fifteenth century, medieval healing had been characterized by mostly non-university trained, itinerant healers. The eventual effects, then, of all the manifestations of the professionalization of medicine included the very physical separation of the elevated medical practitioner from traditional, nonmedical healers. This was accomplished in large part by making reductive theoretical, textual, and physical separations between professionals and nonprofessionals, in an attempt to authorize and ennoble professional mediations over nonprofessional ones. This division was largely established by legal means, whether it meant the prohibition of undesirable healers from university medical faculties, their marginalization from municipal medical practice, or their exclusion from professional guilds. However, this ostensible separation was frequently ambiguous in daily practice. Differentiations between medieval healers of all kinds were unclear well into the early modern period.

One impetus for the professionalization of medicine was to clarify distinctions between medical healers in order to facilitate vocational control. A licensed physician or surgeon was supposed to possess a particular body of knowledge so that the patient could expect specific kinds of remedies and results. However, oblique distinctions existed among learned, semilearned, and nonlearned healers. Historians of medieval medicine have recently questioned the supposed meanings of licit medieval healing professions including physician, surgeon, barber-surgeon, and apothecary. Monica Green is one of several scholars who attest to the tremendous fluidity between these professions and to their imprecise definitions:

> It should be emphasized, however, that these categories were much more fluid and subjectively defined than in the modern, highly regulated medical industry of Westernized societies. (Indeed, even the vocabulary to distinguish these specialties does not begin to take shape until the tenth and eleventh centuries). The possibility of overlap in functions was enormous, hence the intensity with which certain practitioners fought to solidify hazy boundaries.[108]

Licensing and the enforcement of legal regulations made the control of medieval and early modern healing more stringent. Efforts to professionalize medicine in this way signaled an attempt to define and maintain distinctions between professional and nonprofessional practitioners, and between the various ranks of professional healers themselves.

Traditional women healers were seriously and adversely affected by the professionalization of medicine. Officially barred from university entrance, the Iberian emphasis on university study rendered women's licensure as physicians and surgeons illicit. After completing the four-year *studium generale* (which they could not attend) women presumably would have had to be examined by a licensing board, a process from which they routinely were prohibited. However, the latter prohibition was ignored with great frequency in the city of Valencia, more or less simultaneously with the black death in the fourteenth and fifteenth centuries. Moreover, the requirement regarding university study has already been shown to have been applied arbitrarily, as evidenced by the capricious decisions of the Castilian Real Protomedicato.

In many ways, the immediate effects on women healers of fourteenth-century medical regulation was similar to its consequences for men healers: rules and regulations often were overlooked, and many people who did not meet official requirements continued to practice as physicians and surgeons. However, the long-term effects on women were such that by the early fifteenth century they were increasingly maligned, pursued, and prohibited from healing practices that they had traditionally carried out.

Due to the lack of analysis of data, it is impossible to determine the extent to which the Valencian environment resembled that of other Iberian communities. The Valencian statutes (*furs*) of 1329 established an examination board, defined "the route leading through examination to practice whether for physicians, surgeons, or barbers (provisions 1, 2, and 5)," and excluded women (provision 3):[109]

> <3> Alcuna fembra no ús de medicina, ne de dar bouratges, sotz [sic] pena de córrer la vila açotan, mas puxen pensar de infans pochs e de fembres, a les quals, emperò, no donen alcun bouratge.
>
> [3. No woman shall practice medicine or give potions, under penalty of being whipped through the town; but they may care for little children, and women—to whom, however, they may give no potion.][110]

Women then were barred twice in the legislation, implicitly as prohibited from studying at the university, and explicitly in the above provision. Although they were permitted to care for children and women, they could not practice medicine and were prohibited from prescribing medicines.

While the penalty of a public whipping seems harsh, the legal mandates of the statutes contradict the medical reality in Valencia and the entire Crown of Aragon. Documentation about women practitioners actually exists after the enactment of the statutes in 1329. García-Ballester, McVaugh, and Rubio Vela cite concrete instances of women practitioners of every ilk in Barcelona and Valencia, including midwives, specialists in eye ailments, and practitioners of general medicine and surgery who treated both women and men. The examples given earlier in this chapter about women practitioners in Iberia point to a more than one-hundred-year presence of women practicing medicine as a "normal occupation, often without bothering to seek formal exemption from the *furs*." Their presence suggests that the regulatory legislation of 1329 regarding women was "a dead letter."[111]

Three explanations have been offered for the discrepancy between the legislation of 1329 and women's medical practice. First, since in none of the documentation referring to the licensing of women practitioners had women doctors (*metgesses*) received their licenses from the medical examiners or the municipal council (they had always been meted out by the king, Pere IV [1336–87]), it was in the king's best interest to circumvent the examining board for reasons that shall be made clear shortly. Second, due to the fact that the majority of women seeking licenses were Muslim rather than Christian or Jewish, the prohibition against women practitioners was directed mostly at Muslim women seeking to practice medicine on Muslims and Christians in an increasingly Christian society. But, why were women doctors allowed to practice both officially and unofficially in Valencia? The third cause of the contradiction between the statutes and medical reality is the simplest and probably the most accurate. The fact that experienced physicians were sorely needed in Valencia created an environment in which proficient women healers were simply too valuable and needed to be ignored.[112]

While the institutional mechanisms set out to limit the practice of women healers were sometimes ineffective or implausible, the professionalization of medicine had long-term, detrimental effects on traditional women healers. These mechanisms caused an increasing debasement of the formerly legitimate woman healer, and they drove a wedge between women healers and men physicians. The historian Michael McVaugh has attributed the elevation of medicine and the male physician, and the "triumph of bookish medicine" in the late Middle Ages to a "broad public enthusiasm" that welcomed "the learning that medical education seemed to guarantee."[113] Yet, this contention fails to tell the whole story about the eventual establishment of medicine as the most authoritative response to illness. Although one may agree with García-Ballester, McVaugh, and Rubio Vela when they argue that medical science was increasingly considered responsible for health and well-being and for abetting social equilibrium and stability, at the same time it must be recognized that the eminence of medical science was institutionalized by societal groups for whom social control had significant economic and political consequences.[114] Despite McVaugh's suggestion that the "lay public's" support of medicine—municipal governments, courts of law, patients themselves—illustrates a kind of universal enthusiasm for medicine and book learning, many of the advocates of medicine were individuals with vested interests in the exclusion and disempowerment of traditional healers for the establishment of social control and order.[115] The professionalization of medicine coincided with a plethora of societal vicissitudes produced by the impulse toward nationalism in the late fifteenth century. These changes included explorations that led to the colonization of the Americas, the opening of new economic markets, enforced Iberian racism with the expulsion of Jews and Arabs, and zealous, forced conversions to Christianity. This narrowing peninsular homogenization, and the increase in measures implemented for royal and municipal domination of civil life also characterize the professionalization of medicine. For, that process represented the increased objectives of those in positions of authority to control who diagnosed, treated, and remedied illness, pain, and suffering.

Starting as early as the fourteenth century, women began to be regularly penalized throughout Europe for their traditional healing practice. In the famous legal case of 1322, a Parisian healer named Jacqueline Félicie was convicted of civil disobedience for practicing medicine illicitly without university training or a license. Initial charges were brought against her by the dean of the medical faculty in Paris who sought to have her marginalized and punished. In the course of the trial her defense counsel presented witnesses who attested to Jacqueline's competence because she had effectively cured them. Despite the newfound supremacy of the fourteenth-century medical faculties, the defense counsel based Jacqueline's innocence on the fact that the statutes against competent healers were "contrary to the public good."[116]

Clarice de Rothomago was arrested in 1312 on the insistence of the University of Paris's dean of the medical faculty. She was brought to trial with the goal of prohibiting her from illicit medical practice.[117] In another case from around 1330, the woman practitioner Mayrona was fined forty shillings for practicing in the town of Bayons in northern Provence.[118] In fourteenth-century Valencia, four women practitioners—Na Benvenguda ("La Maestra"), Na Blanca, Na Bonfilia, and Jamila—were tried before the court of Valencia for their illicit medical practice.[119] Jamila was particularly singled out and warned not to interfere with the medical profession. Another woman healer, Carinyea, was punished for practicing medicine in 1399 with the severe fine of twenty florins.[120]

Another disparaging effect that the professionalization of medicine had on traditional women healers is exemplified by women's punishment for using conventional, nonmedical techniques. The legitimacy of traditional healing methods such as the conjuration was increasingly called into question. Diocesan archives from Barcelona and Gerona show that traditional women healers were punished when they used the verbal conjuration to heal throat and eye ailments. Na Orpina was subjected to the public punishment of having to stand barefoot and without a cloak one Sunday in August in front of the church door during high mass. The conjurer Na Ramona Guitarda was forced to stand in a public place (presumably in front of the church door) two Sundays in a row, with the conjuration written out and hanging on a rope from her neck.[121]

The professionalization of medicine also brought about women's exclusion from their traditional duties as midwives. After the decimation rendered by the black death in the fourteenth century, the presence of women medical practitioners in Iberian historical documents decreased. The marginalization of women medical healers in Iberia seems to have coincided with a general decline in midwifery throughout Western Europe. Midwifery ironically is one of the healing practices that women were legally permitted to perform in the statutes of 1329, suggesting that women's gradual exclusion from healing was not limited only to medical practice but included obstetrical duties as well.

The institutional mechanisms that were created to marginalize women from licit medical practice also had pejorative implications for their practice of midwifery. The historian Monica Green claims that both men and women healers traditionally practiced on women and men clients. But another scholar, Myriam Greilsammer, believes that men's interest in women's health during the medieval period was a new one, in order to "challenge the existing supremacy of the female practitioners, which they . . . [could not] but acknowledge."[122] In her study of midwifery in the Low Countries, Greilsammer proposes that the decline of midwifery stemmed "not from the alleged primitiveness of midwives, but from the deliberate action of church and state."[123] She suggests that women's exclusion from medicine and midwifery was not due to a lack of knowledge or incompetency on their parts. Rather, their skill and efficacy threatened the hegemony of men medical professionals to such a degree that men sought to replace women in obstetrical and other matters.

However, constraints on midwives' duties were by no means universally enforced in practice, as evidenced by the fifteenth-century expectation of some Iberian physicians that the midwife be responsible for removing the child or fetus from the woman's body by Caesarean surgery.[124] Attempts to block women from authorized healing practice, including semiprofessional surgery and midwifery, were often implausible.

The institutional mechanisms mobilized by the professionalization of medicine to limit women from practicing the healing arts were frequently ineffective. Laws against the licensing of women physicians were regularly overlooked as late as the fifteenth century in the Crown of Aragon. Four main reasons explain the periodic failure of these mechanisms. First, women healers could not be completely marginalized because their skills were sorely needed to treat people afflicted by plagues and other ailments. Second, there was a scarcity of men physicians available to heal the sick. Municipal complaints to royal authorities about the dearth of physicians and surgeons were common in the fourteenth century from Catalan cities and towns such as Barcelona, Rigaborça, and Jérica, and from Valencian municipalities such as Borriana and Morella.[125] When they were available, physicians often charged prohibitive fees for their services. Not only could few individuals pay these high fees, but the sick likely perceived the selfish concerns of some doctors who valued financial gain over efficacious healing.[126]

Third, the public could not rely upon the mediations of men doctors, since early modern men physicians were routinely criticized for being incompetent and ineffective. Their practical skills did not match their study and learning. For instance, syphilitic patients in the late fifteenth century were particularly critical of the ineptitude of men physicians.[127] The afflicted resorted to the services of untrained doctors and charlatans because they believed them to be the only ones capable of curing the disease of syphilis. Complaints against incapable professionals were so pervasive that they became a literary trope in the sixteenth and seventeenth centuries, as evidenced by early modern theater such as Calderón de la Barca's *El médico de su honra.*

Fourth, the institutionalized legal mechanisms designed to professionalize medicine largely failed to translate their written efforts into actual results. This may have been due to power struggles between monarchs, municipal boards, and royal boards, or it may have been caused by the failure of laws and regulating boards to wield any real, centralized control. Fourteenth-century kings such as Pere IV seem to have exercised more authority over the licensing of physicians than municipal regulating boards. In order to license women healers, Pere IV bypassed municipal legislation prohibiting their license. The tension between royal dominion and local, municipal power may have subverted at times the efforts at control by local governing bodies such as the Valencian council.

This battle for power was played out differently in sixteenth-century Castile. Instead of circumventing the strictures and decrees of a municipal body, Felipe had to fight for the management of his own royal entity, the Real Protomedicato. Felipe constantly seemed to have to fend off the potential for corruption and insurrection by the medical examiners.

The failure of the institutional measures to marginalize women healers is evidenced by the fact that women throughout Europe continued to be sought out by the sick as late as the sixteenth and seventeenth centuries. In an example mentioned earlier, in sixteenth-century Madrid, Isabel Pérez de Peromato petitioned the courts to allow her to use the oil that she and her husband had invented for the curing of wounds.[128] The desirability of women healers was recognized in other parts of Europe as demonstrated by a treatise written in 1530 by Cornelius Agrippa of Nettesheim. Agrippa praised the "'old wife' [who] searched wood and field for the individual plants, learning their colors, forms, taste, scent and species, [and] according to her experience of their virtues administers the surest remedy free of charge to everyone."[129] In 1600, Olivier de Serres, lord of Pradel, commended women healers as "more equipped than men" to heal the sick, especially in the countryside where physicians were scarce.[130]

Because of the failures and inconsistencies of the institutional mechanisms designed to elevate medicine and men physicians, the professionalization of medicine required further means to eradicate the active practice of traditional women healers. To that end, men authors complicit with the ideology of the newly authorized male physician attempted to undermine the literary models that promoted women healers. In order to discourage the sick from seeking the assistance of women healers, late medieval and early modern authors employed various strategies to subvert previous literary models of figures such as the Virgin and the physician Trotula. These writers tried to provide the same information to readers as the older medieval texts, concerning whom they should seek out in times of illness. Yet these later works disparaged the interventions of earthly women healers in order to dissuade readers and listeners from seeking relief from them.

The three late medieval and early modern works that I examine in the following chapters, Jaume Roig's *Spill*, Fernando de Rojas's *La Celestina*, and Francisco Delicado's *La Lozana andaluza*, play out the progressive marginalization of traditional women healers from licit medical practice. Each of these authors uses different strategies to denigrate the healing practice of traditional women healers, most of which center on the Virgin, especially on the contrast of the Virgin and ordinary *medianeras*. These three writers altered the nature of the relationship between Marian literature and medieval readers, listeners, and viewers by perverting the expected similarities of gender, work, and character between the paradigmatic Virgin and her mundane, female cohorts.

All of these authors were involved in medical matters and would have been familiar with the professionalization of medicine. Jaume Roig was a physician and medical examiner in Valencia, and wrote a scathing condemnation of women healers in the *Spill*. When Fernando de Rojas likely wrote *La Celestina* in about 1499, he was a law student at the University of Salamanca when the professionalization of medicine was gaining momentum. He was also the close friend of the Castilian physician Francisco López de Villalobos (*Sumario de medicina*). Francisco Delicado wrote a medical treatise on syphilis and is believed to have suffered from the disease for twenty-three years in Rome. His concern with the popularity of uneducated women healers of syphilis undergirds the writing of *La Lozana andaluza*.

The next chapter on Jaume Roig's *Spill* demonstrates the strategies that Roig employed in order to malign ordinary women healers. His main tactic was to create a contrast between the Virgin as the only woman capable of healing and earthly women who only augmented disease. The Virgin was increasingly stylized and abstracted from her previously human interventions, and became a distant icon to be worshipped rather than imitated. Roig's work provided the reader with the hygienic information that the avoidance of earthly women healers facilitated peoples' well-being and the general social order. According to Roig, reliance on the Virgin and men physicians were the only ways in which one could be truly healed.

Through strategies such as these, Roig, Rojas, and Delicado tried to transform and subvert the medieval literary models that had supported the practice of women healers. The failure of institutional mechanisms against these women necessitated new literary paradigms of exclusion that were contrary to the old models in medical treatises, hagiography, and Marian literature.

2
Eva/Ave: *Ramería*, Reproduction, and the Song of Roig in Jaume Roig's *Spill o Llibre de les dones*

Jaume Roig was born in the city of Valencia at around the end of the fourteenth century and died there on April 4, 1478.[1] He worked as a physician in Valencia like his father, and obtained university degrees in both medicine and the arts (*mestre en arts*). As a young man, he apparently studied at the medical faculty in Paris. He was named medical examiner by the council (*consell*) of Valencia in 1435, a job that entailed the licensing and examination of medical professionals, and exercised duties in that capacity until his death in 1478. Roig worked as a doctor in two Valencian hospitals, *l'hospital General* and *l'hospital d'en Bou*, and lended his services as a physician to the Dominican Order and to the Franciscan women's Trinitat Convent. His services extended to the royalty of the period, since he served as physician to Maria, wife of the king of Aragon, Alfons el Magnanim (1416–58).

Roig wrote the *Spill* around 1460 when he was approximately sixty years old. A highly misogynistic and anecdotal work written in five-syllable verse (*copla nova*), the text is written in the first person, and according to the preface, pretends to be a recounting of Roig's life. The main body of the text consists of four books. The first one, "Juventut" [Childhood], retells the narrator's early years at home and his travels to Paris. The second book, "De quant fon casat" [On When I Was Married], narrates his misfortunes in marriage. The third book consists of a dream-sermon by Solomon, and the fourth, "O quarta part principal de enviudat" [The Fourth Main Part on Old Age], is written from the point of view of a centenarian who has adopted the contemplative life.

The *Spill* was read throughout the sixteenth century in three Catalan editions (Valencia 1531; Valencia 1561; Barcelona 1561). One of the reasons for its renown was its fixation on the Virgin, since devotion to her was a popular theme among fifteenth- and sixteenth-century male writers.[2] The title pages of the three sixteenth-century editions of the *Spill* bear this out, each with a different representation of Mary in an elevated position at the top of each illustration.[3] They further maintain that Roig's advice (*consells*) in the text is intended as healthy instruction on how to live a well and ordered life, and that at the same time, he seeks to augment devotion to the Virgin. For instance, the 1531 title page begins: *Libre de consells: fet per lo magnifich mestre Jaume roig/los quals son molt profitosos y saludables axi peral regiment y orde d' ben viure com pa augmentar la d'uocio ala puritat y concepcio dela sacratissima verge Maria* [Book of Advice: by the magnificent doctor Jaume Roig, which is as beneficial and salutary for the ordering of good living as for the increase in devotion of the purity and conception of the most sacred Virgin Mary].[4] The title page of the second edition, Valencia 1561, advances the same concerns: *Libre deles dones, mes verament dit de consells profitosos y saludables, axi per al regiment y orde de la vida humana, con pera aumentar la deuocio de la inmaculada Concepcio de la sacratissima verge Maria, fet per lo magnifich mestre Iaume Roig* [Book on Women, or better called a book on beneficial and salutary advice, as much on the ordering of human life as for the increase in devotion of the immaculate conception of the most sacred Virgin Mary, by the magnificent doctor Jaume Roig].[5] Good living, good health, and devotion to the Virgin are interdependent—one cannot be had without the other. The *Spill* connects them in order to expressly align the Virgin with the reader's good health and well-being.

This strategy is employed in order to praise the Virgin in contrast to all earthly women, who are presented throughout the text as vicious and malevolent. This contrastive technique is Roig's most forceful misogynist strategy, and the *Spill*'s focus on the Virgin differentiates it from other misogynist works that served as its models, namely Alfonso Martínez de Toledo's *Arcipreste de Talavera*, Boccaccio's *Corbaccio*, and Jean Lefèvre's "Lamentations" in Matheolus.[6] The *Spill*'s concentration on the Virgin is ultimately intended to disseminate a range of hygienic information about *earthly women's* evils, as it attacks women as a generic group and focuses on combating their spurious and destructive mediations. The *Spill* posits mediation as the characteristic common to all ordinary women since they negotiate domestic, religious, business, and healing practice. Ordinary women intervene on other people's behalf like the Virgin, but unlike her, their interventions are only malevolent. In order to justify the exclusion of traditional women healers from the licit practice of medicine, the *Spill* must illustrate the great divide between the Virgin and a variety of multivocational *medianeras*, such as healers, procurers, go-betweens, and seamstresses.

The *Spill* thus constitutes not only a veritable guide to increasing devotion to the Virgin, but also a therapeutic manual to improve the male reader's health and well-being.[7] To this end, the *Spill* aims to discourage the reader from pursuing the services of women healers and to encourage him to seek out the mediations of male medical professionals. The *Spill*'s therapeutic information—that women and women healers must be avoided at all costs to ensure men's and society's well-being—also communicates the general effectiveness and beneficence of the male physician, that is, of individuals such as Roig himself.

In order to demonstrate the gap between men and the Virgin, and all earthly women, Roig posits women's destructiveness as stemming from their diseased and contagious nature. Because disease was thought to be a product of or a punishment for sin in the Middle Ages, Roig claims that ordinary women are sinful and diseased because they are birthed from Eve, who is "the primeval source of all men's suffering."[8] Roig seeks to discredit all earthly women by opposing them to the Virgin who represents an uncontaminated channel emanating from God, and tries to edify the immortal Virgin as the only competent female healer. Through this division of Eve and Mary, Roig avoids "the abstracted double" that had long characterized misogynist literature, in which women were depicted as neither entirely evil like Eve nor wholly pure like the Virgin, but paradoxically both.[9] Roig evades this contradictory model in order to establish earthly women as utterly contrary to the Virgin.

By the mid fifteenth century, the Virgin is no longer used to vouch for the analogous connection between her healing powers and those of earthly women. Instead, Roig presents her as superior and competent in contrast to all other women who are not.[10] Roig's singular womanly model becomes not a woman at all but a metaphorical and unique flower, a *lilium inter spinas*, a "lily among thorns," an iconic mother and savior stylized to the point of a disintegrating resemblance to ordinary women in the world, and a "super healer / intercessor" whose feats are so beyond anything an ordinary woman could do that they cannot be confabulated like they had been in the thirteenth century.[11] Far removed from the earlier medieval "super healer" of Alfonso X's *Cantigas* and Gonzalo de Berceo's *Milagros* who had faithfully mediated by example each and every ill of any sinner who asked for her intervention, the renovated Virgin-healer of the fifteenth and sixteenth centuries exists behind the distorting glass of Roig's *Spill* as the one *medianera* who will help men live healthy lives in the world, and help them reach their ultimate goal of eternal life in heaven.

Roig diagnoses the etiology of men's ills as diseased and infectious women. Since the Virgin is not a woman, but rather a female icon, she is the only female they can trust. This contrast still depends upon the resemblance of the Virgin to ordinary women, but now she is distanced from them in ways that were not emphasized in thirteenth- and fourteenth-century Marian works. Her resemblance is based on her gender and the biological potential that all gendered females share. Roig's misogynist opposition is theologically constructed with the Virgin as the generator of anything male, and Eve as the birthing dynamo of all female entities.

Roig refers to women throughout the text as "the daughters of Eve," and in book 3, King Solomon's dream-sermon, Mary's one offspring, Jesus Christ, has the male gender, which is characterized as integral and whole in the paradoxically multiple figures of Jesus the Son of God, and God the Father.[12] By way of the Eva / Ave (Eve / Mary) contrast in book 3, Roig lists Mary's offspring as a series of powerful male figures who are really one: "Ffilla e mare / pari son Pare, / pare e Fill / ... pari Messies / ... pari fill verb / ... pari fill fort / destruynt mort" (11313–42) [Daughter and mother, she gave birth to her Father. Father and Son, she gave birth to the Messiah. She gave birth to the son the word. She gave birth to a strong son, the destructor of death]. All men derive from the stable, integral Mary and apparently possess her same unequivocal characteristics. All women, on the other hand, descend from the sinning, tempting, and diseasing Eve. Hence, Roig's sanction of the male physician as the most capable healer and interpreter of disease is founded upon the male doctor's Marian lineage, as opposed to the Evian lineage of women healers. Roig's therapeutic imperative for the treatment of illness is constituted by the search for the male physician who truly knows how to heal and treat disease without exacerbating the illness. At the same time that Roig denigrates all ordinary women except his wife—and specifically women as healers—he delegates the omnipotent male physician as the individual most competent at healing.

Since men's mediations are aligned with Mary, and women's mediations with Eve, the intercessions of various kinds of earthly women are devalued on every level. According to Roig, the advice of nuns and abbesses is intended to destroy men, and the healing practices of midwives and healers are ruinous. Women who mediate in any other capacity in which they make things for men's consumption, such as cooks, will only try to kill them. Because they derive from Eve, they are tainted with sin and thus with disease. Like Eve, earthly women deviate from the norm which is the Virgin, and instead of healing like the Virgin and the male physician, they intensify the conditions of illness. They increase men's pain, alienate them from their daily routines, and make the threat of death a reality. The medieval reader who looked to the *Spill* for salutary information and advice about alleviating illness may have agreed with the authorized physician Jaume Roig that men were far better healers than women, and that the Virgin was the only female who healed at all.

The Sacred *Ramería*

The *Spill* is framed as Roig's autobiographical recounting of the story of his life with women. In the preliminary "Consulta," written from Callosa where he fled the Valencian plague, he says that he wants to write about women's "natural" and "voluntary" way of being in order to more easily describe the Female One, whose state is completely opposite. He attempts to teach men to resist women as vile, to love only the Female One, and to be able to choose the lily among the thorns. Roig's audience consists of gender-specific impressionable or uninitiated men such as the young and inexperienced, priests who have forgotten their vows of celibacy, and gentlemen. In the preface the narrator tells Roig's nephew Baltasar Bou to pass the *Spill* on to those men so that they will avoid Roig's errors with women (292–322).

Despite the fact that the *Spill* reviles earthly women, it cannot avoid Roig's actual wife, Isabel Pellicer, and thus cryptically mentions her at the book's end as the only ordinary woman able to approximate the Virgin.[13] Not surprisingly, however, in a description that stands out because of its uncharacteristic gender fluidity, the *Spill* claims that this woman with so many favorable qualities seemed more like a man than a woman (15974–76). Rather than representing a purely ironic or sarcastic declaration, the logic of this statement wholly conforms to the *Spill*'s division between men as sons of the Virgin and women as Eve's daughters. Any woman who could be deemed favorable would have to resemble men more than women according to the *Spill*'s argument.

The masculinization of the aberrant, earthly Pellicer also corresponds to the sexual extreme of the homosocial, if men's relations are viewed along a continuum that encompasses their social relations and a different point along that spectrum constituted by their sexual relations.[14] The masculinization of Roig's actual wife has astounding consequences for the extension of his misogynist and homosocial scheme; women who resemble men are less tainted by Eve's sin than feminine women, and hence merit partnership with men. The end result of the *Spill*'s misogynist argument only allows for men to cohabitate with the asexual Virgin, or presumably with others who are like them—men, perhaps, and masculine women. The only other virtuous women mentioned in the work are dead women, that is, saints and biblical women revered by Roig (15216–69).

Roig arrives at these misogynist conclusions by way of a pilgrimage that is prefaced in the first book by the predictable news that Roig's adolescence was miserable because of his mother's callousness, and that she drove his father crazy and finally to death. He then sets out on a pilgrimage through Catalonia and France, where he attempts to fulfill his objectives as set out in the brief "Consulta" that initiates the *Spill*. Because his final aim is to describe the Virgin One, he must first depict all the other women to whom she is contrasted. To this end, he travels in search of a wife and meets up with a host of evil *medianeras*. This constitutes a journey toward the Virgin's shrine by way of a myriad of counterexperiences with ordinary women along the way. The pilgrimage motif is invoked again in the fourth book, at the same time that Roig concludes that men should be monastics, live among themselves, and marry the Virgin (15479–610).

The pilgrimage motif is significant because of its medieval relation to illness and its association with devotion to the Virgin and other saints. In the *Spill* it suggests that Roig's journey toward the Virgin constitutes an effort at self-healing both for the writer and the reader, as it shows that this attempt is always at the expense of earthly women. The pilgrimage and the *Spill*'s first-person narration from the pilgrim's point of view are crucial strategies in the denigration of women healers, because they exemplify for the pilgrim / reader a journey toward self-healing that the reader never has to undertake physically. By way of negative example, the reader identifies with the *Spill*'s first-person narrator, and will agree with him that earthly women must be avoided because they seek to augment men's pain. Roig tries to show that all women, through their shared nature and their shared quality of mediation, threaten men's well-being even if they are not explicit healers. For this reason, the plethora of earthly women in the *Spill* are crucial to Roig's complicity in restrictions against women healers in late medieval Iberia.

Roig's first pilgrimage generates experiences that in turn generate the stories about his medical training and his first wife. The pilgrimage is constantly referred to with regard to the hardships on the road toward the accomplishment of finding the Virgin. Roig only meets duplicitous women whose mediations kill and harm men such as the married Parisian woman who connives with her deceitful chambermaid (*ffalsa terçera*) to kill her husband (1512–1646). This story leads to another in which Roig recounts the New Year's dinner in which he and his friends had found human body parts in their meat pies: a finger and an ear (1647–1741). The *pastissera* or woman pastry cook and her two daughters regularly cut men into pieces for use in their pies, and Roig explains that when discovered, the three evil women were publicly quartered. The end of this story provides Roig with more opportunities to degrade women, as he proceeds to communicate to the reader the fact that on many occasions, he saw women condemned and hung like branches from trees (1742–57).

The pilgrimage motif manifests what Roig advises: one must learn to identify and elect the Virgin from a gamut of women who resemble her, yet whose outer appearances are duplicitous. Instead of avoiding them, however, Roig constantly puts himself in contact with them in the most seemingly routine or benign situations such as a meal.[15] Because of the constant emphasis on women as deceitful *medianeras*, Roig's sacred pilgrimage or *romería* is, in effect, a meretricious pilgrimage or *ramería* in which the object to be avoided is also the object of desire: Roig desires contact with women because he wants to get married. But, in order to reach the perfect wife, the Virgin, the lily among thorns, he must first find and discard those who are thorns.

Roig's self-placement as a pilgrim in the text is supremely important to the book's autobiographical frame, and to its authority regarding its statements on women. The historicity of the experiences is inconsequential in the book. Rather, Roig's self-placement as a male pilgrim and physician on a *ramería* of healing, in search of a wife and of the Virgin One, metaphorically generates the entire text. The *Spill* is explicitly authorized by Roig's self-identification as a physician at the beginning of the book, and despite the fact that Roig never clearly identifies himself as the book's narrator, the authority of what is recounted is garnered through the work's connection to Roig, the medical professional. The narrator even inserts himself in the work as a medical doctor or examiner when he is called upon to verify the diagnosis of four midwives (3462–94).

This association is further underlined by the narrator's inclusion of his own pain, as evidenced by his breaking into tears when faced with the horrors of a woman's outlandish sin, having supposedly tried to burn a child that was miraculously created from the host that she had taken and put in a box at mass:

> Tan lleig peccat
> no'l puch narrar
> sens fort plorar:
> lo paper mulle
> lo ja scrit sulle
> llacrimejant. (3606–11)

[I cannot even talk about such a nefarious sin without crying hard: I wet the paper with my tears and I stain the writing.]

The inclusion of his own pain or illness is designed to create an analogy with the male reader's pain, and a further parallel between women as agents of the conditions of illness on the pilgrimage, and women in everyday life.

This close, analogous relation between narrator and reader, along with the *Spill*'s autobiographical frame, are clearly reminiscent of the fourteenth-century *Libro de buen amor*, written from the point of view of an ostensible archpriest from Hita named Juan Ruiz.[16] Not coincidentally, the *Lba* also includes Iberian literature's most renowned early *medianera*, Trotaconventos, who travels from town to convent to monastery in order to negotiate amorous and sexual liaisons for the archpriest and other clients. Just as the authority of Jaume Roig as physician is more important than the veracity of the *Spill's* events and the "historical" identity of its narrator, the accuracy of the *Lba*'s events and the "truthful" identity of its narrator are less significant than the book's main objective, which is to invoke the ethical response of the reader.

Despite the evident similarities between the *Spill* and the *Lba*, they mediate the reader and the reader's world in different ways. Both works directly appeal to the reader's involvement with the text, but the *Spill* is akin to a manual of sexual well-being as it tries to instruct the reader on how to live an ordered life, and as it seeks to augment devotion to the Virgin. The *Lba*'s objectives are not so evident—it could be considered a manual on relations with women, but the information it tries to transmit to the reader about those relations is highly doubtful. Rather than direct the reader on the correct path to good love (*buen amor*), the *Lba* confounds the notion of good love and gives it various possible meanings, including as it relates to sacred love or to carnal, profane pleasures.[17] The *Lba* forces the reader's ethical response to questions about love and sex rather than providing her or him with definitive answers like the *Spill*. The *Lba* evidences "a powerful and intimate relationship between book and reader," unlike the *Spill* which requires compelling identification between the male *narrator* and his pain, and the male reader.[18] The fluid, narrating *yo* or "I" of the *Lba* moves from the archpriest to the book (v. 70) to the protagonist don Melón, an evident pseudonym for the archpriest.[19] The *Lba* often resists an authoritative, stable first person narrator while the *Spill* establishes its dominance through its association to the intractable physician and medical examiner, Jaume Roig.

Even when the *Spill*'s narrator changes from the initial centenarian who introduces the work in the preface, to the ostensible Jaume Roig himself, and finally to Solomon in book 3, Roig the author relies on the strategy of the confabulator, the authority figure who disseminates valuable and unequivocal information to the male reader.[20] The "clinical function" that characterizes the *Spill* is not present in the *Lba*, that is, the *Lba* does not clearly attempt to ameliorate men's sexual well-being like the *Spill*.[21] The *Spill* may be viewed as a clinical locus that tries to replicate the encounter between authoritative physician (confabulator) and patient, whereas the *Lba*'s authority is mobile and ever-changing.[22]

Each work accomplishes its goals in highly divergent ways, the *Spill* by way of a univocal series of stories recounted while traveling on a pilgrimage, and the *Lba* through the medieval strategies of reading and interpretation, such as the presentation of contraries and the convention of glossing, which recognized the indeterminacy of signs and meaning.[23] Instead of providing readers with a clearly laid path toward their ultimate goal, as Roig does with the *Spill*, Ruiz offers them a series of oblique and often contradictory statements and episodes whose value readers must decide for themselves. The *Lba*'s worth and meaning are dependent upon readers' identities, and vice versa.[24] The inconsistencies and gaps that characterize the *Lba* are not imitated in the *Spill*. The *Spill* is unequivocal in its rebuke of earthly women, and despite the occasional manly Isabel Pellicer or the rare, dead biblical saint, male readers must avoid them in order to preserve their well-being and the social order.

Even the *medianera* Trotaconventos's value in the *Lba* is left to the reader's determination. At the same time that the archpriest tells readers to avoid the mediations of duplicitous old women, such as in 909c, he also praises Trotaconventos's skills and even mourns her death. Unlike Roig's narrator whose sorrowful tears lament the horrors of women's sin, the pain of Ruiz's narrator is due to the loss of the *medianera* (1520–75). Even if the reader agrees that the *Lba* tries to discourage him or her from imitating the archpriest's adventures with women, Ruiz's plaint attests to the desirousness of the *medianera*'s negotiations.

Trotaconventos even becomes connected to *buen amor* itself on two occasions (932–33, 1331), as she incarnates what the *Lba* represents, the indeterminacy of meaning and interpretation.[25] Since she embodies the duplicitous qualities of an Eve / Mary figure so common in misogynist literature, her value is not determined until the reader decides it. But, Trotaconventos's double presentation in the *Lba* is not intended to conform to the conventions of misogynist literature, but rather, results from the exigencies of medieval manuscript culture, which necessitated the existence of contrary elements and opposing systems of value. Her duplicity conforms to the instability of the book itself, rather than to an evident misogynist strategy.

The requirement of contraries is further emphasized in the *Lba* through the differing intercessors presented in the work. Instead of embarking on a pilgrimage to find abstinence with the idealized Virgin, the *Lba*'s archpriest begins a journey toward the ideal secular intercessor, and thus toward sexual gratification. Ruiz employs several intermediaries, and even hires one man, the messenger Ferrand García (115–22), but none compares to the interventions of Trotaconventos. The praise songs to the Virgin found near the beginning and end of the *Lba* (20–43 and 1635–49) may set that holy *medianera* apart from secular negotiators, but more importantly, they present her as one of a number of possible intercessors to whom one could turn. Ruiz incorporates the Virgin into the *Lba* instead of elevating and distancing her from it like Roig does in the *Spill*.

Ruiz emphasizes the mediating qualities of many of the characters, and in the case of the Virgin, Trotaconventos, and doña Venus, he uses similar concepts to describe them:

By using some of the same terms to describe the Virgin, Doña Venus, and the female go-between, he draws attention to the mediating function all three women perform. The Virgin Mary is "comienço e fin del bien" (1626b). Doña Venus is "comienço e fin d'este viaje" (583d). Trotaconventos is "comienço para el santo pasaje" (912d).[26]

Their like, interceding roles stand out more than their differences, as they have similar functions in varying contexts. Trotaconventos is perhaps the most peculiar of all since the sexual *medianera* paradoxically represents the beginning of a sacred trip or passage, presumably meaning either that she initiates sexual bliss, or that she serves as a negative example toward sacred redemption. The reader must know what to avoid before she or he can choose the truly sacred path. Unlike Ruiz, Roig tries to separate these sacred and earthly *medianeras* in the *Spill*.

Both works rely on the recounting of stories to achieve their different goals. Much in the same way as Ruiz's "journey" toward sexual satisfaction, the pilgrimage motif in the *Spill* generates the stories that generate the book. Yet it is the guiding voice of the confabulator Roig, the pilgrim / doctor, that motivates the entire pilgrimage, as he affirms abject descriptions of a distant past, and of a more immediate one. The *Spill*'s meretricious pilgrimage or *ramería* in order to finally idealize the Virgin depends upon the return by way of a story to an ordinary woman who is herself repeated in every woman whom Roig meets. This division between good intercessors and bad ones is not so evident in the *Lba*, since all of Ruiz's go-betweens appear to be separated not by essential qualities of character or person, but by varying degrees of success in arranging unions between two people, and by the appropriateness of their interventions according to differing contexts.

The *Lba* is replete with stories like the *Spill* is, but their meanings are hardly univocal like those in Roig's work, which constantly repeats and returns to the same story: the one that reveals the evils of women. Since the *Spill* is unequivocal in its interpretation of the value of earthly *medianeras*, it is an effort to stabilize the rendering of these women as evil and dangerous. In fact, it is buttressed by a tradition of medieval stories and fables that establish women as agents of contagion, and it replicates this misogynist belief through its own exemplary stories that demonstrate to male readers that the etiology of their ills lies with women.[27] The vast majority of the *Lba*'s fables and *exempla* do not center on this objective, and instead, seek to evoke the reader's ethical response. Despite the fact that some of these stories point to the evils of women (as Michael Solomon shows with Juan Ruiz's fable of the "Garçon que quería casar con tres mugeres" [The Young Man Who Wanted to Marry Three Women]), their aim is broader and not one-dimensional like it is in the *Spill*.[28]

A final characteristic that differentiates the *Spill* from the *Lba* is its use of the repetition-of-stories tactic. Roig's tales about his adventures with women must be univocal not only to justify the separation of the Virgin from earthly women, but because these stories are intended to connect to a biblical world that prefigured and authorized them. Roig tries to link his immediate, worldly past to a similar nostalgic, ancient biblical past in Solomon's dream-speech in book 3, where Solomon's authoritative, biblical diatribe confirms for the reader in the present what Roig says about his own past, that secular women are diseased and evil. Solomon justifies Roig's discourse by making it seem natural through repetition, as he retells stories that parallel Roig's. Solomon's biblical truths about ordinary women are analogous to Roig's, and Roig's experiences and pain are emblematic of this restated truth. Hence, Roig's pilgrimage in search of the Virgin is an attempt to connect to something out of the ordinary, a female who is not a carrier of the disease of male destruction.

In the end, what Roig finds is his own creation, a shrine to the Virgin that is the book itself, a therapeutic manual for distinguishing the lily among the thorns. What the archpriest finds at the end of his book is the difficulty of finding another satisfying intercessor. Hence, he appeals to the reader to amend his book, add episodes to it, enjoy it, and pass it on to other interested readers (1618–25). Unlike Roig's stylized shrine to the Virgin, Juan Ruiz's *Lba* ends as a kind of elegy to mediation, in which the indeterminate book negotiates the meaning and value that the ethical reader gives it. The reader's ethical choice at the end of the *Spill* is no choice at all, since the lily among the thorns on whom the reader must rely has been identified as the Virgin.

Marriage, Reproduction, and Surgery

One of the most compelling ways in which Roig seeks to reach his goals of assuring the reader's well-being and augmenting devotion to the Virgin is by focusing on women's malevolence in marriage and reproduction. He tries to discourage the reader from associations with earthly women by demonstrating that all women, including midwives, doctors, wives, and even nuns seek to harm men in intimate human relationships. According to the *Spill*, one of the consequences of worldly marriage is death, since marriage results in men's eventual destruction, as in the case of the pastry cook's achievements with meat pies (1647–1741). Roig laments the fact that his first wife kept such substances as medicinal compounds, oils, and powders in a chest under lock and key, suggesting that these secret materials could be used to deceive and ultimately destroy men, and most importantly, husbands (2515–35).[29]

Another repercussion of marriage is emasculation, advanced when the reader is told that Roig recovers his manhood after his divorce from his diseased first wife:

Sa malaltia [his first wife's]
ve[e]nt incurable (3036–37)
....
Com carçeller
pres me tenia;
ma homenia
puys fon quitada
he rescatada
yo reposi. (3136–41)

[Seeing that her illness was incurable . . . She had me shackled as if she were my jailer; I lost my manhood, recovered it, and rested.]

This example is further echoed by Solomon in book 3, when he claims that he too had been emasculated by women (7913–23). Another is infidelity, since women cannot stay faithful to their husbands. Roig cites the case of his first wife, whose disease he diagnoses as incurable, but which he attaches to her malicious intentions to divorce her first husband. Consequently, she is married to two men at the same time (3094–114). The last consequence of marriage is that it forces one to live in abject conditions: Roig's first wife also frequently urinates in bed while sleeping (2376–78).

All of Roig's examples and arguments about the evils of women and marriage are based on the problem of women's agency. Women simply say or do too much, and of their own accord. The imperative to marry the Virgin illustrates Roig's need to protect himself against women's agency and to warn other men about their common enemy. Women are dangerous because they exercise tasks that only the Virgin and her male offspring should perform. His first wife, for instance, never sews or knits, but instead possesses all the instruments necessary for writing, and often displays ink-stained hands from writing a text that she keeps hidden from Roig. She goes into the streets with her friends and frequents Magdalen houses like the *Llonga* but he does not know why. She goes to the baths and dances with her friends, which causes him further consternation (2585–721). This series of descriptions suggests that marriage does not tame women and make them stay at home and carry out traditional tasks. Everything that is absent and unknown—the wife on her forays into the world and her written text—threatens Roig in this episode. The areas that he least controls, such as the invisible writing or his wife's unobservable activities, constitute an ineffability that evades his domination.

Roig focuses on marriage because of its link to inheritance rights and patrimony, its connection to legitimate human reproduction, and its compliance in the establishment of the social order. Marriage constituted the licit social paradigm for the attainment of status, societal stability, and financial and physical protection in the fifteenth century, but as Roig tries to show in the *Spill*, women continually tried to undermine it through their maliciousness toward men. Roig seeks to enhance men's well-being by warning them of women's viciousness in marriage, one of the most powerful institutions of the social order.

Roig's focus on marriage and human generation is intended to counter women's potential conjugal and inheritance privileges at this time. For, unlike what is gathered from conventional notions about women in history—that is, their abject, impoverished place in medieval Iberian society—inheritance benefits sometimes made conjugal agreements legally enticing for both women and men in the medieval period.[30] Wives in the Middle Ages were potentially wealthy and perhaps relatively powerful, given that certain communities such as Cuenca were "highly egalitarian" in the legal division between wife and husband of assets acquired during a marriage.[31] Women's "strong legal background" with respect to inheritance rights must have caused further tension in an increasingly centralized and homosocialized medieval society.[32]

Roig's attack on women in marriage is further related to their corrupt deeds in human reproduction. A large part of the *Spill* is devoted to women's evils as mothers, and as midwives and others who counsel and care for them. This aspect of the text is framed by Roig's never-satisfied desire to have a child, so that he depicts women as always characterized by a pathological need to either avoid childbirth altogether, sabotage it, or take it away from men's control. Because women control the means of human reproduction, that is, they physically produce children, and in the fifteenth century still occupy the position of healer in the birthing chamber, they are presented as incompetent and destructive. The argument against women's reproductive rights is motivated in part by medieval women's ability to inherit and also disinherit property and wealth, reflecting the text's matrilineal discomfort and anxiety.[33] Roig believes that women dominate all facets of reproduction since they have access to information about how babies are born, they understand how to manipulate the hetero-coital act in order to satisfy their desires concerning childbirth, and they constitute knowledgeable healers in the birthing chamber.

Hence, he employs a number of arguments in order to weaken their command over human reproduction. Roig claims that women who want to avoid childbirth abort their own fetuses, which he supports with a story about an ex-lay sister who aborts twin fetuses and later becomes an *alcahueta* or pimp (4121–37; 4191–98). Roig's third wife refuses to breastfeed the child she bears with Roig, so that her baby dies after having been nursed by a series of wet nurses (5202–75). In another argument against women's reproductive rights, Roig considers it heinous that nuns who become pregnant refuse to take responsibility for giving birth and find ways to eliminate the fetus. Their transgression is clearly against the norms of the church, but Roig's disgust is less an issue of altruistic Christian morality than it indicates his concern for the nuns' mobility. They have too much freedom since they traffic themselves and end up impregnated, which his third wife, who was educated in a convent, relates to him in a lengthy, painful speech (5330–6315). She tells him that when nuns are pregnant, they play a little game called "Who's the Father?," thus trivializing the contradiction between their vows and their behavior, and thus belittling their irresponsibility. The majority of them prefer to dry out cruelly their breasts in order to avoid caring for their children. These "deplorable" religious women directly contrast the Virgin, whose nutritious milk in several of Alfonso X's *Cantigas* is used to heal sinners.[34] Roig bemoans the fact that mundane women control their breast milk in order to fulfill their own destructive desires against babies and men.

Women's evil command of the realm of childbirth and reproduction is also criticized with regard to their imposition of unsolicited desire to birth babies. Women's sexuality and reproduction become intertwined in a passage in the dream sequence in book 3, where

Solomon is perplexed by how women who are born without a vaginal opening acquire the knowledge about how to give birth (8658–79):

> Be se n'[h]i ha
> de closes nades
> o no passades;
> vergens de dit,
> no de sperit;
> vergens de fet,
> mas contra dret
> dites donzellas:
> ab coçquelles
> ho no se com
> (8658–67)

[I know that there are women who are born closed or unperforated; virgins by name but not by spirit; virgins by act, but called damsels against all right, because through foreplay or I am not sure how]

These women are virgins only by name, not by spirit, because perhaps through foreplay involving tickling they become impregnated despite their physical quality that would otherwise prohibit it. Solomon is less concerned about women's loss of honorable virginity than he is about their apparent potential to manipulate their bodies in such a way as to satisfy their own selfish sexual or reproductive desires. Solomon's anxiety suggests that the consequences could be destructive for men, and so he follows up this warning by justifying invasive measures to open the vagina at birth:

> mas no sens hom
> ni sens plaer,
> ffills saben fer;
> ab natural
> o manual
> cert instrument,
> fforçadament
> se han obrir
> ans del parir:
> les mes ne moren,
> com se desfloren,
> les nades closes. (8668–79)

[but not without men or pleasure they know how to make offspring; by natural methods or with a certain manual instrument they have to be forcibly opened to give birth; hence, the majority of occluded women die when they are deflowered.]

Solomon attempts to discursively control the threat of women's agency with this theory of rather violent manual aid in childbirth, followed by the threat of death upon these women's initial coital experience. Roig also implicitly counteracts the threat of women's sexual desire and reproductive control by warning them that intercourse causes their deaths. Both men imply that coitus is a threatening and dangerous act for "closed" women.

Roig's tirade against women's reproductive domination includes attacks against a variety of women healers. His second wife is unable to become impregnated and consults a *metgessa* or woman doctor whom Roig claims had contaminated all of Aragon, from Rosellón to Valencia (4534–601). The doctor diagnoses Roig's semen as the cause of his wife's difficulties and as therapy offers the wife the use of her laboratory of virile young men as a guarantee of impregnation. But, since the *madrina* (Roig changes the doctor's name to *madrina*, or midwife) practices bad medicine, his wife decides not to pursue the healer's services and so divulges her diagnosis and therapy to Roig. He tells the governor of Valencia, Boyl, and then his successor Rabaça, who decides to have the woman secretly hanged in order to avoid a scandal against Roig.

The woman healer proves perilous for Roig because of her ability "to disease," which can be understood in two ways: as the ability to transfer (infect) illness to another person, and as the capacity to name and diagnose disease, its etiology, and its makeup.[35] Roig claims that women take advantage of healing and diseasing for their own selfish benefit. His objection to the doctor's therapeutic laboratory or stable of male concubines is based on her ability to designate him as the locus of disease, that is, as the carrier of semen insufficiency. Upon identifying him as ineffective, she renders him insignificant and unnecessary since she capably provides a remedy outside the accepted domain of marital coitus. Roig then eradicates her from the text in the same way that she marginalizes him from reproductive coitus and obstetrics, by having someone else mediate the deed: Rabaça in Roig's case, and Roig's wife in the doctor's.

Roig's intolerance of "incompetent" women healers is further illustrated in book 2 where he describes the perpetual pregnancy of a woman from Zaragoza. Having been thrown in jail by her husband who has her arrested on charges of adultery, she is sentenced to death. She postpones her execution for more than three years by repeatedly becoming pregnant, apparently by other prisoners. Roig says that she uses her perpetual pregnancy for her own benefit, since authorities would not kill a pregnant woman (3426–99). One day four midwives examine her and do not find her pregnant. Jaume Roig the physician examines her next, and his prognosis of course reveals the truth, that she is indeed pregnant. But since the midwives' observations are believed over his, the woman dies. Roig creates a stunning connection of cause and effect between the healers' "erroneous" prognosis and the woman's death, attesting to the fact that the examination of the lowly, nonmale, nonuniversity-trained midwives was considered more credible than his. He laments the unnecessary deaths of the woman and her unborn "child," and goes on to say that she could have birthed many more babies had she only lived.

Actually, Roig laments the death of a birthing machine, the loss of a generator of a product in demand, children. The value of the woman's life in itself is secondary to her worth as a procreator and to the value of children in the *Spill*. Another part of the grieving in this episode is based on the physician's lack of control of women's bodies, specifically here in relation to obstetrics. Roig would have saved the lives of the woman and child if his authoritative physician's voice had been respected over the women's. But, since women healers direct the fate of women patients in obstetrical matters, the results are only disastrous.

The invective against women in relation to biological processes of reproduction may seem odd, since women's biology constitutes one of the elements that has come to define the stable and essentializing definition of "woman." But women's most traditional and common functions in society are what present the greatest health risks in the *Spill*. It is precisely because women were so active in medieval healing and exercised a relative amount of self-determination over their practices that they are attacked by Roig, the physician and medical examiner. In her study of late medieval midwifery in the Low Countries, Myriam Greilsammer argues that the decline of midwifery was due to the deliberate action of church and state, and not to "the alleged primitiveness of midwives." The professionalization of medicine reduced the role of midwives to that of medical auxiliaries, stripping them of their previous responsibilities and authority. The many episodes in the *Spill* that depict women's continued participation in the birthing chamber and in obstetrical matters as hazardous to society's well-being portend the transformation of midwives in the seventeenth and eighteenth centuries into "ignorant 'matrons.' "[36]

Other traditional women's occupations, such as those of seamstresses and dressmakers, further threaten men's attempted hegemony over surgical matters in the *Spill*, and even more overtly in *La Celestina*. Women's daily tasks in the clothing professions are analogous to surgical duties such as the use of needle and thread, cutting things off, and opening, closing, and extracting things. The lexicon of tailoring and surgery is further appropriated by Roig and given a common scatological twist in order to degrade women's physiology and his wife's lack of eroticism. While discussing the defects of his fortyish wife, Roig employs sewing terms like *punta* (corner) and *agulla* (needle) to describe her inability to birth children and how disagreeable she is to sleep with:

ni malaltia
no la retia
parir inabil;
mas era llabil,
punta corrible,
ab mi terrible
he desamable,
inacordable
per al conçebre.
    Per lo pesebre
temptant entrar
he sens desgrat
ffos l'acostar. (4486–95)

[neither did she have a disease that made her unable to give birth; rather, she was skilled in fault-finding, terrible and opposed to me; she was disagreeable for acts of conception: it was tempting to enter the bedroom, but sleeping with her was so unpleasant.]

Roig and his wife were unable to procreate because his wife harbored strong feelings against him. Their coital encounters were utterly displeasing, and if they occurred at all, they produced no offspring.

Roig's disparaging of women as obstetrical patients and practitioners is strategically linked to this kind of lexicon, which appears periodically throughout the *Spill*.[37] Due to women's healing activities in the birthing chamber and as illicit surgeons, connections between occupational meanings and scatological ones malign women healers who exercised surgical procedures. Iberian midwives at this time were expected to know how to perform caesarean sections, and surgeons were called in only when the dead fetus had to be removed in pieces, or when there were gynecological problems "of a surgical nature."[38] Physicians intervened only in cases of fever or other illness during the pregnancy, birth, or postpartum care. Thus, women's role in the birthing chamber was active and required skill and knowledge in a variety of areas such as female anatomy and surgery. The more or less unencumbered practice of midwifery became increasingly scrutinized with the installation of the Real Protomedicato and the designation of the male physician as the supervisor of midwives in most kingdoms of the peninsula.[39] Roig's invective against women healers in areas of reproduction must be read in the context of these increased efforts to organize and license differing practitioners of medicine. Women's questionable autonomy in this area until around the middle of the fifteenth century undergirds Roig's anxiety about women midwives, especially in light of the rise of surgery as an organized craft and learned occupation after around 1300 on.[40] Many physicians throughout Europe sought to distance themselves from what they viewed as unlearned surgeons. Roig seems to ignore the figure of the surgeon altogether, and instead seeks to supplant women's work in the birthing chamber with the omnipotent figure of the male physician.

The male physician, in fact, is the only explicit alternative offered in the *Spill* to solve the problem of incompetent obstetrical women healers. Despite the fact that healing alternatives appear throughout the text, such as calling on God the Doctor (10918–43, 12104–28), summoning a confessor such as Vicente Ferrer to purge women of the devil (5790–99), and employing the Great Virgin Intercessor, Ave (11940–63), Roig insists on the male physician's control of reproduction. According to the orthoscopic surgery that he himself performs on the adulterous woman discussed above, he deems himself the only person who can reveal the truth about pregnancy and the sole individual able to expose the incompetence of the deceitful midwives. The physician must do more than simply supervise all specialized surgical and midwife tasks such as examining the pregnant woman, monitoring the child's birth, performing any surgical maneuvers, and providing postpartum care: he must clearly dominate them.

At issue in this command of reproduction is the gender-specific domination of healing techniques and technologies. Since Roig perceives them to be in the hands of women, men become simple devices to be manipulated like the surrogate inseminators in the doctor's genetics laboratory cited above. The *metgessa*'s reproductive techniques in that episode empower motherhood over fatherhood, since women in this case determine lines of inheritance. The imperative to marry for the sake of procreation is rendered null since a woman can be impregnated by one of the doctor's servants. Instead of the modern-day development by male scientists of the necessary scientific technology to realize surrogate motherhood, women in the *Spill* are the "scientists," healers, fertility brokers, and agents who direct and determine the terms of human reproduction.[41] Roig wants that command and the molding of what constitutes motherhood and fatherhood to lie within the exclusive powers of the licensed male physician. Roig does not abdicate women's control over the self, the body, and reproduction; he encourages men to seize it from them.

The Song of Roig

In the *Spill*'s third book, King Solomon approaches Roig in a dream and spends almost half the book convincing him of what he already believes: that ordinary women destroy men. He illustrates the belief with the biblical story of Sara, daughter of Rachel, who married seven men and strangled each one on their wedding night (6782–804). The appropriation of Solomon as narrator is not a coincidental choice. The son of David, he was considered one of the most sagacious men in the Bible and was granted a wise and discerning mind by God (who, not surprisingly, came to Solomon in a dream [1 Kings 3:5–14]) because the young king desired it above material possessions. Solomon's wise discourse in the *Spill* confirms Roig's statements about women, and both stand in an analogous relationship to one another. Solomon's discourse parallels Roig's, making book 3 a kind of "Song of Roig," in an allusion to Solomon's hypothetical narration of the biblical "Song of Songs." Solomon's wisdom serves as a model for Roig's ostensible knowledge, and his methods of royal, social judgment function paradigmatically for procedures of Valencian social control. Roig's ultimate and unspoken goal, which also corresponds to the implicit objective of fifteenth- and sixteenth-century medical licensing, is the control and regulation of healing and of other societal areas, all at women's expense.

Solomon's authoritative claims about the evils of women are legitimated by his seemingly reasonable judgments about them in the Bible. For instance, in 1 Kings 3:15–28, he ordered that a baby be cut in half in order to divide it between two mothers, both of whom claimed it as their own. When one woman agreed by saying that neither then would have the whole baby, while the true mother quickly argued for the other woman to have the child, Solomon wisely decided that the second woman was the real mother since she placed the child's life above her selfish desires. Solomon was likely chosen for the role of narrator in the *Spill* because of biblical accounts asserting his decision-making expertise, especially in light of this story, which deals with issues of motherhood, infanticide, and the ownership of children. The reader would have read Solomon's prowess at conflict-resolution both in the Bible and the *Spill* as analogous to Roig's.

Solomon's dream-speech provides the forum from which to pontificate on the advantages of social control, always to women's disadvantage and disempowerment. Solomon even declares them the cause of the destruction of many a city throughout history (7118–28), a common medieval trope. The control of women in Valencia implies the salvation of the city from threats of disease and other causes of social chaos. Book 3 emphasizes judicial means, and the control of the interpretation of history and the Bible as ways to edify Valencia's foundations and thus gain social domination. It insists on the practical application of a legal apparatus as part of the definition of an edified Valencia. When Solomon addresses Roig's desire to marry in order to have male inheritors, he recounts what happens to adulterous wives in the various regions of the peninsula: according to ancient law, they should be stoned to death; in Castile they should be decapitated, and in Aragon hanged (6867–95). But according to the statute pertaining to Valencia, the woman adulterer only has to pay a monetary sanction. Hence, Valencia's legal codes are too lax, especially when compared to the ostensibly just sentences of the other regions, and they must be fortified in order to achieve stricter control over women adulterers.

Solomon further interprets Valencia's history as clearly heroic and resistant to the plethora of invading peoples who populated parts of the peninsula. When push came to shove, Valencia always maintained a sense of pride in its essential, original identity. It never gave in and paid tribute to the invading Romans, nor did it renounce its legal rights under the Visigothic domination (7156–85). Much like the ordering of history in the Castilian chronicles,

Solomon refers to the same foundational stories repeated there and elsewhere such as the blaming of Cava, Count Julian's daughter, for the peninsula's fall to the Arabs (7198–213). Biblical history and interpretation are also crucial here because they establish the bases on which Roig builds his book, Solomon constructs his dream-speech, and Valencia grasps its present, disruptive social plight. By way of the Bible, Solomon sets out the basis for the whole of Roig's book, which is the contrast of Eve and Mary (10295–332). Unlike Roig's story that focuses on the evils of ordinary women and in which the Virgin rarely appears, Solomon finally edifies her presence in book 3 in order to justify and legitimate Roig's intentions as set out in the "Consulta." Solomon returns to the very beginning of biblical time in order to explain Eve's creation from Adam's rib, and reverts to the beginnings of women's monstrousness as manifested in Eve and Eden.

The Eva / Ave opposition as set out in book 3 emphasizes the main differentiating characteristic between the two female figures to be their birthing production. Men derive from the Virgin and women from Eve. The Virgin's attributes entail the following: she is an ideal female healer because she is not human like mortal women; she never ages; she is the only good spouse; she does not give birth to daughters, only to one chaste son, as opposed to every mortal woman who constitute the horrific "daughters of Eve." Earthly women on the other hand, as derived from Eve, possess evils that only equal the excessive exemplarity of Roig-Solomon's discourse. Their evils only lead to the destruction of men. They turn ordinary routine tasks into evil destructive mediations, like baking, sex, and sewing. They do not follow men's directives, like those of doctors, and so must be roped in and dealt with forcibly. The Eva / Ave contrast constitutes the basis from which all history proceeds, since as the two females physically have generated human beings, so have they generated cities, events, governments, language, and everything else.

The foundations of the city of Valencia, that is, the legal, historical, and biblical means that give way to and support everything that Roig and Solomon claim about Eva and Ave as the city's respective destroyer and savior, further allow for Solomon's lengthy sermon on the ways to control all kinds of women—mothers, wives, magdalens, Beguines, lay sisters, abbesses, pastry cooks, market saleswomen, and healers—in places such as monasteries, jails, hospitals, and private homes. The two narrators are both strongly concerned about women's freedom of movement and direction in all facets of life, including an ostensibly spiritual one. The *Spill* rails against women's spiritual locales, such as Magdalen houses and convents. Roig seems to have a particular hatred for Beguines and lay sisters, who did not lead a cloistered existence in fifteenth- and sixteenth-century Iberia. They enjoyed freedom of movement in cities and towns while also having taken vows to uphold Catholic doctrine and its form of life. But according to Roig-Solomon, they only act to the contrary.

The nun's speech near the end of book 2, which delineates the reasons for Roig-Solomon's antagonism, is supposed to add a great deal of authenticity to the men's claims about the evils of convents and their inhabitants (5346–6306). The nun says that the women there turn their noses at the order. The main cause of anxiety, however, stems from the fact that they spend too much time together. The older women, such as the abbess, train the younger ones to be as rebellious and self-willed as they are. New women are indoctrinated into conventual life by learning to give the evil eye and to practice witchcraft. They learn that abortion and feigned virginity are not sinful, implying that these women mock their vows by acting like virginal whores or whoring virgins. Roig is proposing a virtual genetic theory of gynelineal transmission of behavior in which women inherit their insubordinate behavior from other women. The fact that men are not agents in a convent setting causes him great consternation, especially since women manage everything there, including biological processes. Roig's message to the reader is that if men controlled women's education, reproduction, desire, sex, and everything else, they could biologically and physiologically determine women's place in the world. But, the Eve / Mary contrast depends upon the exclusive Eve-women relation and the Mary-men one, so that deviant, duplicitous women have to exist in order to parallel the edification of the Virgin. Roig's point in this founding of the city is that women have to be isolated in their exclusive spaces and at the same time controlled there.

The Magdalen houses referred to at various times in the *Spill* (e.g., 2611, 7316) correspond to fifteenth- and sixteenth-century attempts to formulate moral order in many Iberian cities by way of the correction of women prostitutes in Magdalen houses and convents.[42] To this end, the profession of urban prostitution underwent a series of alterations intended to ensure stronger municipal control over its management and daily transactions. For instance, brothels became municipally controlled and their managers selected to the detriment of women adminstrators.[43] In fourteenth-century ordinances from Seville, public brothels were largely accepted as a "necessary evil" that accommodated women "who do not want to be good and chaste and want to sell their bodies." The ordinances stated that women could be controlled better there than in the "monasteries of evil women, who use their bodies for evil in the sin of lust, and who have a director, in the manner of an abbess" and who "carry out their lusts and evils, more covertly than the public brothels."[44] The urgency clearly expressed in documents by men to reform public brothels and convert prostitutes coincided with the desire to reform women's convents and monasteries. In the *Spill*, Roig recounts the story of how a count came to build a monastery where "wayward women" could do penance, on account of the rebellious life that his wife, the countess, had led:

> Lo marit comte
> donà per comte
> son exovar,
> he feu obrar
> lo monastir
> per sostenir
> alli tancades
> dones errades,
> d'incontinençia
> ffent penitençia. (7373–82)

[The consort count donated the trousseau for her sake, and ordered the construction of the monastery, which was intended to enclose wayward women to do penitence for their scandalous living.]

Barring marriage, convents were the only places in which prostitutes could be enclosed. Roig points out the clear connection between the money of nobles and the construction of particular structures that responded to the need to enclose and supervise unmarried, "wandering" women.

It is not surprising that Roig's most potent invective against religious women in the *Spill* is directed at Beguines and lay sisters, both of whom constituted two of the least-monitored religious groups for women.[45] Their ease of movement along with the separatist independence of the Beguines helps to fuel Roig's diatribe against all women. His second wife is an ex-lay sister who, after fleeing Roig and returning to her old way of life at a Beguinage, ends up withering away as a go-between who is later punished with lashings and eventually exile: "Son beguinatge, / he beatatge / en mal finaren

/ he s'espletaren / . . . / ffon alcavota. / . . . / ffon acusada; / sentençiada, / be l'açotaren / he bandejaren" (4191–204) [Her freedom (*beguinatge*) and wandering ways (*beatatge*) ended up miserably withering away; . . . she became a go-between . . . she was accused and convicted; they whipped her well and exiled her]. In book 3, after going on incessantly about a veritable life of Christ, Solomon suddenly pauses to discuss how much he despises the Beguines (14494–620). He says that they constitute a plague that moves around freely, but that their most significant transgression or form of "rebellion" is their speech—they ask too many daring questions:

de Deu demana,
puys d'ell emana,
tant virtual
huniversal
he fructuosa,
tan graçiosa
ffont d'aygua viva,
com no's diriva
a tots los vius
per eguals rius,
car molts no'n prenen,
he los que'n tenen,
no per egual (14519–31)

[How is it that God, from whom emanates such a virtual and universal fountain of life, fruitful and full of grace, does not direct such grace to all the living by the same river, since it does not reach many of them, and those who do obtain it do not achieve it in the same way?].

In other words, they wrongly seek out answers to the disparity between earthly inequalities and God's supposed infinite wealth and abundance. Solomon tells them to obey God's orders and to remain silent.

Efforts to control women's speech constitute one of the most common medieval strategies to contain them, and Solomon's dream-speech is no different. In general, the *Spill* is an attempt not only to demonstrate women's evils as daughters of Eve, but also to show that their destructive tendencies are spawned by their wicked, self-generating speech. Roig-Solomon points this out by referring to Eve as a prattler with a goat's tail for a tongue (10333–35; 10414), a popular tale also repeated in Francesc Eiximenis's late-fourteenth-century fable, "De com fou creada llengua a la fembra i què se'n seguí" [How Women's Speech Was Created, and What Followed from It].[46] The metaphor indicates that women's speech and tongue derive from animals, and that they are bestial since the tongue wags aimlessly and unceasingly like a goat's tail. A woman's tongue and speech never stand still or idle. The goat's tail as a prosthetic device implies that it can be removed as easily as it was attached. A woman's tongue and speech are unstable and mutable—remove the tail-tongue device, and she will not be able to speak. The control of her discourse constitutes an attempt to control how she functions in the world, and how she is regarded and dealt with by others. Efforts to silence her are attempts to determine how she will be treated in the world: she will be at best invisible and at worst a reticent object to be manipulated and violated.

The control of women's discourse in the *Spill* is synonymous with determining how they are read. The control of women's desire and agency in the text is as important as controlling the reader's desire for women. Earthly women are rendered utterly repulsive in order to dissuade the reader from consorting with them as mothers, lovers, healers, and workers.

Yet, women also represent an important target of social undesirability because they were increasingly identified as supposed agents of disease. The widespread presence of love-related disease in this period was progressively linked to women's etiologic culpability. Women's speech and human essence were pathologized in order to characterize them as a dangerous source of disease. The third part of Solomon's sermon opens with a list of afflictions suffered by Roig the reader. One of them may be *amor hereos*, the mental, psychological disease of lovesickness that supposedly afflicted a great many nobles at the time: "tens, hereos, / bestial furia / de gran luxuria" (11992–94) [you suffer from lovesickness, a bestial fury caused by great lust]. Its treatment was psychological distraction to take the lover's mind away from thoughts of the beloved. This is exactly the *Spill*'s homosocializing effort; that is, to turn men's thoughts and desires away from ordinary women and toward the Virgin. In order to effect this diversion, earthly women are categorically maligned.

Women healers bear the brunt of an enormous amount of castigation throughout the book; Solomon in book 3 spares them nothing. As women, they constitute the etiology of all disease, essentially causing the pain and illness of the patient they are trying to treat (see 6771–829). Instead of ameliorating the conditions of illness, the mediations of women healers only intensify them, and contact with all other kinds of women will have the same effect. But, women healers also hold the power to pathologize desire, that is, to determine certain symptoms or signs as related to a particular disease. Roig seeks to distract men's attention from earthly women, but the

Spill implies that women will only seek contact with men because they want to disease and destroy them. Just as Roig can point to women as the cause of disease, women healers could point to men as "diseased" subverters of their traditional roles. Women healers must be discredited because, as is made evident by Roig's own practice, the power to name disease and its etiology has forceful implications for entire societies and individual groups of people.

One of Roig's most effective strategies against women in general is to suggest that women's gender and healing go hand in hand. His attack is not exclusively directed at midwives nor at other women who would have worked in birthing chambers. Many of Roig-Solomon's denunciations are directed toward women who are not healers but still carry out the same evil doings based on their positions as wives or girlfriends in domestic settings. Sick men who seek women's remedies and company will make a quick trip from the bed to the grave (8079–97). Women never listen to doctors, so they only follow nonmedical or domestic methods of therapy in order to ultimately kill their husbands, an argument that plays into the efforts of learned professionals such as Roig who were trying to undermine domestic methods by associating them with superstition or witchcraft (7998–8105).

According to Roig-Solomon, no remedy exists for women's diseased plight. Roig the medical doctor says in book two that he is able to cure his wife of everything but her ferocity (4654–65). Solomon claims that there is no cure for women and that their sin makes them all equal (6979–89). Roig's strictest remedy for the general problem of women, particularly women healers, is to kill them by hanging. The public spectacle of their deaths exemplifies the results of civil disobedience, which for women is considered an essential, unavoidable quality. But, how can one disobey when her behavior is categorically predetermined the way it is in the *Spill*? If women are essentially diseased, how can they possibly not disease; and hence, are they not in some ways relieved of responsibility for their ostensibly wicked actions? How does a writer such as Roig justify the disparity between the idea of obedience / disobedience and the inevitable behavior of women? He asserts himself as the diseaser, namely, the individual authorized to identify other people as the carriers of the origins of disease. He pathologizes women and has them killed discursively in his meretricious pilgrimage for violating a social order that Roig himself defines. The staging of punishment is the performance of social order; Roig sublimates potential societal conflict, such as women's resistance to the biased professionalization of medicine, by simply negating it.[47] To affirm the women's deaths is synonymous with negating their lives and thus their potential to undermine the social organization laid out by men. Roig's prescribed punishment is as mobile as he is on the meretricious pilgrimages, so that it is transportable from place to place on the peninsula. It is also as mobile as ordinary women are described as being, unlike the stable Virgin.

Roig's prescribed, mobile punishment of hanging has exemplary significance for the reader, which is fortified by its striking resemblance to a part from the *muger* (woman) entry in Covarrubias's early-seventeenth-century dictionary, *Tesoro de la lengua castellana*: "Vio Diógenes pendientes infamemente de un olivo a unas que la justicia había castigado con aquel suplicio y dijo: ¡Ojalá todos los árboles del mundo llevaran este fruto!: 'Utinam et caeterae arbores similem ferrent fructum!'" [Diogenes saw some women whom the justice system had punished by execution hanging terrifyingly from an olive tree. He said, 'If only every tree in the world bore this kind of fruit!'].[48] Just as these hanged ordinary women are figured as the public example of the "fruits" of disobedience in Diogenes's eyes, so are they illustrated in the *Spill* as the transgressors of official, Roigian rule. In contrast, the Virgin in the *Spill* is figured from the outset as a beautiful lily.

One of the sermons in Castilian by the Valencian preacher Vicente Ferrer sheds light on the weighty significance of women's relation to fruit and trees, and their further connection to the foundation of cities. While Roig refrains for the most part from referring to particular sermons, Ferrer represents a pillar of Church and confessional authority throughout the *Spill*. He delivered the misnamed "Sermón de la *Ave María*, fecho en Santa María de Nieva" [Sermon on the Virgin Mary, given in Santa María de Nieva] at Toledo in 1411.[49] After laying out Mary's edification as consisting of three hierarchies or walls inhabited first by those who love one another with humility, second by chaste individuals, and finally by saintly persons who participate solely in God's service, Ferrer equates her edification with that of the holy city of Jerusalem: "E en esta manera la Virgen santa María fue edificada por tres muros como Iherusalem, que son estas tres virtudes [humilidat cordial, virginitat personal, limpieza de placeres carnales]" (368) [And in this way the Virgin Mary was edified by three hierarchies or levels just like Jerusalem, which are the three virtues (humility, individual virginity, and cleanliness from carnal pleasures)]. He then glosses Psalms 122:3, and describes what David, Solomon's father, said to the Virgin: "'Bienaventurada eres tú, Iherusalem, que eres edificada assí como çiudat, la partiçipaçión de la qual es en ty mesma'" (368)

[Oh, how lucky you are, Jerusalem, to be edified as a city, whose participation is within yourself]. The stunning analogy between the building or construction of the Virgin and the holy Christian city, as two areas or places for the participation of pious, chaste individuals, demonstrates their supposed similitude through their self-containment. Jerusalem's feminization suggests that urban sites take on conventional female qualities such as reproductive processes, and accessibility by way of openings such as paths into the city or orifices in the body. Cities may be described in the same terms that Page DuBois uses to describe women's bodies, as "spaces of reproductive labor."[50] Cities reproduce institutions and women generate children, both of which may be handled and manipulated by authorities who want to control or influence them. Both Ferrer and Roig mold their written material about the Virgin so that their words will have therapeutic effects.[51]

Like David's analogy in Psalms, the foundational attempts in book 3 of the *Spill*—to align Valencia's origins with an almost messianic biblical determinacy and then to create the parallel between the Virgin and the Aragonian city—are efforts at containment and regulation. At the same time that women and cities are figured as unfixed and self-determined throughout the *Spill*, they are also shown by Ferrer-David and Roig-Solomon to be controllable and able to be totalized and transfixed. If regulated by the authority of these men, the generation of people and materials by women and cities will not produce the inevitable line of abject, destructive offspring and materials previously manufactured. Like so much of the earlier medieval Marian production, such as Alfonso X's *Cantigas* and Gonzalo de Berceo's *Milagros*, the monotonous repetition of the same praises to the Virgin will always produce the same, repetitive results. Ferrer gives the reader (listener) six phrases to present to the Virgin in order to raise oneself to her in prayer: "E por quanto nosotros devemos sobir a la Virgen María por devota oración, por esso dize el thema: '*Ecce ascendimus Iherosolimam.*' Dize: 'Catad, que agora nós sobimos a Iherusalem;' es a saber, a la Virgen santa María orando" (368) [And inasmuch as we must rise up to the Virgin Mary for devout prayer, for that reason the phrase says: '*Ecce ascendimus Iherosolimam.*' This means: 'Look, now we are going up to Jerusalem' in order to find the sacred Virgin Mary praying]. Ferrer repeats the Latin line throughout the sermon after the explanation of each of the six *cláusolas* or phrases (368 and passim). Praising the Virgin is equivalent to praising the city; the stability of the praiser's discourse is synonymous with the fixed results from the Virgin-city.

2: EVA/AVE
81

Ferrer's gloss of the devotee's fifth phrase, "*Et benedictus fructus ventris tuy Ihesus*" (375) [And blessed is Jesus, fruit from your womb], is inextricably tied to trees, fruit, healing, and the Virgin. The preacher asks a rhetorical question about the existence of a tree that would bear fruit to heal every sickness and pain. If such a tree existed, Ferrer believes that everyone would say: "¡O bendicha sea tal árbor, e bendycho sea el fructo della!" (375) [Oh, blessed be such a tree, and blessed be her fruit!]. He goes on the explain that the "virginal tree" is truly the Virgin Mary, who bore the most marvelous fruit to cure all sickness, her son Jesus Christ. He tells his audience that when any one of them has an illness, they ought to go to the Virgin and devotedly *take her fruit from her*. The individual should say Jesus's name while devotedly making the sign of the cross and thinking about Christ's passion. In this way, she or he will be cured. Ferrer encourages his audience to teach this healing technique to their children, who, since they are younger and have committed fewer sins, will receive more virtue from the fruit. He finishes his lesson with a gloss of Romans 6:22 that instructs the individual to *take* the fruit that is Christ, who will cure body and soul. Ferrer finally closes where he started, with his own praise to the Virgin-tree: "Señora Virgen María, bendicho es el fructo del vuestro vientre, que es Ihesú Christo" (375) [Sacred Virgin Mary, blessed is the fruit from your womb, which is Jesus Christ].

The passage reinforces exactly what Roig is trying to do in the *Spill,* and can only be understood in contrast to Eve and the sinful fruit from the tree in the Garden of Eden. Eve's offspring are generated from her relations with the devil, and Mary's offspring-fruit from her direct contact with God. While Eve's fruit (women) intensifies the conditions of illness, Mary's fruit (Jesus and all men) cures all infirmities. The opposition is also significant because of the issue current at the time regarding parental or reproductive rights over children. Ferrer encourages his audience to violate the Virgin's integrity by taking her son, unlike the ordinary women in fifteenth-century society who would have gained financial and economic benefit from giving birth to and rearing children.[52] In reading the passage analogously with secular women, the Virgin's willingness to abdicate possession of and control over her son stands in stark opposition to women in secular society who would have sought to retain the rights to raise their children. Jesus's unequivocal ability to heal stands in clear contrast to the female offspring of Roig's characters, such as the daughters of the pastry cook in book 2 who collude with their mother in order to destroy men. The Virgin is a pure, chaste mother who gladly gives up her son for the sake of the health and welfare of Christian individuals.[53] Unlike ordinary women, she never claims ownership of her child. Not only does this image work against the mediations of earthly women healers, since the Virgin and her offspring (men) are presented as the only capable healers of body and soul, but it works against the rights of ordinary women to privately determine the fate of their children. It combats matrilineal inheritance rights, and mothers' rights and agency after childbirth.

Ferrer's sermon seeks to achieve the same goal as Roig's, the effort toward the naturalization of the Eva / Ave contrast in order to ultimately justify the imposition of legal regulations for the sake of urban establishment and social order. Both men deal with particular images that, by way of the analogous tendency of the reader, have potentially significant ramifications for mortal human beings. Roig and Ferrer promote images of motherhood for the clear benefit of male citizens; mothers are only useful to society when they produce men and when men control all facets of their reproductive processes. The fruit borne by the Virgin is only salutary and good insofar as it stands in opposition to the Edenic tree of knowledge, and to Diogenes's hanging fruit of the olive trees, the scores of nameless healers, *alcahuetas*, and other *medianeras* encountered by Roig-Solomon on his journey toward the Virgin.

This required contrastive distance between the Virgin and ordinary women is crucial for Roig's idea of men's well-being, for at the same time that it allows Roig to discredit earthly women, it also permits him to exalt the Virgin as superior to Eve's daughters. While ordinary women's mediations parallel the Virgin's in the *Spill*, they cannot possibly hope to meet and replicate them. As the next chapter demonstrates, this discursive strategy by authors complicit with the ideology of the male physician will change in nature with the approach of the sixteenth century.

The fifteenth-century *Spill* drove a wedge between women healers and the male physician. It aligned the Virgin and her son, the male physician, and opposed them to secular women healers who were derived from Eve. It relied on this theory of genealogy in order to demonstrate women's evil disruptive nature, and to illustrate their participation in individual and social breakdown. Women healers such as doctors and midwives were deprecated at every turn in the *Spill*, as their Evian origin only portended disastrous outcomes in their efforts to heal and care for others. Roig carried this characterization one step further and showed that women of all kinds threatened well-being and good living. All earthly women were linked by mediation and their Evian heritage, so that women, "antihealth," and "antihealing" became synonymous in the *Spill*. Roig had to maintain women's distance from the Virgin because their mediations were antithetical to hers, and because he attempted to intensify Marian devotion.

The *Spill* illustrated the tremendous gap between the Virgin and women healers in order to dissuade readers from seeking the services of ordinary women healers. This contrastive strategy between the Virgin and all other women changes dramatically in the later *La Celestina*. Fernando de Rojas presents the Eve / Mary relationship in a very different light from Roig. Instead of contrasting the Virgin like two equal weights that balance a scale, Celestina tries to become the Virgin incarnate. She attempts to do what was expected of women at this time, that is, to emulate the work and mediations of the Virgin. Yet since she cannot possibly imitate those interventions, and because her horizontal distance from the Virgin cannot be maintained the way it was in the *Spill*, Celestina and her mediations must be eradicated.

3
Eva and Not Ave: Marginalization and the Palimpsest Principle in Fernando de Rojas's *La Celestina*

The highly acclaimed *Tragicomedia de Calisto y Melibea* (*La Celestina*, 1499), attributed to Fernando de Rojas, continues to receive some of the most prodigious critical outpourings of any work related to Hispanic cultural studies. Regaled for its formal ingenuity and unique content, *La Celestina* constitutes the first text of its kind to specifically focus on the movements and work of the earthly *medianera*.[1] It spawned and influenced a variety of sixteenth- and seventeenth-century texts, such as Francisco Delicado's *La Lozana andaluza* (Venice 1528), Feliciano de Silva's *Segunda Celestina* (1530), and Alonso J. de Salas Barbadillo's *La hija de Celestina* (Zaragoza 1612).

La Celestina's extensive, sixteenth-century influence and notoriety coincide with one of the most pivotal periods for the professionalization of medicine. Rojas is likely to have been familiar with the professionalization of medicine since he studied at the University of Salamanca at about the time the medical faculty was established there in the late fifteenth century. His studies in Salamanca also coincided with the activities of physicians and medical writers, such as those of his friend Francisco López de Villalobos (*Sumario de medicina*, Salamanca 1498), who came to the new medical faculty in order to teach, write, and study.

The continual reference in *La Celestina* to disease, pain, healers, and remedies must be considered within Castile's late-fifteenth- and early-sixteenth-century medical atmosphere. Like Jaume Roig's *Spill*, *La Celestina* enjoyed sixteenth-century acclaim because it responded to cultural anxiety about the woman healer and *medianera*. At the same time that a reader would have been entertained by the work, it also imparted information about the incapacities of the woman healer and the dangers of her healing techniques.[2] Since the reader would have recognized an analogy between Celestina and women healers in her or his own society, Celestina's pejorative portrayal had significant implications for the reader's own hygiene and well-being. Through Celestina's unappealing characterization, the text tries to demonstrate that ordinary women healers, such as Celestina, only intensify the reader's pain and illness. Hence, it attempts to discourage the reader from seeking the healing services of evil, incompetent women.

Celestina's incongruous relationship to healing and well-being is established from the outset of the work. In act 1, the lovesick Calisto declares to his servant Pármeno that his meeting with the *alcahueta* (go-between or bawd) Celestina portends an encounter with health (*salud*), the ostensibly desired opposition to his illness: "Y no más, sino vamos a ver la salud" (1.114) [Well, no more, but let us proceed to my healing] (1.37).[3] Yet the text constantly tries to prove the *alcahueta* otherwise, so that Celestina is presented again and again as an ex-prostitute and current *alcahueta* / healer incapable of remedying Calisto's lovesickness. Instead of relieving Calisto's pain, she only intensifies it and ultimately leads many of the characters to their deaths. The work tries to discredit the *medianera* and her interventions at every turn, and in this way attempts to disprove Calisto's remark.

For as *La Celestina* demonstrates, womankind is the originating agent of disease. The *medianera* Celestina is the ultimate *puta madre* (mother whore) of canonized Iberian literature of this era who, like Eve in contrast to the Virgin, constitutes and represents the evil, diseased generator of humankind. Depicted as if she were Eve's daughter, Celestina prolongs her "mother's" legacy and is referred to as a generative *madre* throughout the work, by Sempronio, for instance, in act 1 ("Madre bendita, qué desseo traygo!" [1.104] [Blessed Mother! How gladly do I come!] [1.29]) and by Celestina herself in the same act: "Y yo ansí como verdadera madre tuya" (1.122) [As a real mother to you] (1.44). Her repeated connection to *motherhood* emphasizes her generative abilities, which are increasingly linked to her work in all vocational areas such as prostitution, sewing, matchmaking, and healing. Yet, motherhood in *La Celestina* has less to do with the procreation of actual children than it does with Celestina's birthing of whoring, Eve-like (Evian) women such as herself, whom she produces through her work as an intercessor.[4] Celestina trains younger women in the art of being "celestine." Her association with motherhood and the creation of artisan and human products intensifies rather than domesticizes her work in the late medieval and early modern sex industry, where she works as a brothel owner, house mother, trafficker of women, producer of sex, and perpetuator of the Evian lineage.

Missing from *La Celestina* is the contrastive paradigm of the Virgin, whose metaphysical intercessions play no part in the story. Instead, Celestina is a parody of the Virgin, a palimpsest or a visible figure covering the erasure of the paradigmatic, sacred *medianera* before her. At the same time that the work constantly tries to demonstrate Celestina's distance from the Virgin, it must also invoke the reader's complicity with both images. In order to subvert Celestina's successes as a healer and in other areas, the text tries to combine Marian and Evian qualities in her. The other characters repeatedly react to Celestina in the same way that they would to Mary: "Calisto is so gratified by her presence that he kisses the ground on which she walks. Later he kneels before the old bawd when she brings him news of her successful 'intercession' before his other goddess, Melibea."[5] After establishing what appears to be this Marian / Evian combination, the text clearly works to undermine it.

Manuel da Costa Fontes has convincingly argued that Celestina's resemblance to the Virgin is intended as a parody and criticism of the Marian cult by Rojas the converted Jew (*converso*) who, like many other converts at the time, did not accept the doctrine of Mary's virginity.[6] Yet at the same time that Rojas's parody demonstrates a possible critique of Christian doctrine, it also evinces social and cultural consequences. Costa Fontes identifies Celestina as a "parodic parallel" to the Virgin, which suggests that, similar to the *Spill*, the work allows for distance between them.[7] However, the Eva / Ave relationship in *La Celestina* is very different from the *Spill*'s. In the same way that Roig's contrast requires a vast horizontal distance between Eve and Mary in order to keep them apart, Rojas's parody necessitates shared codes between the "encoder" (author) and the "decoder" (reader) in order for the reader to recognize the parodic gesture.[8] In *La Celestina*, distance is not achieved spatially the way it is in the *Spill*, but through the structural coexistence of two repeated but different texts. *La Celestina*'s message is not that the Virgin and Celestina are homologous, but rather that Celestina can never replicate the Virgin's image behind her. The other characters in the text plainly err in equating her with the Virgin.

The parody of Eva and Ave in *La Celestina* is what Hutcheon calls a "bitextual synthesis," as opposed to the monotextual strategy used in pastiche.[9] The bitextual synthesis that characterizes parody creates a linkage between two texts that requires ironic distance. Parody activates the two images, the Virgin and Celestina, through their difference and not through their correspondence.[10] Hence, *La Celestina*'s parodic intent and veritable attack focuses less on the Marian figure than it does on the incapacities of the mundane go-between. The characters in the text treat Celestina in the same way that Berceo's and Alfonso X's characters treat the Virgin in early medieval Marian literature—they invoke the go-between's services. But as *La Celestina* clearly demonstrates, the earthly go-between can never replicate Mary's intercessions to provoke the same result. She is the antithesis of the Virgin.

Like the *Spill*, *La Celestina* functions pejoratively against women and *medianeras* in a variety of professions and circumstances such as mothers, seamstresses, healers, and go-betweens. It presents a range of arguments and justifications for the exclusion of traditional women workers from society's professional ranks, including that of the woman healer from professionalized medicine. The text tries to illustrate the disastrous effects that result from women's attempts to imitate the Virgin in order to malign them in opposition to the able and licit professional worker. For instance, Melibea questions Celestina's legitimacy and authenticity when Celestina acts as a healer in act 10. After Celestina asks Melibea for her monetary recompense or permission (*licencia*) in order to be able to tell her the cause of her ill, Melibea gets angry:

¿Cómo, Celestina, qué es esse nuevo salario que pides? ¿De licencia tienes tú necessidad para me dar la salud? ¿Quál médico jamás pidió tal seguro para curar al paciente? (10.241)

[How, Celestina? Is this not a strange request? Need you leave to repair my health? What physician has ever required permission to effect a cure?] (10.157)

The passage suggests that since Celestina has no *license* or *permission* to heal people (*dar la salud*), she cannot possibly require Melibea to give her any kind of *licencia*, neither in the form of money nor as permission. Celestina's image must be familiar to the reader in order for her to be cast as an ineffective imitator of the erased image that she covers.

The palimpsest principle is used in this text, as Celestina is constantly portrayed as recognizable yet different from the erased image behind her. This principle allows the work to have a forceful connection with historical and cultural events in sixteenth-century

Iberian society because the erased image on the paper may consist of traditional female icons such as the Virgin, women healers, knitters, and seamstresses. The palimpsest principle permits her parodic linkage to the Virgin Mary and her further association to women who actually worked in medieval society. They all converge and resemble one another in the ubiquitous *alcahueta*, Celestina. Thus, instead of an ambiguous or favorable interpretation of Celestina's role in the work, her mediations on behalf of the other characters are ultimately ludicrous, chaotic, and destructive.[11] Celestina tries to exercise the role of cultural intercessor that had been patently linked to women in the early medieval Marian literature. But the parodic element allows the work to demonstrate the ample breadth between the inept interventions of the earthly *medianera* and the consummate mediations of her model, the Virgin.

Medianeras were increasingly maligned in a society in which the traditional bases of social organization (or lack thereof) were in flux. *La Celestina* responds to and participates in this greatly shifting society. Implicit attempts to persecute undesirable members of society took on an increasingly violent tenor in fifteenth- and sixteenth-century Iberia. The founding of the repressive tribunals of the Inquisition by Fernando and Isabel (enacted by Pope Sixtus IV in 1478) and their increased activity in Iberian society only fomented and championed the chorus of vitriolic discourse, both oral and written, against women in general and women healers in particular.[12] Legal mechanisms against women and others were strengthened. Professionalizing efforts in fields such as medicine, prostitution, and other trades were ostensibly intended to improve the quality of the service provided. However, all of these measures served to regulate a process of differentiation between social sectors and groups of people that ultimately resulted in increased methods of control without the benefits of greater social order.

STRATEGIES FOR DISPARAGING A *MEDIANERA* IN *LA CELESTINA*

The many strategies that Rojas uses to discredit *medianeras* and women workers include their supposed predilection for controlling birth, abortion, and virginity, their mobility and instability, their unruly desire to dominate husbands and other men, and the trope of women's duplicitous language. But, perhaps the most powerful textual strategy employed in the text is Celestina's demonization and bewitching, which is especially meant to alter the reader's perception of traditional women healers and their practice in order to correlate their methods with those of the devil.

Celestina invokes the assistance of the devil throughout the work. For instance, in act 4 she alludes to the use of a conjuration, a traditional healing method, only in this case it is supposed to relay diabolical powers. In another example, Pármeno describes the items kept in Celestina's laboratory as ingredients for secret potions and spells. But, many of the items are the same as those distributed by apothecaries of the time.[13] By way of such depictions, Rojas tries to show that in the hands of women, traditional healing practices such as herbal remedies, the use of amulets and charms, and the invocation of otherwise pious prayers, become disruptive, demonic, and heretical.

The demonization of traditional women healers and their practice by those who held the means to establish regulatory norms—that is, writers, lawyers, doctors, judges, and royalty—constituted one significant way in which such authorities justified women's prohibition from professional medicine and other fields. Most twentieth-century Hispanists have not recognized Celestina's demonization as a strategy of denigration on Rojas's part, and instead have chosen to interpret her as reflective of communities of witches who actually lived in European society at the time.[14] Julio Caro Baroja, for instance, believes that Rojas's depiction of Celestina corresponds perfectly to individuals who lived in fifteenth- and sixteenth-century urban Iberia:

> resultó que su dibujo correspondía tan perfectamente con tipos reales que podían encontrarse en la [sic] ciudades españolas (Toledo, Salamanca, Sevilla . . .) en los siglos XV y XVI, que dio un patrón excelente a los cultivadores de la literatura realista.[15]
>
> [it turned out that her depiction corresponded so perfectly to real people who could be found in fifteenth- and sixteenth-century Spanish cities (Toledo, Salamanca, Seville . . .), that it provided an excellent model to the creators of realist literature.]

According to Caro Baroja, Celestina is an archetypal figure who represents the numerous witches later exposed by the inquisitorial tribunals at Cuenca and Toledo.[16]

Hispanists who interpret Celestina as a "witch" and her activities as "real withchcraft" evince misguided assumptions about traditional healing and medicine and about the early modern phenomenon commonly referred to as "the witch trials" (approximately 1450–1750), which in Spain were supervised by the Inquisition. Recent historians have begun to evaluate the witch hunts anew and have called them more precisely an early modern rather than a medieval occurrence.[17] They generally point out that the numbers of convicted "witches" have been inflated, and that the witch hunts were motivated and justified by cultural changes, biases, and prejudices.[18] They were officially motivated by the need to combat heretics and heretical practice. Individuals were frequently pursued according to reports from neighbors and townspeople who suspected questionable activity, suggesting that the identification of these people received a certain degree of support within communities.

In showing that women accounted for about 75 percent of those persecuted throughout Europe, Anne Llewellyn Barstow demonstrates that gender played a significant role in this heinous activity.[19] In chapter 6 of her book, "From Healers to Witches," she argues that the practices of traditional women healers were often targeted, despite the fact that their healing practice was largely indistinguishable from that of doctors.[20] Ritual healing that included the use of herbs, incantations, charms, and amulets was universally recognized as common healing practice in the medieval period. Medicinal recipes often included incantations such as the Lord's Prayer and Hail Mary in order for remedies to take effect: "In order for herbs to be efficacious, as one gathered them one must say five Lord's Prayers, five Hail Mary's, and the Creed."[21] Thus, Barstow suggests that only in the early modern era did it become necessary to attempt to differentiate between natural and supernatural methods, and between religious and "magical" demonic ritual.

Many medieval Hispanists have not noted this early modern change. Dorothy S. Severin has argued that Celestina is empowered by the use of "magic" and "sorcery:" "Witchcraft, sorcery, and bawdry empower Celestina in her society and make her the dominant character not just in the work but in her social milieu."[22] Celestina is certainly a powerful figure in her circle of acquaintances and ultimately sets in motion the deaths of most of the book's main characters. However, that which Severin regards as witchcraft and sorcery was considered conventional healing practice even into the sixteenth century. Despite Severin's claim that the heretical practices make Celestina a dominant figure, the nonheretical work of traditional women healers often resembled hers. Like many scholars before her, Severin reads Celestina as if she were heretical rather than conventional. Hence, Celestina is "empowered" not by the devil nor even solely by her ability to manipulate language, but by her skill in effectively employing traditional healing methods. Her "magical" practice is often quite the same as that which would have been exercised by licit physicians, priests, midwives, or apothecaries of the day.

During the early modern period, various societal authorities such as medical examiners, priests, and judges sought to undermine the occupational skills that traditional women healers had developed as imitators of the Virgin and holy women. Like the textual figure of Celestina, mundane women were trapped by authorities who sought to malign them for traditional practices that they had been taught to follow. In one of Barstow's examples, a woman healer from Modena, Chiara Signorini, was tortured because she admitted that the Virgin visited her frequently in order to protect her from her enemies, such as family members who did not pay her after she healed them. Chiara also admitted to holding her newborn baby up in her arms in order to turn its protection and care over to the Virgin. This admission incriminated her further since "witch-midwives" were believed to offer babies in this way to the devil.[23]

Like Celestina's palimpsest parody of the Virgin, Chiara's inquisitor evidently perceived her devotion to the Virgin as antithetical to acceptable behavior. What both Chiara and Celestina make manifest, however, are the existent social anxieties with respect to ordinary women's relationship to the Virgin as both women figures and healers. They illustrate the tremendous disturbance caused by textual and ordinary women's imitation of the Virgin and the ensuing success of their methods. It is precisely this success and "power" that Rojas seeks to discredit by bewitching Celestina and her healing techniques.[24] Rojas tries to portray Celestina as a destructive, pagan sorcerer in order to clearly distinguish between false charlatans like her who intensify illness, and true healers, such as the male medical professional.

La Celestina further reviles *medianeras* by negatively associating them all to *alcahuetería* (pandering); and by extension, womankind in general becomes whorelike. The term *alcahueta* begins to broaden in meaning during this period. As is evident in *La Celestina*, the term starts to be applied to women of all kinds, even if their tasks were unrelated to prostitution. Celestina's countless jobs and activities clearly bear this out. Rojas collapses two kinds of conventional representations in Celestina: medieval literature that supported women's healing practice, and other popular works that depicted go-betweens and prostitutes such as the fourteenth-century *Sendebar* and the *Calila e Digna* collection. Many of these portayals were misogynist, and correspond to the influential tradition of fables and stories that characterized women as agents of disease, and as sources of illness and disorder. Rojas recognized the strength of medieval stories and *exempla* to naturalize social conditions, and in this case, to make women's supposedly evil state appear intrinsic and inborn.[25]

Go-betweens in many medieval stories were characterized as multivocational, working in a variety of occupations as seamstresses, perfumers, cosmetic-makers, gynecologists, procurers, matchmakers, and witches.[26] Sometimes they were presented as old, obscene hags experienced in several healing and sexual activities.[27] Rojas's conflation of these two kinds of depictions is intended to associate women healers with prostitution in order to malign traditional women healers and undermine medieval models that had previously supported them.

One of the most forceful ways in which *medianeras* are vilified in *La Celestina* is by associating them with disease. In describing herself as an old woman, Celestina states that old age is nothing but a *mesón de enfermedades* (an inn of illnesses):

> Que a la mi fe, la vegez no es sino mesón de enfermedades, posada de pensamientos, amiga de renzillas, congoxa continua, llaga incurable, manzilla de lo passado, pena de lo presente, cuydado triste de lo porvenir, vezina de la muerte. (4.154)

> [For—and I speak truly from my experience—old age is but an inn that houses all infirmities—a lodging-place of recollections; it is fond of bickerings—a continuous misery, an incurable wound, a regret for times past, it is a discomfiture in the present, deep care for what's to come; death's neighbor.] (4.73)

Celestina represents disease itself in this sense, as an old woman who ironically tries to cure others of their diseases. "Close" to death herself according to her rhetoric, the text suggests that a person such as Celestina could not possibly restore or augment the vitality and well-being of others.

In one instance, Celestina is a healer of the uterine disease referred to as *mal de la madre* (wandering womb and suffocation of the womb), whereby the detachable uterus was thought to stray from its correct place in a woman's body. The belief in the disease stemmed from the classical writers Hippocrates and Plato, and continued through the medieval and early modern periods:

> The womb was thought of as a kind of animal, a frog or a toad, and it was believed that this being could at certain times wander about within the body of a woman producing a number of unpleasant symptoms such as shortness of breath, aphonia, pain, paralysis, choking and suffocation as well as a violent seizure of the senses.[28]

The proper remedy for the malady consisted of giving the patient strong odors at first, although it was believed that it could only truly be cured by excessive sex and eventual motherhood.[29] The *mal de la madre* has powerful ramifications for women, sexuality, and motherhood. It not only connects women's biology to disease, but it designates motherhood itself, Eve's punishment, as the generating force of sin, disease, and pain. Even though motherhood was believed to cure the malady, giving birth also denotes the continuation and regeneration of Eve's disease. Motherhood as a remedy is ironic because at the same time that it perpetuates sin, it also supposedly transforms women's *nature, condition,* or *sin,* and restores women's well-being.

In act 7, Celestina prescribes the proper remedies for Areúsa's *mal de la madre.* But, they are summarily discredited because women's diseased nature and Eve's curse are emphasized in the passage. They suggest that Celestina's mediations serve to restore a dangerous, "natural order" in the form of Areúsa's well-being, which only portends the breakdown of societal integrity. Motherhood restores Areúsa's health, but coitus and procreation perpetuate disease.

In a later act, Areúsa denies Sempronio's exaltation of noble lineage, and articulates the ultimate, dismal outcome of human reproduction: "Ruyn sea quien por ruyn se tiene; las obras hazen linaje, que al fin todos somos hijos de Adam y Eva" (9.229) [Low is as low does, boy. It is works that constitute aristocracy, for in the final analysis we are all children of Adam and Eve] (9.144–45). The *mal de la madre* is Eve's punishment passed down to both Celestina and Areúsa. Its implications in the text are more significant for Celestina than for Areúsa because the disease constitutes the *mal de Celestina,* or the disease that is Celestina—she is the text's matrix / mother who moves around unrestrained, causing and augmenting pain. Although she bears no children herself, Celestina the *medianera* commands the generation of disease, sin, and sexual promiscuity.[30] It is her lineage that perpetuates the destruction in the text. In act 7, when Areúsa says, "ha quatro horas que muero de la madre, que la tengo sobida en los pechos, que me quiere sacar del mundo" (7.202) [For the last four hours I've been dying with the hysterical passion. It has now moved up into my breasts and it's murdering me] (7.120), she refers to a disease whose etiology and matrix Celestina represents as a daughter of Eve. The *mal de la madre*'s cure is paradoxically humankind's curse because motherhood constitutes the unrelenting production by way of sexual indulgence of transgressive Eves and victimized Adams.[31]

La Celestina further vilifies *medianeras* through the trope of women's duplicitous speech. Aside from the text's more general concerns with rhetorical issues, classical works, and the insufficiency of language, *La Celestina* renders speech and language from women's mouths—especially Celestina's—unsurprisingly mendacious and false. When Celestina tries to seduce Melibea for Calisto, the young woman responds angrily:

> ¿Qué te parece? Si me hallaras sin sospecha desse loco, con qué palabras me entravas. No se dize en vano que el más empecible miembro del mal hombre o muger es la lengua. Quemada seas, alcahueta falsa, hechizera, enemiga de honestidad, causadora de secretos yerros. (4.161)
>
> [What else do you think it could be? If you had not found me on guard against him, I wonder just what kind of argument you would have used to win me over. How exact it is to say that the most dangerous organ of an evil man or woman is the tongue! May you be burned—false procuress, you witch, you enemy of all virtue and the cause of secret errors!] (4.80)

Melibea's insults contrast sharply to Celestina's preceding discourse, in which the old woman had informed Melibea that with "sola una palabra" (4.159) [only a word or two] (4.78), her smooth speech would heal the ailing Calisto. But, Celestina manages to convince Melibea that her (Celestina's) motivations are sincere. Celestina employs the exact remedy that would have been appropriate in this situation according to the remedies handed out by many healers of the day for Calisto's supposed toothache (4.164). She requests a prayer from Melibea, and asks the young woman for a small ribbon or cord (*cordón*), attesting to her belief in the power of reliquaries. By the end of the scene, in a sleight of "tongue" on the part of

Celestina, Melibea apologizes to the old woman for becoming angry and for disbelieving her:

> ¡O quánto me pesa con la falta de mi paciencia!, porque siendo él ignorante y tú innocente, havés padescido las alteraciones de mi ayrada lengua. (4.168)
>
> [Oh, how I regret having lost my temper! I see now that he had no evil intention and that you were innocent too. And yet I made you suffer the outbursts of my wrathful tongue.] (4.86)

She also agrees to give her ribbon in the hopes of carrying out the pious and sacred act of healing that she had referred to earlier (4.166). The scene reinforces the duplicity and irony of Celestina's words, as noted by Lucrecia in an aside (4.168). But it also demonstrates Celestina's ability to manipulate the rhetoric of healing for her own ends. She refers to religious objects and activity (Santa Polonia's prayer for toothaches and reliquaries) in a blasphemous way; not in order to heal a toothache, but to win Melibea over to Calisto's cause, which is the healing of his lovesickness.

She further subverts the value of traditional healing remedies as she exposes the way in which *medianeras* manipulate the role of the confabulator for their own purposes. As the intermediary between Calisto and Melibea, she will relay Melibea's healing words to the lovesick Calisto, ultimately not in order to heal his toothache, but to persuade Melibea that she should have sex with him. Thus, the therapeutic role of the medieval confabulator, the individual who provided relief through her or his words, is radically altered. Under the auspices of Celestina, the confabulator's role becomes most destructive and pain inducing. Melibea's participation in Celestina's scheme, as she who possesses the healing words, results in her and Calisto's death.

La Celestina also denigrates the *medianera* through the text's wide-ranging attention to audio and visual perception, which is again connected to Celestina's duplicity. Her speech and actions do not signify literally, and they are never as they appear. Her speech and actions mask deceitful motivations and intentions. The *medianera* becomes the focus of and the scapegoat for the traditional medieval concern with the *integumentum*, which is the outer cover that must be broken or cracked in order to discern the truth behind or beyond it.[32]

This anxiety about appearances and perception, about how one can be certain that what she or he sees and hears is as it seems, partially answers itself in the text: the *medianera* must be avoided. This is evident in Calisto's ironic statement alluded to earlier, about going to see *health* in the form of Celestina (1.114). In speaking with Pármeno in the same act, Celestina refers to her "mind's eye" (*intellectuales ojos*), a reference that can only be interpreted as paradoxical if not ridiculous:

> Bien te oy, y no pienses que el oyr con los otros exteriores sesos mi vejez aya perdido. Que no sólo lo que veo, oyo y cognozco, mas aun lo intrínsico con los intellectuales ojos penetro. Has de saber Pármeno, que Calisto anda de amor quexoso. (1.117)
>
> [Yes, indeed, I heard you quite clearly. Do not for a moment think that because of my age these old ears have lost their ability to hear. I preserve my other senses, too. Oh, yes, I can see and grasp very well indeed, and furthermore, with my mind's eye, so to speak, I can pierce right through to the very heart of a matter. Now, you must realize, Pármeno, that Calisto is battling with love.] (1.40)

This passage represents the social conundrum of the *medianera's* keen perception according to her access to information and people. Celestina alludes to a kind of "intellectual" eye that enables her to perceive interiors, to bypass the outer cover and to enter directly into that which is truest and most important, the interior part of whatever is at hand—in this case Calisto's disease. Calisto on the other hand, delirious in act 1, continues to believe that outer appearances correspond to interiority:

> ¿Qué hazes, llave de mi vida? Abre. ¡O Pármeno, ya la veo; sano soy, bivo soy! ¡Mira[s] qué reverenda persona, qué acatamiento! Por la mayor parte, por la filosomía es conoscida la virtud interior. ¡O vejez virtuosa, o virtud envejecida! (1.116)
>
> [What do you do, key to my life? Open!—Oh, Pármeno, I see her! I am whole again, I am alive. Do you not observe what a reverend person she is? Mark you not her dignity? We are generally aware of the inner nature of persons from their external appearance, you know. O virtuous and venerable lady!] (1.39)[33]

It becomes evident in the work that Calisto is ill, not well (*sano*), and that events are not as they appear. One of the main concerns in the text is Celestina's control over not simply what is seen, heard, or perceived, but over how things are interpreted. Like the medical professional, she looks into people's bodies and diagnoses their ills. Her perceptions must be maligned in order to authorize the sight, hearing, and diagnosis of the male physician.

Celestina is able to keenly perceive because of her ubiquitous social role, which is also denigrated in the text. Her free access and easy movement through the city / town is meant to illustrate her dangerous instability. But instead it demonstrates some of the reasons why people desire her services, and why she poses a threat to the perhaps less widely connected medical professional. Everyone recognizes and knows her. She gains access to people's homes, monasteries, and churches, and travels within and between social classes and ranks. She conducts business as easily in the street as she does within buildings. Celestina has what every medical professional desires, ready access to men and women alike, notoriety around town, frequent meetings with women and men, and a clientele that requests her services and trusts her abilities. People turn to her to remedy their ills because they know her and they believe that she heals. Hence, she also possesses the necessary means for gaining new clients if needed. All of these advantages in Celestina's favor are eroded in the text.

Lovesickness and Its Prostituting Cure at the Margins

La Celestina treats and responds to various medieval discourses about love, some of which encouraged different kinds of relations with women as remedies for pain. Ranging from Marian literature to courtly love poetry, and from medical discourse to didactic moralizing about the body, love was construed in many ways in the medieval period. It was sublime as an expression of devotion toward God or the Virgin, yet it was also thought to be a disease, a sexual remedy, a signifier for sin, and a ludic diversion.

Distinctions between medieval discourses on love were frequently unclear, so that many discursive practices of Iberian Marian devotion, for instance, were indistinguishable at times from erotic love discourse. Many of these different kinds of love-discourses collapse in the figure of Celestina the *medianera*. Her roles as a healer, a pimp, and an arranger of sexual encounters connect her to several different discourses about love and sex, such as those of the disease of lovesickness, medical imperatives about coitus, and legal decrees related to municipal prostitution. The *medianera* was also a conspicuous target for moralizing discourse such as Roig's in the *Spill*.

In *La Celestina*, the diseased *alcahueta*'s seemingly paradoxical participation in both healing and prostitution exemplifies love's variety of functions, and illustrates the complicated relationship between love, sex, medicine, and the body. But in the early modern period, the collapse of love discourses and functions in Celestina also serve to fix the *medianera*'s identity as unstable, chaotic, and duplicitous. The broadening of the *alcahueta*'s signification to include and refer to many kinds of women otherwise unrelated to prostitution is part of the strategy to discredit the worldly *medianera*, and was effected by changing the cultural perception of her traditional connection to sex, healing, and the body. Instead of effectively healing illness like the woman healer in the *Speculum al foderi*, Celestina only intensifies it.

The pathologizing of love in the late Middle Ages was constituted by several discourses: medical texts of antiquity, classical literature, Christian sources, the new Christ as model of love and suffering, and popular love.[34] Lovesickness, called *amor eros* and *amor hereos* during the Middle Ages, was considered an affliction of the mental and imaginative faculties. Discussed in many of the popular medical treatises disseminated in the fourteenth and fifteenth centuries, it was thought to afflict the noble classes and to be remedied by psychological distraction.[35] Michael Solomon has convincingly argued that one of *La Celestina*'s parodic objectives is its portrayal of the curing of lovesickness. Instead of applying the medically prescribed cure of psychological distraction, Calisto invents a counterdiagnosis or a form of self-therapy in which he decides to enlist Celestina's services as healer: "The medieval reader with even the most rudimentary knowledge of lovesickness would sense the parodic tension which emerges between diagnosis and counter-diagnosis as Calisto attempts to cure his illness using a therapy that will only intensify his ailment."[36] Celestina's mediations between Calisto and Melibea will only exacerbate his already ailing condition.[37]

The intensification of Calisto's condition is due in part to Celestina's work as an *alcahueta*. One of the strongest criticisms against Celestina's work as a healer in the text is that it cannot be separated from her work as an *alcahueta*. She promotes disease in a number of ways, both insofar as sex was considered sinful at the time, and with respect to her mediations, which encourage the disease of lovesickness. In act 1, Celestina even suggests that she must reopen

Calisto's wound in order to heal him, thereby increasing his pain. She aligns herself ironically with surgical pain in order to emphasize the certainty of her cure:

> Digo que me alegro destas nuevas, como los cirujanos de los descalabrados; y como aquéllos dañan en los principios las llagas, y encarescen el prometimiento de la salud, ansí entiendo yo hazer a Calisto. Alargarle he la certinidad del remedio, porque como dizen, el esperança luenga aflige el coraçon, y quanto él la perdiere, tanto gela promete. ¡Bien me entiendes! (1.107)

> [Well, I am delighted with this news, as doctors are when people crack their skulls. And just as in the beginning those physicians make the patient's wound seem more painful than it really is in order to make their promises of restoring his health seem more impressive, so shall I likewise do in the case of Calisto. I will make him believe that his cure will take place far in the future, and, as folks say, long hoping afflicts the heart—so the more hopeless he is, the more opportunity there is for me to encourage him. And now you get *my* drift.] (1.32)

She seeks to reassure Sempronio of her competency, but the surgical example that she chooses would have made a reader of the period reluctant to accept her as a capable healer. Instead of selecting an example that would illustrate how an illness was abated, thereby solidifying her expertise as a healer of Calisto's ill, Celestina alludes to the augmented pain and harm created by surgeons. A reader would have recognized her allusion to surgeons since surgical methods and the pain they brought on were objectionable to many people of the time. As surgeons increasingly tried to organize and legitimize themselves as medical professionals in this period, they largely avoided any mention of pain in their stories and treatises.[38] Hence, Celestina's statement suggests that she associates herself with surgeons if not specifically as an augmentor of Calisto's illness, then certainly as an intensifier of his pain.

Celestina's ironic remark contributes to her characterization as an incompetent healer. Since she is presented at once as a healer and promoter of the disease of love, her supposed worthlessness as a healer is made increasingly manifest throughout the text. Her ineptitude is inextricably linked to her occupation as an *alcahueta*, a go-between and brothel owner. The idea that an ex-prostitute (*puta vieja*) and current pimp could aid a man's well-being is portrayed in *La Celestina* as ludicrous, dangerous, and destructive. The text pathologizes the very individual who supposedly provides remedies, cures, and good health. Not only does she promote disease through her work, but like earthly women in the *Spill,* her Evian gender determines her disease. Women's reproductive biology also causes them to produce sin, disease, and every other ill imaginable.

Celestina's unfavorable portrayal is especially directed toward her mediations as a healer of lovesickness, since this role was justified by medical instruction in at least two medieval treatises that dealt with the disease, Bernard of Gordon's *Lilio de medicina* (1305) and the Christian commentator Peter of Spain's (d. 1277) thirteenth-century *Questions on the Viaticum.* Medical writers, in other words, recognized the value of women's salutary intercessions for relief from lovesickness, and recommended their use.

Before the thirteenth century, Constantine the African's twelfth-century therapies for lovesickness had been based on "tempering the humoral composition with baths, lectuaries, enemas, and herbal-dietary regimentation."[39] But as early as the thirteenth century, Peter of Spain recommended the employment of *medianeras* to distract the lover's excessive contemplation of the beloved. In the *Questions on the Viaticum,* he posed questions about whether or not ugly and beautiful women should be brought before the beloved. He agreed with Avicenna that ugly women must not be employed for hygienic purposes, and that the presence of beautiful women before the lover would represent a higher form of beauty to distract him from his previous object of desire.[40]

By the fifteenth century, medical writers more commonly prescribed psychological cures associated with mental distraction. It was thought that a preoccupied mind could be diverted by language and verbal therapy, including diatribes against women, admonitions, logical arguments, and harsh words.[41] When such customary therapies did not assuage the affliction, Bernard of Gordon declared in the *Lilio* that the help of an old, ugly, bearded woman (like Celestina) should be sought:

> Porende busque se una vieja de muy feo acatamiento con grandes dientes y barvas y con fea y vil vestidura.[42]
>
> [On account of that, look for an old woman with a hideous countenance, big teeth, a beard, and ugly, vile clothing.]

Bernard believed that the old woman should present herself before the afflicted, hiding a rag soaked in a woman's menstrual blood. She should proceed to disparage the beloved, attributing derogatory characteristics to her such as drunkard, bed wetter, epileptic, and dirty. According to Bernard, this should be sufficient to discourage the man from his preoccupation with the beloved, but if not, the old woman should take out the bloodied cloth and place it directly before the man's face:

> E si por aquestas fealdades non la quisiere dexar saque el paño dela sangre de su costumbre de baxo de sy: y muestre gelo subitamente delante su cara: y de le grandes bozes diziendo: mira que tal es tu amiga commo este paño. (fol. 58r)

> [And if those epithets do not prompt him to leave his beloved, take out an old cloth soaked with menstrual blood, and present it to him lifting it right up to his face. Shout at him saying: "Look, your beloved is just like this cloth!"]

According to Bernard, the *medianera* acts as the abject confabulator who provides therapeutic relief to another person. Her abjection should encourage avoidance of the beloved, since the *medianera* constitutes her monstrous antithesis. In the same kind of distant recognition required of parody, due to her gender, the *medianera* is placed over the image of the beloved only to violate it. This undesirable woman-monster is what Bernard indicates should be sought in order to relieve the affliction of lovesickness.

But, Celestina's mediations only seem to prolong the illness. Her remedy of bringing Calisto and Melibea together is countertherapeutic to Bernard's authoritative medical remedy of distraction and demonstrates her general incompetence. Although she resembles Bernard's abject woman healer, she does not deflect the lover's cogitations, and instead tries to advance Calisto and Melibea's union. Moreover, Celestina's depiction clearly grates against Peter of Spain's advice about women's role in distracting the lover's contemplation. She is not beautiful, but rather is old, ugly, and bearded.

As I mentioned in chapter 1, coital remedies such as Celestina's were considered legitimate and salutary by medical writers of the medieval period. Galenic medicine considered moderate intercourse or sexual stimulation necessary for the emission of excess seed stored in the body.[43] According to medical writers, lack of intercourse could have detrimental effects, such as suffocation of the womb in women. When intercourse was impossible, as it was deemed for widows, masturbation was explicitly recommended.[44]

Sex in moderation was thus considered salutary in late medieval medical works such as Bernard's *Lilio*, and in the practical guide on sexual hygiene that I discussed in chapter 1, the *Speculum al foderi* (but it was not appropriate for the healing of lovesickness). Unlike Bernard and Peter of Spain's advice about the woman healer's role in the remedy of lovesickness as a deflector of excessive cogitation on the beloved, her role in the *Speculum al foderi* required that she effect the lovers' union in order to restore the lover's well-being and satiate his desire.

Rojas's depiction of the abject healer Celestina who prescribes the mistaken remedy of sexual union of the lovers undermines the favorable representation of the messenger / healer in the *Speculum al foderi*, just as it subverts Bernard and Peter's women healers. The *Speculum*'s instructions to the woman healer even allude to lovesickness when they explain that the messenger / healer should tell the beloved that the lover is crazy and dying for the woman's love. Yet this does not compromise the positive and desirable role of the woman healer in fomenting the lovers' union in the *Speculum*. Celestina's depiction, however, is utterly contrary to the messenger / healer whom she vaguely resembles but whose favorable depiction she subverts.

Nothing about Celestina is appealing. The messenger's eight respectable qualifications in the *Speculum* become pejorative in *La Celestina*. The messenger's discretion and unmarried status in the *Speculum* are altered in Celestina who is portrayed as dangerously independent and conniving. Her many gatherings with other women are only malicious because of the web of contagion sown from their meetings and activities as seamstresses. Furthermore, Celestina is aged, unattractive, scarred, and bearded, and her forays into households are achieved through duplicitous means. She pretends to accomplish some task such as the selling of thread in act 4, but its banality only disguises her true, evil objectives and motivations. The characteristics that are desirable in the *Speculum* are repugnant in *La Celestina*.

Celestina's depiction attempts to fix the woman healer as quintessentially diseased and dangerous. She subverts the favorable models of women healers in medical texts, and she can only be interpreted as inherently evil. The denigration of Celestina's role in curing lovesickness is further maintained by the ways in which she is related to sex, erotics, and love as a prostitute and *alcahueta*. This connection is one of the most compelling reasons for designating *La Celestina* as an instrument that ultimately justified the practical control of women healers and other workers.

La Celestina plays out and participates in social processes that increasingly relied on the conflation of sex workers and healers in order to discredit and control both. Women's traditional roles as negotiators of salutary coitus and as healers of love-related diseases such as lovesickness caused them to be increasingly allied with prostitution and new formulations of love-diseases such as syphilis. The collapse of healing and prostitution in the figure of Celestina is analogous to the same linkage between them in the social networks of everyday life as a strategy to exclude women from previous healing functions. The regulation of healing practices at this time occurred simultaneously with the sanctioning of municipal controls over prostitution, forcing women out of traditional roles as *alcahuetas* and brothel managers or owners and into more lowly positions as clandestine prostitutes or illicit *alcahuetas*.

The professionalizations of both prostitution and medicine are connected by the fact that the places where women healers and women love arranger-prostitutes practiced sometimes coincided. Eva Carrasco and Ismael Almazán have pointed out four sites in which prostitutes have been regularly identified from about the fifteenth century on: prisons, hospitals, streets or brothels, and shelters (*las casas de refugio*).[45] The parallels and connections between these places and those who frequented or worked in them are unavoidable. For instance, in the early medieval hospitals, that is, the charitable refuges for travelers and the poor, owners and managers hired prostitutes to work one night on a regular basis, suggesting that coitus constituted one of the services provided in hospitals of the time along with care of the poor. Furthermore, the regulation of prostitutes in Barcelona dates from the regulations (*Usatges*) of 1150 and entails the rigid separation of prostitutes from other women.[46] The separation of women in this occupation parallels the separation and containment of the sick in late medieval hospitals, suggesting that prostitution represents a kind of transaction that must be marginalized and contained because of its connection to illness. Along with the older convention of locating prostitutes in medieval hospitals, this indicates that the *association* of illness, morality, and prostitution was established in tandem with the regulation of prostitutes themselves. Hence, it is not accidental that the progressive professionalization of medicine coincided with increased attention to the regulation and institutionalization of prostitution.

One way in which prostitution was controlled was through the establishment of municipal and / or monarchical bordellos in an effort to combat the problem of clandestine prostitution. Jaume II of Aragon conceded one of the first of such brothels to the city of Valencia at the beginning of the fourteenth century.[47] During the fifteenth century and under the reign of the Catholic kings, clandestine prostitution was prohibited throughout the peninsula for reasons including moral concerns, disease, and economic domination. In this way, the monarchs sought to control and insure monetary gain to the crown, and to protect society from disorder and immorality in three ways: first, to protect upstanding women from the deceits of women go-betweens who operated brothels; second, to avoid arguments and murders in the streets between pimps or go-betweens and prostitutes; and third, to diminish homosexual practices that were increasing at an intensive rate.[48]

These protective interests helped to spawn the kind of sixteenth-century representation of the *medianera* exemplified by Celestina. Celestina works alone, apart from municipal control, and asserts the type of commercial autonomy that the Catholic crown of Fernando tried to control by way of sanctioned prostitution. But during Fernando's reign, a woman's gender became another reason for institutional attempts at her suppression. This is evident in the vast discrepancy between men and women go-betweens in late-fifteenth-century, Valencian municipal prostitution. Pablo Pérez García claims that the literary archetype of Celestina was hardly recognizable in Valencia, where out of 123 go-betweens recorded at around the end of the fifteenth century and the beginning of the sixteenth, only 23 were women.[49]

This institutional gender disparity with respect to the proprietors of brothels probably constitutes at least one of the reasons for the existence of vast clandestine prostitution in Valencia, which forced women to find ways to work independently.[50] The discrepancy between the extant statistics about the scant number of *alcahuetas* in Iberian society and the seemingly ubiquitous figure of Celestina attests to an already professionalized society in which measures for the control of municipal prostitution were dictated and "successfully" implemented by men. In other words, by 1499, *alcahuetas* were either virtually obsolete or working clandestinely.[51]

Hence, Celestina's characterization as a marginalized *alcahueta* constitutes one of the many ways in which she responds to diverse practices on love. The conflation of love discourse and Celestina's body is motivated by the evident need at this time to socialize love and sex, to facilitate it and make it licit, and contain it in hospitals, brothels, and other similar places. It is also generated from the different kinds of discourses such as that of ecclesiastical writers and preachers, which argued against carnal knowledge for reasons of moral and physical well-being. Most importantly, however, the collapse of a discourse about love in the figure of Celestina responds to the multiple formulations of love as either beneficial or destructive to men's well-being.

Late medieval medical discourse about lovesickness was undergirded by discourses about men's ability to control their own sexuality, sexual behavior, and that of others for the purpose of well-being. Men's command of their own bodies was contingent upon their control and regulation of women's bodies, which is one effect of the municipal regulation of prostitution.[52] Moreover, medical thought about lovesickness allowed its theorists and commentators to "master . . . powerful collective anxieties over erotic love," which were also reflected in the creation of late medieval courtly love.[53] The basis for the collective anxieties about erotic love lay in the perception that erotic love threatened normative or naturalizing gender relations: "[the lover's malady] offered a way of controlling a historically- and socially-conditioned experience of eros that was felt to threaten the normative hierarchy of gender and power."[54] Mary Wack proposes that lovesickness was necessary for the maintenance of the "normative hierarchy of gender and power," since that order was reinforced by the disease. The creation and use of disease as a means of social control, that is, to support normative ideas about the hierarchy of gender, may explain in part why men *alcahuetes* replaced women *alcahuetas* in Valencian brothels. The management of prostitutes by male procurers suggests that women were excluded not only from the economic command of that occupation, but also from a kind of *prostituting control* of disease.

A woman like Celestina who either exacerbates or remedies a pathologized eros (lovesickness) exercises some degree of control over it, and so subverts to an extent the hierarchy of gender that lovesickness was meant to guard. As she intensifies lovesickness, Celestina strengthens women's control over men in two ways: Melibea takes over Calisto's mental faculties; and Celestina herself wields force over Calisto because, deluded, he believes that she will provide the means to facilitate his own well-being and survival.

Calisto seeks her services because medical imperatives in treatises and guides such as the *Speculum* encouraged the employment of a woman healer, and because the labors of women healers were readily available. But, *La Celestina* works against Calisto's insistence on Celestina's abilities to heal him: "Seguro soy, pues quien dio la herida, la cura" (6.188) [I am safe, for she who gave the wound now likewise gives the cure] (6.107). Although Calisto literally refers to his own wounding by love's arrow, *La Celestina*'s entire handling of lovesickness also alludes to the generic infliction of that disease by women whose simple image makes men ill. In other words, because of her gender, Melibea stands for the cause of Calisto's wound and for the wound's cure. In turn, because of Celestina's gender, she stands for the same thing. But, like her palimpsest relationship to the Virgin, Celestina cannot replicate Melibea's beauty nor her desirability.

However, a striking contradiction in the text that must be constantly addressed is the fact that Celestina *is* desired by many of the other characters. Calisto does not regard her in the same way that he does Melibea, but Celestina certainly represents one of the cogs in the machinery of desire and love. Celestina's "attraction" in this regard, and the text's accompanying discouragement of being deceived by her is intricately connected to her gender and biology. The text suggests that women's gender / biology makes them both the etiology of the disease and supposedly the disease's cure, whether that cure be construed as the avoidance of the beloved by the *medianera*'s abject example, or as the realization of sexual pleasure by means concocted by the *medianera*. The text tries to undermine the *medianera* by showing that the web and net of disease that Celestina weaves and represents is ultimately contingent upon her connection to a prostituting cure in which women's bodies are exchanged, traded, and used not for therapeutic reasons such as those elucidated in the *Speculum*, the *Lilio*, or according to Peter of Spain's *Questions*, but for men's destruction. Instead of serving as the *medianera* who goes between the lover and the beloved and facilitates their shared pleasure, the *alcahueta* becomes a commanding agent of disease, chaos, and death.

The Biology of Work on the Margins

Efforts to exalt professional medicine as Iberian society's most sublime form of healing were intensified throughout the fifteenth and sixteenth centuries. The legal, royal, and municipal emphasis on licit medicine and licensed practitioners, and thus the increasing focus on temperaments, complexion theory, humoral balance and the humoral theory of personality and psychology, coincided with extraordinary efforts during this period to link physiology and biology to an individual's living conditions.[55] These physiological ideas largely held that human bodies were composed in a particular way due to the balance of the "humors," i.e., the bodily fluids of blood, phlegm, choler (bile), and black bile, or to the predominance of one over another. Medical thinkers also described the body according to four possible qualities: heat, cold, wetness, and dryness.

These theories had always allowed for biological arguments used in describing and defining the world. From the earliest medical writings of Galen and Hippocrates to the medieval medical theories of Bernard of Gordon, biology was used to distinguish between the two normative genders of woman and man as they were elaborated on by ancient and medieval writers.[56] All of these writers posited the coldness of women's bodies, their reproductive qualities, and their menstrual blood as that which distinguished them from men. Men medical writers further used humoral theory to justify the preeminence of men's strength over women's, and thus men's categorical superiority over women. Even nonmedical discourse such as Aristotle's *Economics* indicated that the division of labor and gender roles were natural to the body's composition.[57]

In a popular treatise from mid-thirteenth-century England, the friar Bartholomew the Englishman established the link between behavioral actions and temperamental conditions, which were determined by heat differences in the two genders:

> The male passeth the female in perfect complection, in working, in wit, in discretion, in might and in lordship. In perfect complection, for in comparison the male is hotter and dryer, and the female the contrary.[58]

The consequences of Bartholomew's connection of gendered biology and human capabilities pervade many areas of social life, including work and individual personality. Moreover, his thoughts about men's biological superiority over women go hand in hand with increased attempts to establish men's occupational superiority over women through the sixteenth century. The gendered exclusion of women from licit medical practice, guilds, and management positions in municipal prostitution during this period confirms the type of connection between biology and work that Bartholomew presents.

Physiognomy is another field of medieval thought and study that played a crucial role in the medieval formation of the body, by linking physical characteristics with moral and behavioral traits. Unlike the physiologically rooted humoral and complexion theory, physiognomy describes external features such as facial traits and voice as indicators of character, attitude, and behavior.[59] Aside from the numerous citations about complexion and humoral theory in medieval medical treatises, some medical thinkers such as Peter of Abano and al-Razi devoted entire treatises to physiognomy, frequently basing them on the *Physiognomicorum* attributed to Aristotle.[60] They normally began their description of the human body at the top of the head and proceeded down the body to the feet. For instance, al-Razi began his chapter on the eyes in the following way:

> Cuius oculi sunt magni, piger est. cuius [sic] quoque oculi in profundo sunt, callidus est et deceptor. Cuius oculi foris prominent, inverecundus est et loquax ac stolidus.[61]
>
> [Whoever has large eyes is dull. Whoever has deep-set eyes is crafty and deceitful. Whoever's eyes project outwards is shameless, talkative, and stupid.]

Hence, the size and setting of one's eyes were signs of his or her character; deep-set eyes would tell of a crafty and deceptive person.

These treatises also generally demarcated male and female genders, attributing less positive features to the female than to the male. Although Cadden believes that complexion theory and physiognomy produced different descriptions of sex and gender differences, she also demonstrates that they agreed that "group differences in personality and behavior are grounded in innate constitutional differences between the sexes."[62] Physiognomy provided the method for defending the prohibition of individuals from areas of social practice, helping to set the stage for women's exclusion from fields such as medicine and management positions in municipal prostitution. Following the lead of medical writers, authorities could point to women and base their judgments on physical features of the female gender.

Iberian medical writers in the medieval period had frequently linked women to specific jobs and vocations in their writings. Both Bernard of Gordon (*Lilio de medicina*) and the anonymous *Tratado de patología general* named midwives as crucial to the healing of suffocation of the womb (*mal de la madre*).[63] The *Tratado de patología general* also gave instructions on neonatal care, including the physical indicators of an appropriate wet nurse (fol. 113v). In a passage from the *Lilio de medicina* that inextricably linked a characteristic of women's bodies to biology and work, Bernard of Gordon claimed that men had nipples and breasts for aesthetic reasons while women had them in order to nurse children: "Pero los ombres las tienen [tetas] por fermosura tan solamente: por que no parezcan menguados: no por la obra saluo por la fermosura" (fol. 116r) [But men have them (nipples) only for aesthetic reasons, in order for them not to seem lacking in anything. They are not for work, but for beauty's sake]. He believed that women's breasts grew in adolescence so that they could fill with milk and nurse children, in contrast to men's breasts that did not grow as much. Hence, treatises such as these connected the work of women healers with women clients through birthing and illnesses associated with women, as they frequently linked women's bodies to particular kinds of jobs.

These kinds of connections and arguments, which had always existed in medical discourse, were readily employed in late medieval and early modern medical writings. The progressive restricting of women's traditional tasks in medicine and other fields was justified and bolstered by biological arguments against them, which culminate in Juan Huarte de San Juan's *Examen de ingenios para las ciencias* (1575; 1594), where the Spanish physician argues that people's occupational abilities are determined by their humoral constitution or balance.[64] Although Huarte writes some seventy-five years after Rojas's *La Celestina*, his views do not represent the beginning of this type of thinking, but rather its culmination in the early modern period. Huarte ascribes the theory of humoral balance to Aristotle, and describes it as the "temperamento de las cuatro calidades primeras (calor, frialdad, humidad y sequedad)" [the temperature of the four first qualities (hot, cold, moist, and dry)].[65] Huarte's contention throughout the treatise is that work is *biologized*, that occupations require certain predetermined traits and abilities that individuals are born with. For instance, in chapter 11 on jurisprudence, he insists that lawyers, judges, legislators and legal theorists must possess certain characteristics in order to function correctly according to the exigencies of the job, and more importantly, for the good of the republic.[66] Huarte's theory about the biology of work argues that the human temperament determines one's job for the good of all society. In chapter 12, he advocates the medical skill of Jewish and converted doctors and invariably proposes a seed-genetics theory that upholds the belief that race determines occupational competence.[67]

The emphatic early modern linkage of human physiology and social conditions (the relationship between human traits, the correct occupation, and societal harmony) went hand in hand with the professionalization of medicine and the simultaneous attempt to privilege medical practice over other forms of healing.[68] The connection between human physiology and social conditions further points to the late medieval and early modern change in focus from local, individual control over people's immediate environment (that is, the six nonnaturals, environmental factors such as food or rest and sleep that were thought to affect people's health) to "state" and municipal control of the civic or communal environment, in order to guide and direct people.[69]

Another salient characteristic of Huarte's theory about the biology of work is the absence of women. Their elision corresponds to attempts at their exclusion from the increasingly professional ranks of society. As a means of social control, the professionalization of medicine aimed to institutionally dictate society's legal medical practitioners, which resulted in the marginalization of numerous traditional healers such as Jews, Muslims, and women.[70] The professionalization of medicine coincided with the professionalization or reorganization of other occupations in late medieval and early modern Iberia. The creation of society's professional strata progressively stripped the licit right to work from women and others. As discussed in chapters 1 and 2, the separation of occupational tasks along gender lines was frequently unclear during the medieval period especially with regard to the practice of healers and artisans. Women and men often worked alongside one another in markets, apothecary shops, and delivery rooms. The later Middle Ages and the early modern period mark the point at which juridical means were employed more tenaciously than before in order to differentiate professionals from nonprofessionals, that is, to sanction the licit practitioners of fields such as medicine and prostitution. Society's juridical arm was employed most actively to determine those practitioners according to ethnic, gender, and class differences. Although ethnic and gender difference certainly existed before this period, medieval alterity was also articulated differently.[71] The patrol and enforcement of ethnic and gender difference intensified along with the distinction between professionals and nonprofessionals, and simultaneously with the establishment of regulating boards such as the Real Protomedicato and the inquisitorial tribunals.

One of the strategies employed to facilitate the separation and distinction between professionals and nonprofessionals was the legal recognition of official trades (*oficios* such as those of physician and surgeon), which were informally opposed to the societally pervasive tasks (*funciones*) carried out by persons of unofficial and often illicit status. Individuals who performed licit trades were regularly recorded in extant documents, while practitioners who exercised tasks were at worst invisible and at best unclearly alluded to in documents. The hierarchical distinction between trades and tasks constituted an attempt at social control, although the differentiation was often hypothetical and not always apparent in daily life. The establishment of regulating boards, legislation, and the Inquisition attest to the actual lack of control over the workforce that seems to have existed up to that time. With regard to healers and healing practice, the obscured differences between trades and tasks illustrate the lack of control that characterized the relationship between regulating boards and healers of all kinds.

The ambiguous relationship between trades and tasks in *La Celestina* as text and in the main character herself represents the occupational confusion that was present in contemporary daily life. It also reinforces what the professionalization of medicine was trying to carry out: the prohibition of women from medical practice. The ways in which Celestina's jobs are discussed, described, and exercised in the work all attempt to support the exclusion of women from professional arenas. Furthermore, *La Celestina* is an active participant in pervasive societal efforts to *biologize* work according to, in part, binary physiological difference. Huarte's medical treatise crystallizes the biologizing attempts that preceded it. Biology undergirds not only texts such as *La Celestina*, but also society's professionalizing efforts and the marginalization and expulsion of heretics from the fifteenth century onwards. Hence, the maligning of women's work in *La Celestina* is predicated on the discrediting of women's biology. Like the *Spill*, *La Celestina* proposes that women cannot adequately heal or work in many other fields because they constitute the original source of disease and are incompetent.[72]

In act 1, Pármeno claims that Celestina once had six trades, but his list represents the confluence of trades and tasks rather than their clear separation. Even her evidently low-brow jobs appear licit and authorized under the rubric of trades:

Ella tenía seys officios, conviene [a] saber: labrandera, perfumera, maestra de hazer afeytes y de hazer virgos, alcahueta y un poco hechizera. Era el primero officio cobertura de los otros, so color del qual muchas moças destas sirvientes entravan en su casa a labrarse y a labrar camisas y gorgueras y muchas otras cosas. (1.110)

[She has had six trades: seamstress, perfumer, cosmetic maker, repairer of maidenheads, go-between, and a bit of witch. The first of these has always been a cover-up for all the rest. Thus protected, she has brought many girls of the working classes to her house to be repaired, to make shirts and gorgets and many other things.] (1.34)

The fact that Celestina worked in myriad occupational fields was not considered unusual for medieval and early modern women of the working classes. The traditional male model of a lifelong career is not usually helpful when studying women's occupations during this period because women traditionally held more than one job in a lifetime.[73] However, all of Celestina's tasks relate to the two overriding functions that she has in the text, as an *alcahueta*-brothel owner / procurer of prostitution, and as a mediating agent for the healing of disease.[74] When Celestina appears performing tasks other than those of an *alcahueta* and healer, as in act 4 where she is a saleswoman of thread, the seemingly benign occupation belies more ominous objectives, which in that case are her functions as an *alcahueta*. Celestina and other characters frequently refer to a multitude of occupations and tasks that she notably exercised in the past.

Pármeno's list of trades is noteworthy for what it fails to say. He neglects to mention Celestina's past activity as an old whore, although he names the ambiguous "restorer of virgins" as if it were a legitimate trade. Although he later alludes to medical practices, such as "Hazíase física de niños" (1.111) [She acted as a doctor for children] (1.35), he only uses the term *oficio* to describe the six occupations listed above. Two of them, the restorer of virgins and the witch, were not official licit occupations. However, it has been shown that women who worked in some of the other occupational areas that he mentions, such as the seamstress, the perfumer, and the cosmetic-maker, achieved at least partial official legal status through their activities in guilds during the medieval period.[75]

In spite of the fact that information about women's participation in Iberian guilds continues to be scant, it is certain that they took part in some artisan guilds as widows or daughters of male members.[76] This familial condition, however, is not asserted in the description of Galician women's participation in a medieval guild for artisans of *azabache* (jet, a compact, black coal used for jewelry), called the *gremio de acibecheiros de Santiago* (jet-workers guild of Santiago), suggesting the possibility that women joined on their own.[77] Although contemporary historians are as yet unable to develop more extensively the history of women's participation in Iberian guilds, through their work with medieval ordinances they have recently shown that women were present in many areas of public life. In fifteenth-century Cordova and Seville, for example, women worked independently in a number of occupations, including as wheat traders (*alfondigueras*), goat herders (*cabriteras*), butchers (*carniceras*), fruit vendors (*fruteras*), orchard growers (*hortelanas*), innkeepers (*mesoneras*), bakers (*panaderas*), fisherwomen (*pescaderas*), tavernkeepers (*taberneras*), and commercial businesswomen (*tenderas*).[78] In fifteenth-century Cuenca, women's work included that of wet nurse (*ama*), physician (*física*), hospital official (*hospitalaria*), agricultural laborer (*labradora*), washerwoman (*lavandera*), and midwife (*partera*).[79]

With regard to women's matriculation in healing guilds, so far there is no documentation indicating the existence of midwives' guilds.[80] Yet, the skills of women surgeons were probably recognized by the medieval surgical guild of Paris, which seems to have included them as members.[81] Towler and Bramall also contend that several women apprentices were admitted to the thirteenth-century barber-surgeons' guilds in Britain.[82] Furthermore, Katharine Park has pointed to six women doctors who matriculated in the Florentine Guild of Doctors, Apothecaries, and Grocers.[83] At least two of them were daughters of doctors, and as Park suggests, they probably learned their trade from their fathers. Park also believes that there were other women listed in other "distributions." The fact that no women appear in the Florentine records before 1353 and after 1408 confirms scholars' interpretations of the guild statutes, that the field was somewhat more flexible during the years immediately following the outbreak of the first plague epidemic. Women's skills were simply too valuable and needed to be disallowed.[84]

I have been unable to locate any documentation about the participation of women healers in Iberian guilds, although in chapter 1 I outlined the different kinds of women healers who have been documented. Nevertheless, the relationship between Celestina and women workers in Iberian society is very evident. Despite the frequent requirement of the matriculation of men family members, the licit participation of Iberian women in nonhealing guilds demonstrates the sort of legal, societal recognition of women's work against which *La Celestina* is written. Women's public, economic presence and their liberal, independent movements are clearly undermined in *La Celestina* since the text discourages women's licit participation in all occupational fields, whether they were considered unquestionable trades or not.

In Pármeno's list of six trades, it is also odd that he only hints at

Celestina's healing services in passing, despite the fact that the reader first meets her as a healer in act 1 when she is enlisted to remedy Calisto's lovesickness (she is not approached to explicitly serve as a go-between of amorous relations). Although none of the occupations he lists directly refers to a highly skilled, professional healing activity, Celestina's duties as a cosmetics manufacturer and as a restorer of women's virginity point to more lowly and even ambiguous forms of medical practice. Pármeno emphasizes the unskilled, cosmetic aspect of the barber's profession as one who shaved hair or applied makeup, and avoids more complicated responsibilities that barbers frequently carried out such as bloodletting or simple surgical procedures.[85]

The "trade" described as restorer of virgins was one of the most incriminating characterizations attributed to women go-betweens during this period. It was damaging because it acknowledged that go-betweens were capable of deceiving men, and because their dubious deeds affected such a wide variety of areas of cultural life. The routine discussion and debate about virginity from antiquity on stresses the cultural anxieties that the topic produced. With regard to theological and religious importance, virginity constituted that which both aligned mundane women with the Virgin Mary and set them apart from her. It assured sinners of the purity of the channel (the Virgin) who mediated the world and God.[86] Its practical utility was based on the belief that virginity insured the integrity of the female body clearly for men's and, in certain early instances, for women's benefit. In medieval Castile, for example, the potential for virgins to gain more property and wealth (*arras* or endowments) upon marrying was sometimes far greater than for nonvirgins.[87] In other words, virginity represented tremendous benefit and certain prestige for both women and men. For that reason, it was societally important to be able to distinguish true virgins from false, restored ones, which is one of the foundations that motivates the implicit argument in *La Celestina* against women's work.

Various discourse alluded to the restoration of virgins throughout the medieval and early modern periods. Medical treatises, however, were largely silent on the subject, although William of Saliceto (*Summa conservationis et curationis*, Bologna 1285), Pseudo-Albertus Magnus (*De Secretis Mulierum*, late thirteenth or early fourteenth century), and the Trotula corpus (twelfth century and beyond) discuss the signs of virginity and how to tell whether a woman has been "corrupted." Although both William and Pseudo-Albertus take skeptical, mistrustful tones against the feasibility of testing accurately women's virginity, they nonetheless suggest various methods of evaluation. Urine inspection, they claim, can be used to establish virginity or lack thereof, although some people prefer obstetrical examinations that, according to William of Saliceto, "will disclose whether the knot of virginity is tightly tied and wrinkled with veins and arteries that stand out like creases on a chickpea, and whether the mouth of the womb is firmly closed."[88] These writers guard against assuming that blood during intercourse points to a woman's chastity, for it could be caused by menstruation. They also believe the size of the vaginal opening to be an accurate measure of a woman's virginity. Like the Trotula works, William also offers a method for remedying the loss of virginity: the corrupted woman should "wash the mouth of the vulva, sit in a hot bath, rub on certain prescribed ointments, and place in the vulva a dove's intestine that she has filled with blood."[89] The medical works maintain that despite virginity's cultural significance, its veracity is nearly impossible to determine.

Hence, Celestina's duties as a virgin-maker correspond to these anxieties about the status of women's virginity, insofar as virginity has ramifications for men's well-being and social control. Celestina's expertise is directed toward prostitutes so that they can work again as virgins, and toward nonprostitutes so that they can marry as virgins. In effect, Celestina invents whoring virgins, a paradox that defies efforts to separate virgins from other women. Pármeno claims that Celestina sold the same woman servant three times as a virgin: "quando vino por aquí el embaxador francés, tres vezes vendió por virgen una criada que tenía" (1.112) [when the French ambassador was here she sold him as a virgin three times over the same one of her servants] (1.36). Seemingly, Celestina was able to sell the servant three times to the same French ambassador, suggesting that her success as a "virgin-maker" depends upon her ability to deceive the same man. Costa Fontes has stated that virginity ultimately "does not matter much" in *La Celestina*: "for, after all, Celestina is able to restore it through her technical ability, as if she could also perform her own 'miracles'; no one seems to be able to detect the difference, anyway."[90] However, it is precisely her skill at restoring virginity that exemplifies Celestina's duplicitous nature as a deceiver of men. Celestina defies the attempts in late medieval textual discourse to create solid divisions between virgins and nonvirgins and between pairs of other opposite terms. By restoring women's virginity, she threatens the entire rhetorical machinery deployed throughout the late Middle Ages and the early modern period that sought to naturalize virginity for the edification of gender-based hierarchies of power.

Like the arguments against women's domination of reproductive procedures in the *Spill*, *La Celestina* argues against women's access to other women's bodies because the outcome will only be the deceit and deception of men. It is not merely that Celestina's restoration of virginity constitutes an ability to create illusions, but more importantly, she truly remakes and restores virgins. Her complete restoration of the female body to a pure, integral state sunders that which is culturally valued in this case, i.e., men's control over women's sexual activity and over how their bodies signify. She manipulates women's bodies to such a degree that they signify according to her own desire. Her control of materials, of women's bodies, and of signification itself makes her a most disruptive figure for the book's contemporary, male, Castilian readership and society.

Celestina's virgin-making is also specious because it erases the trace of disease and contagion. With the outbreak of syphilis in the 1490s, disease was increasingly associated with sexual behavior and prostitution.[91] The threat of disease contagion and through it, the potential destruction of men, was eliminated by Celestina's skill at destroying the signs of nonvirginity. If a man thought that a woman was a virgin, then it was unlikely that she would transmit disease to him.

Celestina's methods for virgin-making are connected to both sewing and surgery. Pármeno relates two methods by which Celestina the surgeon / seamstress restores the female body to an integral state:

> Esto de los virgos, unos hazía de bexiga y otros curava de punto. Tenía en un tabladillo, en una caxuela pintada, unas agujas delgadas y peligeros, y hilos de seda encerados, y colgadas allí raízes de hojaplasma y fuste sanguino, cebolla albarrana y cepacaballo. Hazía con esto maravillas. (1.112)

> [In the matter of maidenheads—some she made of bladder, some she sewed. In a little painted chest on a stand she had some thin needles, such as leatherworkers use, and waxed silk threads, and there were roots of *hojaplasma* and *fuste sanguino*, squill, and cardoon. She worked wonders with these.] (1.36)

Women's work is not innocuous in this text, as the two methods pertain to both sewing and medical surgery. In the same way that William of Saliceto had prescribed the use of an animal part to remake virgins (the dove's intestine), Pármeno suggests that renewed virgins were made from animal bladders ("unos hazía de bexiga" [some she made of bladder]). Pármeno's second reference to surgical procedure ("y otros curava de punto" [and some she sewed]) is significant because surgeons at this time actively organized guilds in order to combat doctors' perceptions that they were incompetent healers.[92] Medical doctors had reason to malign surgeons in order to promote their own profession. Thus, the figure of an *alcahueta* who exercises surgical procedures would have been read at this time as ineffective and incompetent because of her gender and due to the kind of procedural tactics that she employed.

But Celestina clearly and ironically demonstrates her *competence* as a virgin-maker in the text. The book suggests that she should be avoided not because of her incompetence in this regard, but rather because her abilities are in fact superior. She achieves that which the medical profession claimed to possess—the ability to restore the body to a previous state of wholeness, integrity, and "health." She is completely adept at eliminating external agents that threaten the body's integrity, which in terms of her abilities as restorer of virgins means that she eliminates the vestiges of men's presence altogether from women's bodies. The most imperiled outside agents in this case are men, whose physical violations of the limits of the female body are simply made invisible by Celestina's stitching. Men's lack of control over the determinations of women's virginity and other qualities would have made Celestina a disturbing figure to the reader of the sixteenth century, for, among other reasons, Celestina has the best access to women.

Her channel to other women includes not just clients, but also those with whom she teaches and works. Women stream in and out of her house supposedly to sew (*labrar*) under her auspices as seamstresses and knitters. According to Antonio de Nebrija's dictionary of 1492, the verb *labrar* signifies *bordar* and *boslar*, both meaning to embroider.[93] In Alfonso de Palencia's dictionary of 1490, *labrar* is linked to wool-working in the entry for the Greek goddess Minerva.[94] Hence, stitching defines Celestina's work from the innocent work of the *labrandera* (seamstress) to the more formidable work of sewing-related virgin-surgery. But the jobs also suggest another way in which Celestina's relations with other women needed to be derided at the time. In an analogous way to the weaving of thread-like materials in embroidery, knitting, or dress-making, Celestina's supervision of the work of young women is characterized by a threatening lineage of knowledge passed down to her students. The text suggests that the source of knowledge, the *medianera* Celestina, requires surveillance or eradication.

Despite Celestina's access and mobility, however, she is everywhere and nowhere. Her work within the text reflects a very different period in her life from many of the tasks that she clearly exercised in the past, such as the six trades that Pármeno describes. By the time the reader meets her in act 1, Celestina has been occupationally and physically marginalized in society. She is the first Iberian go-between who is marginalized textually in the modern sense, having been forced to move her brothel to an area near the river, apparently on the outskirts of the larger urban community. Belonging to a poor economic class, her presence is ubiquitous both on the streets and in people's homes. Geographically, she seems to be present everywhere, but economically and socially her status has only declined.

Her societal marginality ironically allows her constant movement within the city and her virtually unimpeded access to women's bodies and people's homes. Old, ugly, and bearded in act 4, she appears at Alisa's house and announces to the servant Lucrecia that she is selling thread: "Y tanbién, como a las viejas nunca nos fallecen necessidades, mayormente a mí, que tengo de mantener hijas ajenas, ando a vender un poco de hilado" (4.151) [Since we old ladies perennially have our necessities—I especially have them, supporting other people's daughters, as I do—I am going around selling a bit of thread] (4.70). Celestina has practiced too many trades and tasks to name, as is made clear throughout the text. In this act, Lucrecia ironically reveals to Alisa that Celestina has more than thirty occupations:

> Señora, perfuma tocas, haze solimán, y otros treynta officios; conosce mucho en yervas, cura niños, y aun algunos la llaman la vieja lapidaria. (4.152)
>
> [Her work, my lady? Why, she perfumes bonnets, makes cosmetics like corrosive sublimate, for example—and does thirty other miscellaneous things. She is well-versed, too, in the lore of herbs, and at times she acts as a physician to children. Some people even call her the old lapidary.] (4.71)

Lucrecia explicitly refers to a gamut of healing functions. Besides Celestina's vast knowledge of herbal and stone remedies, she also cures children and makes *solimán* (mercuric chloride; corrosive sublimate [obsolete]), an odorless, white crystal or powder. The Castilian physician Andrés Laguna (1499–1559) noted its strength and uses as a form of medical treatment in book five, chapter 49 of his *Comentarios*. Mercuric chloride, or mercury, was commonly mixed with wine to fight pain caused by syphilis, but some physicians believed the substance to be poisonous and toxic. Laguna associates the misuse of the substance with incompetent women healers who kill children:

> Una cosa puedo yo testificar del azogue [solimán], que muchas veces le he visto dar a cucharadas en España a los niños, por mano de ciertas hechiceras pestilenciales, contra el Alfirer; de los cuales no me acuerdo que alguno con el tal remedio escapase... Por eso las matronas cuerdas y honradas no confían de semejantes furias la salud de sus dulces hijos que tanto importa, sino llaman a excelentísimos médicos, que con experiencia y juicio hagan lo que el arte y la razón ordena.[95]

> [There is one thing I can attest to about mercuric chloride, that many times in Spain I have seen certain pestilential witches give it to children by the tablespoon, against a children's disease called *Alfirer*.[96] I do not remember any children escaping from that remedy... For that reason wise and honorable ladies do not entrust their sweet children's health, which is so important to them, to such monsters. Rather, they call on most honorable doctors who will carry out, with their vast experience and good judgment, that which is reasonable and appropriate to their profession.]

Laguna then repeats that mercuric chloride mixed in water may be safely consumed, unlike the witches' lethal remedy of tablespoons of pure chemical. Laguna's clear message in the above passage is that witches poison and kill children because of their incompetence. He forces a second moral corollary to the story: that honorable women who are sound of mind (unlike mothers who seek the care of witches) call on the services of "most honorable doctors" who, with their experience and sound judgment, are guided by reason and according to the exigencies of the medical profession. Laguna's audience in this case seems to be a class of women who value honor and a sound mind, especially with regard to the care of their children. The moral of his story should have affected women, whether literate or not, who possessed the means to call on a medical professional.

In *La Celestina*, Lucrecia's seemingly ingenuous list of occupations is neither naive nor coincidental. In the same way, Celestina's care of children as cited by Lucrecia and Pármeno, juxtaposed to her activities as a fabricator of a potential poison, is neither random nor casual. The occupations go hand in hand with Laguna's similar, albeit later, contrast of the incompetent woman healer (with her supposedly evil link to witchcraft) and the only viable and sane alternative to the care of children, the male medical professional. Lucrecia's choice of occupations is especially provocative in this act because she recounts them to Melibea's mother, Alisa, suggesting that the woman healer's incompetence could carry over into her dealings with Melibea.

Celestina's role as one who sells thread is only a mask for her true objectives. Duplicity is the characteristic that allows her access to women's bodies and into people's homes. Celestina's ostensible role as an itinerant saleswoman is a pretext for the real motivation of her visit, to persuade Melibea to relieve Calisto of the disease of lovesickness by way of sexual relations. The other supposed reason for her visit is to collect money from Alisa as relief from Celestina's impoverished state. It is significant that two kinds of work go hand in hand here, both because the benign sales task camouflages another more evil objective, and because women's healing is linked to sewing. In Pármeno's quote from act 1, he says that the occupation of seamstress is that which entwines or covers them all. It serves as the engendering rubric from which all the other occupations emerge; it is the net or web in which all other occupations are woven together and captured. The network or system that Celestina's jobs represent is probably best recognized by Celestina herself:

> Pocas virgines, a Dios gracias, has tu visto en esta ciudad que hayan abierto tienda a vender, de quien yo no haya sido corredora de su primer hilado. En nasciendo la mochacha, la hago scrivir en mi registro, y esto para que yo sepa quántas se me salen de la red. ¿Qué pensavas, Sempronio? ¿Havíame de mantener del viento? ¿Heredé otra herencia? ¿Tengo otra casa o viña? ¿Conóscesme otra hazienda, más deste officio de que como y bevo, de que visto y calço? En esta ciudad nascida, en ella criada, manteniendo honrra, como todo el mundo sabe, ¿conoçida, pues, no soy? Quien no supiere mi nombre y mi casa, tenle por estrangero. (3.141–42)

> [There are few virgins in this town who have opened up shop without my help in selling their first yarn. Whenever a baby girl is born around here I have her name inscribed in my register so that I will know how many of them have escaped my net. Did you think I lived on wind? What other patrimony do I have?—what other house or vineyard? Do you know of any source of income I have besides this business? Where

else do my food and drink come from—my clothes and my shoes? Born in this city, brought up here, trying to keep up appearances, as everyone knows—am I not universally known? My son, if any man knows not my name or where my dwelling is—hold him to be a stranger in the land.] (3.61)

Not only does the passage illustrate Celestina's social importance through her notoriety and recognition by others, but it emphasizes the existence of a women's network for both the maintenance of honor, and for the mutual maintenance of women themselves. Women work in whatever way they can, Celestina in her way, and other women either in shops or in brothels.[97]

Women not only sew, knit, manipulate materials, and put pieces together, but they also sell sex, earn money for it, and corrupt other women in the process. Celestina's inevitable corruption of Melibea had already been articulated and established by Lucrecia in act 4. Like Celestina's guise as a saleswoman of thread, the emphasis on Melibea's honor and loss of virginity in act 4 and throughout the work only disguises a more threatening and disturbing social fear, i.e. the literal corruption, destruction, and disintegration of men by diseased and contagious women. Celestina devises nets and webs of various kinds, such as the circuit her movements made through the city, her visits to monasteries where friars give her money (4.154), or her movements from one house to another.[98] Furthermore, just as her sewing and knitting efforts manifest themselves as whole pieces of fabric and other items, the network of women who work at her house / brothel, both as prostitutes and seamstresses, belies an interconnected circuit of contagious disease intending to destroy the fabric of society—the male, Christian, Castilian body.

Despite the seeming normality of many of her trades and tasks, the meanings and values that they generate frequently deviate from the expected. For instance, much of the lexicon related to the trades and tasks of sewing and stitching carry with them another entire register of erotic signification. Despite the fact that in themselves such double meanings do not evoke images of seditious acts, in the figure of Celestina, the combination of meanings in such language makes her volatile. Several studies have demonstrated the erotic meaning of the lexicon related to stitching, such as the metaphorical significance of thread, or skein of thread or yarn (*hilado*), as cupidity, and as lust.[99] The verb *labrar*, as it pertains to ploughing, has also been shown to mean "to fornicate deeply and vigorously."[100] Celestina actively exercises that role in her occupation as a *labrandera*, which designates two kinds of work, that of seamstress and prostitute. According to Costa Fontes, the following terms signify in two ways: *alfiletero* refers to vagina and needle cushion; *aguja* (needle) and *alfiler* (pin) both signify phallus; and *dedal* points to vulva and thimble.[101]

Benign tasks also make Celestina appear deviant because of her close proximity to other women, which converts her otherwise innocuous jobs into potentially radical and rebellious acts. In act 7, for instance, her efforts to heal Areúsa's illness of suffocation of the womb are indistinguishable from attempts to seduce her for Celestina's own pleasure:

> Areúsa: Más arriba la siento sobre el estómago.
> Celestina: ¡Bendígate Dios y el señor Sant Miguel Ángel, y qué gorda y fresca que estás; qué pechos y qué gentileza! Por hermosa te tenía hasta agora, viendo lo que todos podían ver. Pero agora te digo que no ay en la cibdad tres cuerpos tales como el tuyo en quanto yo conozco; no paresce que ayas quinze años. ¡O quién fuera hombre y tanta parte alcançara de ti para gozar tal vista! (7.202)

> [Areúsa: I feel hurt a little up over my stomach.
> Celestina: Lord love you, and may the blessed Angel Michael prosper you! How fat and fresh you are! What breasts! What loveliness! I have known all along how beautiful you were from seeing what everybody else can see; but now I can tell you that as far as I know there are not in this whole town three girls as well formed as you are. You don't look a day over fifteen. Oh, if I were only a man to be allowed thus to enjoy the sight of you!] (7.121)

What makes Celestina's maligning even more transparent in the text is the fact that the supposedly deviant woman-to-woman seduction constitutes a previously accepted mode of healing for the disease of *mal de la madre*.[102] With Areúsa in this scene, Celestina carries out in a sense the remedy prescribed by older medical writers such as Galen and Avicenna.[103] In *On the Affected Parts* (*De locis affectibus*), Galen reported a case in which a midwife informed him that a widow he was treating was afflicted with a retracted uterus. He pronounced the woman cured when the midwife administered hot remedies to her vulva by hand:

> On application the heat of this medicine and the contact with her sexual organs provoked [uterine] contractions associated with the pain and pleasure similar to that experienced during intercourse. As a result the

woman secreted a large quantity of heavy semen and thus lost the bothersome complaints.[104]

Since suffocation of the womb was thought to be caused by retained seed, medical doctors prescribed sexual remedies in order for seed to be emitted at the point of orgasm. For this reason, coitus with husbands was prescribed as the most effective and readily available cure. However, as Galen, Avicenna, and others implicitly and explicitly suggested, manual treatments such as masturbation and the digital therapies of midwives were encouraged for the patient's well-being.

Many later Christians hesitated to repeat the digital remedy. William of Saliceto, for instance, did not discuss manual manipulation as a cure for the disease, although he recognized its cause as retained seed. In the *De secretis mulierum*, Albertus Magnus was even more prudish, as he avoided elaborating on the Galenic case.[105] Yet in a medieval Castilian allusion to the manual therapy, Bernard of Gordon declared in the *Lilio de medicina* that a midwife's digital remedies constituted one step in the cure of *mal de la madre* when an "uncorrupted" woman found herself in a state of paroxysm. After applying certain compounds such as salt and vinegar to her extremities, binding her arms and legs, and introducing a series of fetid smelling salts to the woman's nostrils, Gordon gave the following instructions:

> E despues la partera vnte su dedo en olio muscelino o de balsamo: o de espicanardi. E sy fuere la muger corrompida meta el dedo aqui e ay e meneelo fuertemente aqui e ay: como la materia veninosa salga a las partes de fuera. E despues faga cosas para estornudar con vinagre e castoreo, pimienta, mostaza e eleboro. (fol. 173r)

> [And then the midwife should lubricate her finger with *muscelino* balm,[106] balsam oil, or spikenard balm. And if the woman is not a virgin, the midwife must move her finger around vigorously here and there until the injurious seed comes out. And then she ought to apply substances so the woman will sneeze, such as vinegar and castor, pepper, mustard, and hellebore.]

Gordon called for an application of similar medical / sexual therapies that Galen had described in the case of the midwife. After lubricating her finger with oil, the midwife should shake her finger around the woman's vaginal area (*aqui e ay*) in such a way that would stimulate the evacuation of the injurious seed, that is, sperm or menses. It is unclear whether or not Gordon expects that it will simply fall out due to the midwife's finger movement, or whether the woman client will experience the physical effects of sexual orgasm.

The anonymous *Tratado de patología general* claimed that after applying balm to her finger, the midwife should introduce it into the uterus and clean it of the coagulated blood if there was any there. Next, she should insert a suppository into the uterus, and in this way apparently heal the woman of her affliction (fol. 101v). In another Castilian treatise, Rojas's doctor friend Francisco López de Villalobos, in his *Sumario de medicina*, described most of the same remedies as Gordon and the *Tratado de patología general* for curing what he called *prefocación de la madre*.[107] López de Villalobos began with prescribing marriage, but said that if the afflicted woman wanted to remain a virgin that her extremities should be bound, and that she ought to be given noxious smelling salts. This author omits all mention of manual contact with the uterus or the vagina (fol. 17r).

The Iberian Hebrew treatise, "A Record of the Diseases Occurring in the Genital Members," prescribes two methods involving the midwife for remedying suffocation of the uterus. First, she should place "drying things such as a cumin electuary" in the womb, after lubricating her fingers with laurel and ebony oils. If the illness has reached a more serious stage, then the woman's hands and knees should be tightly bound and the midwife ought to "massage the orifice of her womb" with materials such as ebony oil.[108] While none of these treatises attaches an erotic or sexual connotation to the midwife's manual manipulation, the infrequency of its appearance in medical treatises, and its alteration from Galen's original account suggest that part of the *medianera*'s threat in medieval Iberian society consisted of her potential for administering sexual, hygienic services to women patients.

In *La Celestina*, if the ultimate cure for Areúsa's disease is the emission of seed through orgasm, then Celestina's "seduction" is the impetus for relief. But, the method clearly fails since Celestina later prescribes coitus. The prevalent omission and modification of the midwife's method by Christian medical writers indicates that part of the medical profession's anxiety about women healers is the ambiguous distinction between their hygienic and sexual practice.

Celestina's sexual and erotic overtures toward the younger Areúsa are preceded in the same act by her odd references to her friend Claudina, Pármeno's mother:[109]

¿Quién sabía mis secretos? ¿A quién descobría mi coraçón? ¿Quién era todo mi bien y descanso, sino tu madre, más que mi hermana y comadre? ¡O qué graciosa era, o qué desembuelta, limpia, varonil! (7.196)

[Who knew my secrets? *Who* was my bosom friend, if not your mother? *Who* in all the world was my treasure and repose? Who, indeed, but your mother—so much more to me than sister or companion! Oh, how deft she was! How open and clean-cut! How spirited!] (7.115)[110]

The masculinization of a woman in both passages suggests another way in which Celestina's various jobs are deprecated in the text. In her exchange with Areúsa, only a man could take pleasure in the young woman in the same way that Celestina does ironically as a woman. In the second quote, Claudina is called manly or *varonil*, a paradoxically masculine woman who worked alongside Celestina in prostitution (1.120). As in the episode between Areúsa and Celestina, the exchange between Celestina and Pármeno illustrates a larger concern with the role of the *alcahueta / medianera*: her potential sexual activity with other women.

Furthermore, the masculinization of the *medianera* constitutes another strategy to malign her as one who transgresses socially acceptable boundaries. Celestina is referred to as bearded on several occasions (1.103, 3.138). The constant double-meaning of the terminology related to sewing, coupled with Celestina's proximity to other women and what she does with them, are developed in order to cast her as deviant from regulatory norms about women's place in society. They are meant to demonstrate why women should be excluded from so-called professions such as medicine and from trade groups such as guilds. At the same time that the text defines the *medianera* as one who exercises innumerable tasks within a variety of fields, it also tries to systematically dismantle any worth or respectability that she might have as, for instance, a healer, a seamstress, or a pimp.

These strategies to discredit women's work in *La Celestina* are inextricably linked to the palimpsest principle that marks Celestina's characterization. Pármeno's comment about her trades in act 1 indicates the parodic distance maintained between Celestina's vocational activities and those of effective professionals who should be carrying them out in society. The resemblance between her jobs and those of women in society are maligned by way of their distance from the Virgin's and from those of the supposedly capable men professionals in society. Celestina fatally imitates the practice of these trades, which Pármeno parodically describes.

This parody suggests that if Celestina's trades were conducted by the most adept people, then damaging consequences for social order could be avoided. Like Celestina's parodic imitation of the erased Virgin, the parody of these cultural trades necessitates Celestina's simultaneous resemblance and distance from the objects of the parody. Her jobs and tasks would have been recognized by many sixteenth-century readers as those that men were trying to dominate or alter in Castilian society. The parody of these trades hinges on imitation and distance, the latter of which is most compellingly focused on Celestina's biology and biological functions. Celestina diverges from normative biology, which is unambiguously masculine.

The entire text of *La Celestina* can be characterized as a series of attempts to shape the *medianera* as divergent and divisive in all aspects of her being. Celestina's otherness, her divergence from static norms, is constituted by her continual presentation as a threat to the social order. On a practical, quotidian level, she works independently and apart from municipal regulation, so that she escapes the control of judicial process and governmental sanction. A large part of her character depends upon her relation to disease, gender, and sexuality. The continued need to textually present women as chaotic threats is only intensified in the object of the next chapter, *La Lozana andaluza*, where disease, gender, and sexuality continue to determine the features of the woman healer and intercessor.[111]

Rojas uses a number of strategies in *La Celestina* to subvert medieval textual models that supported women healers. He employs the strategy of parody to show that Celestina is incapable of imitating the beneficent, healing mediations of the erased image of the Virgin. He undermines Celestina's attempts to emulate the Virgin by depicting her as a witch who colludes with the devil by way of conjurations. Rojas also undermines women's conventional, multivocational status by linking Celestina's healing tasks with prostitution, which suggests that women healers and prostitutes are synonymous.

Rojas alludes to favorable models of women healers in medical texts to erode the credibility of the woman healer. Celestina tries to effect the lovers' union as a remedy for lovesickness instead of attempting to distract Calisto from his excessive cogitations. And unlike the favorable model of the *Speculum al foderi*'s messenger / healer who successfully restores men's well-being and satiates their desires, Celestina eventually brings about Calisto's death. Rojas also relies on medical theories of his day that linked biology with occupations. He tries to show that multivocational, women workers threaten social integrity and well-being because their biology and biological functions are inherently suspect. Evil women generate more corrupt women biologically and through their conventional vocations as healers, seamstresses, and *alcahuetas*. Celestina is a palimpsest with the Virgin in the background who will only reproduce more women who will try to imitate her (Celestina), thereby threatening the individual and social order.

This Evian / Celestine lineage and reproduction extends to the possible generation of Celestina-like texts, which is what Francisco Delicado's sixteenth-century *La Lozana andaluza* represents. But instead of the parodic overlapping that characterizes Celestina, Lozana is an ironic double of herself. She is monstrous and diseased, and simultaneously desirable. Delicado shifts from parody to irony as a strategy to discredit the sixteenth-century woman healer. *La Lozana andaluza* plays out the ironic status of women healers in sixteenth-century society because the institutionalized mechanisms of the professionalization of medicine were frequently ineffective in curbing the popular appeal of women healers.

La Lozana andaluza further reflects the newfound stratification of textual representations of women in Iberian society evidenced by the cultural dialogue about the status of women that men promoted in the fifteenth and sixteenth centuries.[112] A profeminist and antifeminist dialogue developed among men writers and demonstrated men's widening, dualistic division of opinion about the status of women. This division is evident in the ironic *La Lozana andaluza*. It was apparent in *La Celestina* that the mediations that Celestina exercised through her parody of the Virgin only engendered chaos and death. Yet, almost thirty years later, as women healers continued to be sought out for their healing services despite attempts to malign them, Lozana's intercessions are not so transparent. She cannot be depicted as simply good or evil because Lozana is ironically and plainly both.

4
Eva and Not Eva: The Irony of Well-Being in Francisco Delicado's *La Lozana andaluza*

The *Retrato de la Loçana andaluza* (*La Lozana andaluza*) was published anonymously in Venice in 1528. It is attributed to Francisco Delicado, a syphilitic converted (*converso*) priest from Cordova who either sought refuge in Italy after the Jewish expulsion from Spain in 1492, or went to Rome hoping to obtain an ecclesiastical post.[1] He exiled himself to Venice in 1527 because of indictments by Romans toward Spaniards. Delicado's interests ranged from the writing of both "recreational" and more sober texts to book publishing. He generated a prolific and broad textual output during his lifetime including four original works and six edited ones.[2] Besides *La Lozana*, he composed a handbook for clerics, called the *Spechio vulgare per li sacerdoti che administraranno li sacramenti in ciascheduna parrochia* (Rome 1526?). In addition, it is believed that he wrote two treatises about disease, the lost *De consolatione infirmorum*, probably written in Rome in 1525, and *El modo de adoperare el legno de India occidentale*, again probably written in Rome in 1525 and republished in Venice in 1529.[3]

His publications include two editions of the *Tragicomedia de Calisto y Melibea* (1531; Venice 1534), the second of which contains his original treatise the "Introducción que muestra el Delicado a pronunciar la lengua española." He published two chivalry novels, the *Amadís de Gaula* (Venice 1533) and *Los tres libros del muy esforçado caballero Primaleón et Polendos su hermano* (Venice 1534), an edition of Diego de San Pedro's *Cárcel de amor* (Venice 1531), and a treatise called *Questión de amor de dos enamorados* (Venice 1533).[4] Like many writers and publishers of his day, Delicado added his own framing, explanatory writings to at least two of his published editions. According to Tatiana Bubnova, he substituted the existing prologue of the original edition for his own in the *Amadís*, and in the *Primaleón*, he wrote his own introduction to each of the three books.[5]

Delicado's works demonstrate a constant preoccupation with the reader's understanding of the text, and with his or her well-being. Not surprisingly, then, Delicado's works are further marked by a keen interest in healing and disease, which characterizes three of his four authored works, *La Lozana andaluza, El modo de adoperare el legno de India occidentale,* and the *De consolatione infirmorum.* They all employ women healers in different ways, if the latter can be assumed to parallel its apparent model, Boethius's sixth-century *De consolatione philosophiae* in which the feminized Philosophy serves as the healer of Boethius's ills and pain. Furthermore, Delicado's editions of the *Tragicomedia de Calisto y Melibea* are significant in this regard because they further demonstrate his interest in *medianeras.*

Until quite recently, Delicado was more well-known as a medical writer than for his "literary" output. Eighteenth- and nineteenth-century physicians often cited his treatise on the gaiac remedy for syphilis, *El modo de adoperare,* and included him in medical encyclopedias. Not until *La Lozana andaluza* reappeared in 1875 and received a wider circulation were his "literary" talents recognized. He was sometimes listed twice in encyclopedic collections of the nineteenth century, once as "a man of letters" and again as a scholar, physician, and priest.[6]

Delicado's concern with disease and healing is connected to his own affliction with syphilis, which he says he suffered for 23 years.[7] Two scholars agree that he spent a great part of that time at the *Hospital de Santiago de las Carretas* in Rome where he wrote *La Lozana andaluza.*[8] *La Lozana* and *El modo de adoperare* employ the disease of syphilis as the basis for their discourse about disease. *El modo de adoperare* is a treatise on the curative value of gaiac wood (*palo guayaco*), which was imported from Hispaniola and proved to be one of the most effective yet short-term remedies for syphilis, along with the curative uses of mercury. In contrast, the racy, comic *La Lozana* resists the conventions and clarity of the standard treatise, and mimics for the most part the concentration on the woman healer, and the dramatic structure of *La Celestina.*[9] It is divided into *mamotretos* instead of acts or chapters. *Mamotreto* evokes the customarily staid meanings of *memorandum* (*memo / mamo*—bring to memory) and *chapter,* but also alerts the reader to the text's eroto-sexual level of meaning as it signifies both *ejaculation* and *orgasm.*[10]

Despite the fact that *La Lozana* deals with many other topics and issues besides sex and syphilis, coitus and the disease plainly inform every aspect of the text. *La Lozana* focuses on the movements and activities of the name-changing main character, Aldonza / Lozana / Vellida, the prototypical *medianera* of the sixteenth century. She is a prostitute who works mostly in Rome, although she has also toiled in a variety of Mediterranean ports. Noseless and disfigured from syphilis, she apparently spreads disease to all her clients. The relationship between Lozana and syphilis is one of analogy because they share a facility for moving within cities and between ports. Disease accompanies the prostitute in *La Lozana* and vice versa. Since prostitutes and disease are mobile, and together they infect individuals with incomparable ease, from its very first appearance in Western Europe in the 1490s, syphilis was immediately formulated as an urban, sexual disease associated with prostitution and coitus.

Syphilitic discourse also permeates *La Lozana* at the level of nationalities, nationalisms, and origins. Syphilis's disputed geographical and hence "national" etiology parallels the geographic, ethnic, and national instability of Lozana herself.[11] Theories about syphilis's contagion have largely been motivated by national bias. For instance, when the disease first appeared in the 1490s, a minority of individuals thought that it originated with the Arabs, who were only fully dispossessed of their power on the peninsula in 1492 with the defeat of the last Muslim government at Granada. As time went on, more theories were offered to explain its etiology and means of contagion, all of which manifested clear national, political, or ethnic biases against groups of people. The two major theories still debated today contend that it originated in either America or Italy (depending upon one's national allegiance, it was brought to Italy by the French, or it originated with the Italians).[12] The American theory asserts that the Castilian conquistadors brought the disease back to Europe with them after their forays in the Americas. The Italian theory holds that when Charles VIII of France set out to conquer the kingdom of Naples in 1494 and 1495, his troops contracted what they called "the Neopolitan disease." The Italian theory was even further elaborated so that depending on one's national loyalties, the disease was attributed to either the French or the Italians. Even common references to syphilis were cast in national terms. The Flemish, Dutch, and Northwest Africans, for instance, called it "the Spanish sickness" due to the excesses of the Spanish conquistadors. The Portuguese were more specific in designating it "the Castilian sickness." Much of the nomenclature for syphilis in *La Lozana* attests to the effort to link it to national origins. Among other things, it is referred to as *mal francés* (French illness), *mal napolitano* (Neopolitan illness), and *morbus gallicus* or *morbo gallico* (Gallic disease).[13]

Delicado was not alone in his concern with the disease, nor with his writings about it. Many treatises were written by Valencians, Italians, Germans, and Castilians about its horrors and potential remedies. Joseph Grunpeck's (Augsburg) treatise of 1498 underscores the inability of the medications and remedies of erudite physicians to cure the disease.[14] No universal cure existed for all the afflicted, but two substances were found to be relatively effective in combating the disease: mercury, and powder made from the gaiac tree. Despite the fact that both substances were associated with the remedies of lowly charlatans, bewildered physicians without any other recourse immediately began to avail themselves of such alternative remedies. Afflicted with syphilis himself, Grunpeck ended up rejecting such remedies from trained physicians and resorted to the services of untrained doctors and charlatans whom he believed were the only ones capable of curing the disease.

Castilian and Valencian writers were the most prolific writers on syphilis at the end of the fifteenth and the beginning of the sixteenth centuries. Their works were more than likely available to someone like Delicado, since they were often published both in Italy and Iberia.[15] Because Iberian physicians such as Gaspar Torella and Pedro Pintor served popes in Italy, and others such as Francisco López de Villalobos served in the courts of Italian kings, their works were disseminated and read in both regions.[16] In the same way that Delicado's two syphilitic texts represent different formal structures, works on syphilis by other writers appeared in a variety of generic modes as well. Not only did physicians such as Torella, Pintor, Juan Almenar, and Juan de Vigo compose prose treatises in Castilian and Latin, but in 1498, López de Villalobos published the first work on syphilis in Castilian as a 2,500-line medical poem. The disease got its name in 1530 from a poem written by the Italian doctor Girolamo Fracastoro, *Syphilis sive morbus gallicus*, in which syphilis is the name given to a shepherd.[17]

Hence, the connection between written therapeutic information about syphilis and "literary" texts was established from the outset of the disease's identification. Delicado certainly recognized that information about illness and healing was not required to be composed and disseminated in treatise format, as evidenced by the scatalogical *La Lozana andaluza*, which deals extensively with syphilis and its contradictory partner, pleasurable sex.[18] At the same time, however, *La Lozana*'s "Prólogo" (called a *dedication* in the English translation) claims that the text is therapeutic since the author indicates that it relieves his pain, demonstrating that the ludic, "funny," and recreational text belies a serious preoccupation with disease and healing. Like *La Celestina*, *La Lozana* is concerned with *medianeras* and the kinds of diseases that most typified them. *La Lozana* shares a variety of similarities with *La Celestina* such as its primary focus on the single *medianera*, her relationship to healing and prostitution, and her "marginalized" social status.[19] One of the most salient likenesses is the fact that both texts deal with a particular disease generated by the earthly go-between. The *amor hereos* (lovesickness) and the *mal de la madre* (suffocation of the womb) of the earlier *La Celestina* are often substituted for the syphilis of the later *La Lozana*.[20]

With the appearance of syphilis in Iberia (perhaps the case could be made for Western Europe), the focus of the ludic and recreational texts of the time shifts from courtly love and lovesickness to rampant sexual behavior and venereal disease, from the love-disease of the imagination to the sex-disease of the genitals. María Luisa García Verdugo has argued that, "La sífilis es la metáfora del castigo al engaño de Cupiditas en la literatura española de los siglos XVI y XVII" [Syphilis is the metaphor for the punishment of cupidity's deception in sixteenth- and seventeenth-century Spanish literature].[21] This claim is supported in part by the plethora of writing that sprung from a preoccupation with the sexually constructed disease, works such as the parodic "Chiste de la Cofradía del Grillemón [greñimón=syphilis]" (1552; Cuenca 1602; Barcelona and Valencia 1610), Sebastián de Horozco's "Los privilegios de la Cofradía del Grillimon" (Toledo, early seventeenth century), López de Ubeda's *La pícara Justina* (1605), and Miguel de Cervantes's *El casamiento engañoso* (1613).[22] *La Lozana andaluza* certainly joins this cadre of texts.

Indeed, much of the Western European literature of the early sixteenth century "seized on a theme [syphilis] which provided ample opportunities for social satire or for moralizing in the narrow sense of the word."[23] Syphilis's moral significance as a punishment of the afflicted individual is a result of the way the disease was constructed and made to signify in European cultures. Quétel claims that the identification of "high-risk" groups, notably prostitutes, was a prophylactic measure carried out since the earliest identifications of the disease.[24] Clearly, such hygienic measures are not as innocent or beneficent as they appear, since the identification of disease and high-risk groups is not innocuous. The effort to classify groups as most likely to catch and spread disease has two possible results. At the same time that people can be more effectively treated and "educated" if they are deemed "at risk," the naming of high-risk groups is often highly charged with bias based on race, class, gender, and sexual identification. For instance, Cindy Patton has shown how the identification of high-risk AIDS groups (gay men, the poor, intravenous drug users) further stigmatizes those groups as sickly, pathological, contagious, and seemingly dangerous and threatening to society.[25] While it could be argued that Delicado's *La Lozana* lacks a stable moral code and a clear condemnation of the disease, the association of syphilis, women's bodies, *medianeras*, and prostitution directs the way in which the reader thinks about syphilis, women, prostitutes and their attendant connections. In the late-fifteenth- and early-sixteenth-century medical treatises about syphilis, women were routinely cast in the role of contaminator and men were advised to avoid sexual contact with them, especially when they were prostitutes.[26] Thus, syphilis's overarching behavioral / moral lesson in the sixteenth century would have been recognized by anyone familiar with the disease: avoid sexual contact with infected women, especially prostitutes.

In the same way that lovesickness allowed medical writers to "master" society's most compelling anxieties about eros, syphilis articulates many of the social and political anxieties of the sixteenth and seventeenth centuries, including sexual behavior; criminality; prostitution; women's work and worth in society; the need to build clear distinctions between people based on class, religion, gender, race, and profession; and issues of centralized social control. This is the very broad importance of syphilis in *La Lozana andaluza*. Like Lozana, the disease is difficult to control and is founded on the ironic contradiction that it proceeds from the pleasurable act of sexual intercourse. Contradiction is probably one of the few attributes that can be said to unequivocally constitute *La Lozana andaluza*, as has been pointed out and discussed in Claude Allaigre's introduction to a recent edition.[27]

But the characteristic that most forcefully describes *La Lozana* is that of irony. Irony is used in the work as a discursive strategy at the levels of language, form, and visual application in the woodcuts that accompany the text, some of which are reproduced in Allaigre's edition. Irony gives the contradictions and inconsistencies of the text a strong political force because they reside in the main character Lozana, who is figured as a site of social contention. She is the main object of irony in the text, although most of the other characters are ironic as well.

Linda Hutcheon has observed that irony is always problematic and often frustrating and confounding.[28] Its "edge" is constituted by the fact that it only makes its material more complicated instead of less ambiguous.[29] No matter what role an ironist or an audience grants it, Hutcheon claims that there will always be both "a negative and a positive perspective on it," suggesting the impossibility of reaching a decided conclusion about an ironic work.[30] Irony has long been a "weapon in the arsenal" of the powerless and disenfranchised, but has also been used to "reinforce rather than question established attitudes" and authority.[31] It can have many faces and may function in a plethora of ways, including as a reinforcing device. It may be ludic, distancing, and aggregative, that is, it can create and be created by communities.[32] Yet, irony can only exist as part of a communicative process between author or ironist, and audience. It is not merely a static, rhetorical tool to be deployed by an encoding ironist, but arises as a result of "relations between meanings, . . . people and utterances and, sometimes, between intentions and interpretations."[33] Hutcheon points out that discursive communities make irony possible, indicating that it does not exist in itself beyond the confines of history and culture.[34]

As evidenced by the contradictory depiction of Lozana in Delicado's text, that is, as a syphilitic, deformed prostitute and healer who is simultaneously desired and desirable, irony often arises from formal or semantic juxtaposition and incompatibility. Since this oppositional, contrastive gesture also characterizes theories of humor, irony is likely to provoke the affective response of laughter from its audience.[35] But it also "invokes notions of hierarchy and subordination, judgment and perhaps even moral superiority," indicating that what is at stake in irony is *power*.[36] In *La Lozana*, Delicado's text sometimes avoids a clear moral and ethical stance in regard to prostitutes and syphilis. It often appears to work partially against the kind of steady denouncing of women that so forcefully characterizes other works such as *La Celestina* and the *Spill*. But, the pejorative representation of Lozana is thinly guised, if it is hidden at all, since the connection between disease, *medianeras*, and sex is not unproblematic in *La Lozana*. The supposed sexual pleasure that men experience with women actually produces bodily disfigurement, pain, and disease.

Lozana's hypothetical generation of disease parallels her predecessor Celestina's, who intensifies illness and makes the threat of death a reality for many of *La Celestina*'s characters. This parodic gesture of *La Lozana andaluza* is completely compatible with its stronger relationship to irony. Linda Hutcheon explains that the bitextual synthesis of parody requires an ironic distance, and that the two levels of meaning created out of the parodic palimpsest must coexist in irony, which makes them consistent textual partners.[37] Because *La Lozana* is a parody of a parody, *La Celestina*, it is more complicated than if it were a transparent parody using the strategy of irony. For, *La Lozana* is a layer over the erased image of *La Celestina*, which is the image that itself covers the Virgin. It is as if irony were the only useful strategy left during this period to attack women healers, since the layers of textual *medianeras* have surely multiplied with *La Lozana*. And since irony allows for what seems to be unlimited polymorphism and endless multivalence, it is an appropriate discursive strategy for the *medianera* who covers Celestina, who herself erased the by now completely absent Virgin.

But irony is also the element that makes *La Lozana andaluza* so disturbing. For the text fails to overtly position itself in favor of or against Lozana, nor does it manifest itself clearly as either funny or mournful. This ambivalence renders it a kind of transideological tool, like the strategy of irony itself. This is further troubling because the text comes out of a Mediterranean society within which race, gender, class, disease, sex, and profession were in the accelerated process of becoming more restrictive and condemning than they were before. This difficulty in interpreting Lozana's worth in the work, the polyvalent double and triple meanings of words, Lozana's rather free movements through various Mediterranean ports, and the circulation of her body and disease, make her portrayal distressing at a time when the social consequences of being gendered a woman prostitute or healer were often far more grave than they appear to be in the text.

Because the work is founded on a series of contrasts, contradictions, and inconsistencies, it might be argued that *La Lozana* resists an adverse depiction of the *medianera* and in contrast, paints her as more ambiguous than she is in the *Spill* and *La Celestina*. But, Hutcheon argues that irony is different from ambiguity because it has an edge—it makes an ambiguous situation more complicated.[38] For it is not that the reader cannot figure out how to read Lozana as either "good" or "bad," but that instead the reader must decide how to put her inconsistent portrayals together. Lozana's depiction is more complicated than in the *Spill* or *La Celestina* because it is not entirely based on opposition or parody, but on the ironic contradictions and incoherences that characterize the disease of syphilis.

What Delicado has pinpointed and elaborated on in *La Lozana andaluza* is a series of questions and contradictions at issue in the society of his time about disease, healing, and general cultural organization. He articulates what Roig and Rojas completely avoid, that is, why it is that women, supposedly monstrous, diseased, and disfigured, are still pursued as sexual partners and healers. Unlike Roig, Delicado does not insist on the hegemony of the male physician, who according to the *Spill* is the only healer besides the Virgin capable of truly and effectively ameliorating a patient's health. And unlike Rojas's text, Delicado's does not always signify in the same way, that is, as overtly debasing the woman healer. However, even the seemingly approving parts and episodes of the work are based on a most undesirable and ironic *medianera*, the diseased prostitute Lozana.

Despite the contradictory and ironic nature of *La Lozana*, Delicado insists on its therapeutic value. He claims that it will relieve his own pain and entertain the reader. The work implies that the reader takes pleasure in it by seeing what he wants to see and ignoring the rest, which Hutcheon suggests is a characteristic of irony as discussed above. The text is therapeutic because it makes the reader laugh, thereby relieving pain. It also gives the reader pleasure, sexual and otherwise, so that he need not suffer alone. But, since coitus engenders syphilis, Delicado proposes that the reader continue reading to heal the disease that Lozana causes. In the essay after the "Retrato" (Portrait), the "Cómo se escusa el autor" (How the Author Apologizes), Delicado tells the reader to read his two other texts about healing if the reader truly wants to remedy disease.[39]

Although *La Lozana andaluza* constitutes an ironic source of hygienic information, it is not a remedy for disease. Insofar as *La Lozana* argues that coitus is enjoyable and worthwhile, the main character and the work itself are also depicted as disease producing and unstable. And while Delicado's other two works about disease are meant to remedy if not dominate the damage that Lozana and *La Lozana andaluza* cause, they also contrast to the Lozanas as nondiseasing, *medianera* works. While it may be argued that the implicit eroticism of certain sections or *mamotretos* impels the reader to seek out sexual relations with prostitutes instead of dissuading him from doing so, one of Delicado's points in writing the book seems to be that the reader need not venture beyond the limits of the text in order to gain relief, since the book itself is sexually therapeutic.

Books for Delicado are the most reliable intercessors for the relief of illness. Delicado's tripartite formulation of healing and disease in *La Lozana*, *De consolatione*, and *El modo* indicates that the act of reading takes on a different kind of therapeutic importance than it did in the early Middle Ages. For, the concomitant late-fifteenth-century inventions of the printing press and syphilis begin to alter the oral, communal aspects of reading, thereby changing it into a solitary act. Books were immediately present and mobile at a time when syphilis sometimes demanded the isolation of the afflicted. Delicado sets the book-as-mediator in ironic contrast to a pathologized, disfigured, ordinary *medianera* such as Lozana, who incarnates contradiction and intensifies disease and illness. And, he seems to conclude that the book is the most superior healing intercessor of all. Rather than doing something akin to vindicating the woman healer, *La Lozana andaluza* fixes her as ironically pathological and monstrous. But, on the other hand, Delicado suggests that Lozana and her book are sick, and encourages the reader who truly wishes relief to read Delicado's works on disease and its remedy.

Delicado's Three-Pronged Notion of Disease

Manuel da Costa Fontes has argued that a tripartite organization motivates *La Lozana andaluza* and lays the foundation for Delicado's attempt to parody the logic of the Holy Trinity.[40] The text is divided into three parts consisting of sixty-six *mamotretos* that are evenly divisible by three. Costa Fontes cites Lozana's three-fold identity as a convincing example of Delicado's parodic intent. She is created three times in the work, first in Andalusia as Aldonza, next in Rome as Lozana, and third on the Italian island of Lipari as Vellida. Costa Fontes believes that Delicado's status as a convert caused him to mock the idea of three as equal to one, and of one as equal to three: "Jews and Muslims have always considered Trinitarian Christians to be polytheists because of their belief in the Father, Son, and the Holy Ghost, despite the fact that such Christians regard the three as being in fact only one."[41] Costa Fontes argues that Delicado seeks to demonstrate that three parts are not one, but separate and different.

Costa Fontes's suggestion of parody as a discursive strategy in *La Lozana* is provocative, given the fact that irony is so often a strategy of parody, and that irony so completely characterizes *La Lozana*. Yet, while Costa Fontes's parodic, triadic suggestion is convincing, it lends itself to a further tripartite concern that is even more evident in the text than the theological matter of the Holy Trinity. Delicado indicates a three-pronged approach to disease and illness, which includes his three hygienic texts, *La Lozana andaluza*, *De consolatione infirmorum*, and *El modo de adoperare el legno de India occidentale*. He refers to them all in the "Cómo se escusa el autor," where he further repeats the theme of three in the discussion about Lozana's tripartite identity. The proximity of these two tripartite discussions suggests that just as Lozana possesses a three-way identity, so too does disease and its remedy. Each text represents a different branch of the general preoccupation with disease and illness.

Delicado's three-pronged preoccupation with disease is both a serious attempt to respond to and explain the complexities of healing and disease in the sixteenth century, and a comic effort to discredit the woman healer. *La Lozana andaluza* is the text of intervention, the *De consolatione* presents a kind of moral medication to the sufferer, and *El modo de adoperare* outlines the mechanics of cure. *La Lozana*'s ludic, ironic qualities are glaring in contrast to the two straightforward treatises. Yet, these works allude to questions that perplexed authorities during the early sixteenth century, such as those regarding the efficacy of supposedly inept "empirics" who were sought out for remedies over and above the ostensibly infallible medical professional.[42] In addition, the three texts examine the significance and worth of different kinds of *medianeras* in varying contexts. In the same way that disease, cure, and healing were valued differently during this period, texts functioned in different ways according to their cultural worth and appropriateness for the occasion, and in consort with diverse healers.

Medical theorists of the time proposed that entities such as books, people, and cures were important according to their use-value, that is, their effectiveness and propriety. In chapter 12 of the *Examen de ingenios*, Juan Huarte de San Juan tackles the problem of how to rectify the distinction between medical theory and practice. He contends that the individual's success with medical theory and university training is due to the strength of his (for Huarte, male is paradigmatic) faculties of knowledge (*entendimiento*) and memory (*memoria*), whereas the effective healer possesses a powerful imagination (*imaginativa*). Huarte asks about the value, then, of university study and medical training, if they are antithetical to the success of the imaginative healer.[43] Of course, schooling for Huarte is a requirement for medical practice, so that he must find a way of combining imagination, knowledge, and memory:

Y los hombres de grande imaginativa no están totalmente privados de entendimiento ni memoria; y, así, con la remisión que tienen de estas dos potencias, pueden aprender lo más necesario de la medicina por ser lo más claro, y, con la buena imaginativa que tienen, conocer mejor la enfermedad y su causa que los muy racionales.

[And men of great imagination, are not altogether deprived of understanding, nor of memory. Where-through, by having these two powers in some measure they are able to learn the most necessary points of Physic: for that they are plainest, and with the good imagination which they have, can better look into the disease and the cause thereof, than the cunningest doctors.][44]

Thus, the presence of the knowledge and memory faculties only has to be strong enough for the individual to use them to complete the most perfunctory of tasks. Huarte not only stresses the importance of "imaginative" practice over the acquisition of medical information learned by rote, but he suggests that what makes medical practice effective is the way in which information is put to use.

Huarte cites Galen's idea that the physician is the *inventor occasionis* (the inventor of appropriate occasions) because the imagination "es la que alcanza la ocasión del remedio que se ha de aplicar, en la cual gracia consiste la mayor parte de la práctica" [is that which findeth out the occasion of the remedy that ought to be applied, in which grace the greatest part of the practice consisteth].[45] As the inventor of occasions, the successful physician knows which remedy to apply at the right time, just as the capable reader knows which of Delicado's texts to read in order to alleviate a particular kind of pain. Hence, in the same way that the physician is trained to discern between remedies, Delicado's three-pronged approach to disease and illness tries to isolate distinctions between different classes of healers. Each healer treats a different kind of pain focused on in the three works, moral / metaphysical pain in the *De consolatione infirmorum*, physical pain in *El modo de adoperare el legno*, and sexual / erotic pain in *La Lozana andaluza*.

Because Delicado's *De consolatione infirmorum* has never been found, its significance can only be inferred from its title and from its evident model, Boethius's *De consolatione philosophiae*. Boethius's (c. 480–524 A.D.) approach to learning parallels Delicado's tripartite formulation of remedies for disease. In the same vein as Delicado's layering of the three-fold notion of disease, Boethius thought of learning as a multifaceted activity leading to one goal. He invented the Latin *quadrivium* which signaled a four-fold constellation of the disciplines of philosophy. Just as Delicado suggests that disease and illness have three separate but interrelated mediations, Boethius believed that the disciplines of philosophy had to be considered in a four-part way.[46]

The *consolatio* "genre" transmitted information about moral medication to alleviate a metaphysical type of pain, which Boethius seeks to vent by writing. Boethius's text was extremely popular in the medieval period and continued to be widely read in the sixteenth century as it circulated in several Castilian translations. Fray Alberto de Aguayo produced one of those translations in Seville in 1518. He added a prologue and an argument section to Boethius's text, but the entire first book, like Boethius's original, deals with Boethius's illness (pain) and his conversation with Philosophy about how to mitigate it. When Philosophy sees the muses of poetry by Boethius's bed ("estaban junto a mi cama notando mis tristes quexas") [the muses of Poetry standing by my bed, helping me to find words for my grief], she calls them *rameras oscuras* (dark whores), claims their incompetency in healing, and finally drives them away.[47]

Much like Roig's Virgin, Philosophy is an icon, the antithesis of mundane *medianeras* such as the prostitutes. She is a stylized ideal who believes herself the only one capable of relieving Boethius's pain. It turns out that his "moral" pain results from a severe political and social disconnection that leaves Boethius banished far from home, possessionless, and accused of treason. More important than his physical displacement, Philosophy explains, is the fact that Boethius is an instrument of his own kind of self-banishment: "E si piensas que te echaron, tu mesmo te desterraste. Porque ninguna persona tuvo poder para esto" [if you prefer to be thought of as driven, then how far have you driven yourself! For in your case it could never have rightly been possible for anyone else to do this].[48] Only when a person stops wanting to live in a community, Philosophy explains, can she or he be stripped of the rights and protection of that community. Philosophy says that instead of thinking that thieves rule the world, and that things happen chaotically and haphazardly, Boethius's steadfast faith (*sentimiento*) in the divine order and guidance of the world will be his true remedy. Since truth becomes dark and cloudy sometimes, Philosophy will try to get rid of the clouds little by little so that Boethius can see the light of truth:

Mas pues los entendimientos tienen esta condicion que en dexando la verdad se hinchen de falsedades: de donde suele salir una niebla de passiones que escurecen la clareza de la verdadera vista. No te dare que no es tiempo medicinas eficaces: mas provare poco a poco de adelgazar esta niebla con axaraves medianos: porque lancadas las malas y engañosas afeciones puedas ver la claridad de la verdadera luz.

[Men's minds are obviously such that when they lose true opinions they have to take up false ones, and then a fog arises from these false ideas, which obscures that true vision. So I shall try for a while with gentle and moderate applications to lessen that fog, so that when the darkness of those deceptive ideas is removed, you may be able to recognize the glory of the light of truth.][49]

Philosophy's task consists of slowly thinning out the mass of cloudy *passiones* (diseases) that fog Boethius's ability to think and see clearly.

By analogy, the proper and conventional use for Delicado's *De consolatione infirmorum* is in times of moral weakness, isolation, or depravity. Boethius's text clearly defines such an illness as both a physical and metaphysical disconnection from self and community. This text responds to doubts about where one turns when isolation and banishment are both ruthlessly self-imposed and imposed by others. Or, as Philosophy puts it, it consoles an individual when his or her memory of the truth—that there exists a larger plan that guides the world's events—is so clouded that everything seems malleable and chaotic. Boethius's text responds by suggesting a remedy that combines reading and writing. It indicates that one must know Philosophy's truths from books, store them in his or her mind, and have faith that they can heal. Then, one needs to write in order to engage Philosophy in conversation and evoke her remedies.

In light of Boethius's stated objective, Delicado's later, parallel text, *De consolatione infirmorum,* may respond to the concern about how the syphilitic sufferer relieves the pain caused by the banishment and sequestration of being tucked away for days at a time in a hospital. Whether or not Delicado's text even existed, it at least symbolically embodies the kind of guide that an ill person turned to for the alleviation of the anguish of isolation. Instead of presenting Philosophy's soothing words, the title of Delicado's work implies that ill people heal this specific kind of pain themselves.

Hence, the *De consolatione infirmorum* is to be used by a syphilitic individual in times of isolated quarantine and disconnection from the larger society. Delicado's own stated illness and withdrawal (whether real or metaphorical, and keeping in mind his life as an expatriate in Italy), and the remedy through writing, attest to the same kind of occasion and remedy that Boethius proposes in the *De consolatione philosophiae*. The only reference to Delicado's treatise on this kind of pain exists in *La Lozana*'s "Cómo se escusa el autor," where he informs the reader about the information that can be gleaned from his works on healing and curing:

> Y si por ventura os veniere por las manos un otro tratado *De consolatione infirmorum*, podéis ver en él mis pasiones para consolar a los que la fortuna hizo apasionados como a mí. (485)

> [And if by chance another treatise, *On the Consolation of the Infirm*, should pass through your hands, you could see in it my desire to console those people whom fortune made passionate as it did me.] (280)

Hence, the sick writer heals the sick reader. But, Delicado uses *apasionados* ("passionate" ones) and *pasión* (passion) throughout *La Lozana* in an ambiguous way, to mean both disease and erotic desire. Delicado is afflicted with syphilis and its attendant pains, and with burning sexual desire that connotes another kind of anguish. These divergent sorts of passions are united, however, in the sexually transmitted disease of syphilis, which causes different kinds of pain and thus requires different types of texts to read and write. Syphilis demands, then, a variety of *medianeras*, be they textual or human.

The second branch of Delicado's tripartite establishment of disease is his manual about one of syphilis's most effective remedies, *El modo de adoperare el legno de India occidentale*. In the "Cómo se escusa el autor," Delicado implores the reader to pick up and read the treatise if the reader wants to learn about the remedy that contributed to Delicado's health:

> Y en el tratado que hice del leño del India, sabréis el remedio mediante el cual me fue contribuida la sanidad, y conoceréis el autor no haber perdido todo el tiempo [in writing the capricious *La Lozana*], porque, como vi coger los ramos y las hojas del árbol de la vanidad a tantos, yo que soy de chica estatura, no alcancé más alto: asentéme al pie hasta pasar, como pasé, mi enfermedad. (485)

> [And in the treatise I wrote about the wood of the Indies, you will find out the remedy which gave me back my health, and you will know that the author has not completely wasted his time, because, since I saw so

many people gathering the branches and the leaves from the Tree of Vanity, I could not reach very high because I am short in stature. I sat down at its foot until my illness passed, as indeed it did.] (280)

Like the early mercury treatments, the gaiac powder (*leño de India*) became one of the few effective remedies for syphilis. Many doctors warned of the dangerous effects of mercury, especially when it was prescribed and used by "charlatans" and "empirics," but since it proved a sufficient remedy, medical practitioners started to employ it as well.[50] Gaiac was heralded as a prudent alternative to mercury, although the two substances were often used in tandem. Reduced to a powder, infused, and made into a decoction, gaiac had sudorific effects when drunk. After a thirty-day regimen that included limitations in food intake, the administration of mild purgatives, the consumption of the gaiac decoction, and blanket wraps in order to generate profuse perspiration, it was believed that the disease had been rooted out and expelled.[51] After Paracelsus's attack on gaiac in 1529, however, it was increasingly substituted by other woods and roots with sudorific properties.[52]

Delicado's treatise on gaiac exists in two manuscripts, one at the Marciana Library in Venice, and another at the Mazarine Library in Paris.[53] Unlike the *De consolatione infirmorum*, which must be assumed to have been written in Latin, *El modo de adoperare* is composed in Latin, Italian, and Castilian. Like the writing of *La Lozana*, Delicado wrote this work in order to alleviate the suffering of those who, like him, suffered from syphilis. It is a conventional sixteenth-century medical treatise. The woodcut on the first page portrays the gaiac wood ("holy wood," according to Damiani) being crowned by the Virgin Mary, who is flanked by Santiago on one side and St. Martha on the other. A cleric kneels before Santiago with the nearby inscription: "Francisco Delicado composuit in alma urbe, anno 1525" [Francisco Delicado composed this work in the holy city, in the year 1525].[54] Damiani believes that the cleric represents Delicado himself, who with an agonized expression on his face, appeals for healing mercy to the great Iberian healer Santiago. The famous medieval pilgrim's route to witness and be healed by Santiago's relics is made all the more emblematic with the depiction of a shell. The Virgin as queen is also invoked as a figure assigned with the authority to exalt the gaiac as a royal, Christian remedy.

The main body of the work consists of a description of what Delicado calls solely the "French disease," a discussion of its etiology, and the recourse for its remedy. It also contains a letter by the natural historian Gonzalo Fernández de Oviedo, which closely corresponds to the section on gaiac in his natural history, the *Historia general y natural de las Indias* (Toledo 1526). Oviedo's letter is followed by an epilogue written in Castilian instead of Italian because "en este legno da muncha autoridad la nuestra lengua romance" [our Spanish language grants great authority to this wood].[55] Hence, Delicado links the gaiac remedy to the opinions and expertise of several authority figures, the Virgin, Santiago, St. Martha, and Oviedo, the Iberian specialist associated with the American conquest. For, this treatise represents the text to turn to when in need of instruction on how to heal and care for the pustules (*bubas*) that appear on the body as symptoms of syphilis. The treatise indicates that the authorized guidance from the *medianeras* above insures the healing of the symptoms.

Delicado's use of different languages in all three of his texts on healing is analogous to the employment of different codes on diverse occasions for varying objectives. In his transcription of *El modo de adoperare*, Damiani alludes to Delicado's linguistic and stylistic theories, and suggests that his "ostensible preference for the vulgar languages" points to a concern with *utilitas*, that is "communicating something which has an intrinsic usefulness."[56] However, Delicado is also interested in using the appropriate language / code on the correct occasion, so that his use of Latin in *El modo de adoperare* is appropriate to its contexts, which are that of a formal letter to several physicians, and the papal copyright of Clement VII.[57] In the *De consolatione infirmorum*, the exclusive use of Latin corresponds to the moral therapies of the *consolatio* genre, while the pedestrian languages of Castilian and Italian are connected to the mechanics of curing in *El modo*. This mediating role of language corresponds to the intercessors contained in each text.

Mediation at the levels of reading, writing, language, and healing links all three of these works that depict intercessors. Philosophy, the Virgin, Santiago, and St. Martha are all presented as authentic *medianera* healers who truly alleviate the conditions of illness. In Boethius's paradigmatic *De consolatione philosophiae*, philosophy is the female intellectual and moral *medianera* and guide who is contrasted to the discredited prostitutes. Whether or not Delicado followed Boethius's lead and designed the healer-guide of the *De consolatione infirmorum* as female is, of course, impossible to know. What is verifiable and accurate about this nonextant text, however, is the ubiquitous paradigm of the woman intercessor present in Boethius's treatise and shared by Delicado's other two works about disease and healing.

Delicado's second kind of *medianera* is the religious one, illustrated by the Virgin and St. Martha at the start of *El modo de adoperare el legno de India occidentale*. The Virgin constitutes the quintessential *medianera* in contrast to evil, mundane go-betweens and healers, and is both a restorer of an individual's physical integrity and health and a spiritual healer. It is also possible that the sometimes womanized Santiago, often depicted as delicate and fragile in early modern iconography, joins the two woman icons because of his "effeminate" qualities.[58] The stability of these *medianeras* stands in marked contrast to Delicado's third kind of *medianera*, the ironic prostitute Lozana.

All of Delicado's *medianeras* are analogous to the ways the writing functions. Just as Delicado suggests that a different woman intercessor exists for every kind of healing, there are also distinct texts for diverse healing functions. At best, Lozana is a "viable" healer as a provider of sexual services, which is ironic because she intensifies disease and illness. And as discussed earlier, even this slightly favorable assessment of her healing abilities is always tempered in the work by her monstrous physical qualities. Her disfigurement and disease bring into question the extent to which her sexual efficacy can be considered desirable or therapeutic. Unlike the other *medianeras* (Philosophy, the Virgin, St. Martha, and Santiago), Lozana is unstable and does not always signify in the same way. Even the division of linguistic codes that marks the other two treatises is lost in *La Lozana*, where Italian and Castilian are often mixed.

Lozana is the most problematic and dubious "healer" of all because her sexual methods cause more disease, in opposition to the other two *medianeras* and texts that supposedly prevent and heal the conditions of illness. Her portrayal as a syphilitic prostitute and all-around *medianera* is especially perplexing given the fact that Delicado claims that the text relieves pain. Delicado first characterizes *La Lozana* as therapeutic in the "Prólogo," where he claims to write the book in order to forget about his pain: "Y como dice el coronista Fernando el Pulgar, 'así daré olvido al dolor'" (170) [As the historian Fernando del Pulgar said: "In this way shall all my suffering be forgotten"] (2).[59] But, the reader does not discover the medical nature of Delicado's pain until his syphilitic illness is later revealed. The "Prólogo's" statement alludes to an ambiguous pain whose instability is only fortified by the other effort to establish the text as therapeutic. In the letter-essay after the main part of the book, the "Epístola del autor" (Epilogue), Delicado pleads with the reader to pay attention not to his lack of knowledge (*mi poco saber*), but to his good intentions (*sana intención*) (492). Like so much of the language that Delicado employs, his choice of the word for the adjective "good," *sana*, had ironic meanings in the sixteenth century. Along with its reference to *healing*, the noun *sanidad* (health) was connected to physical manifestations of sexual activity such as the erection.[60] Part of the reason that these two meanings are confounding is that they are not completely incompatible. As discussed in chapter 3, sexual activity was traditionally recognized as therapeutic according to Galenic medical theory. By the sixteenth century, however, the compatibility between healing and sex is ironic because of the appearance of syphilis. This tension between traditional sexual therapies and sexually generated disease helps to make Delicado's text and syphilitic *medianera* such powerful signifiers at this time.

Delicado alludes to two kinds of healing in the work, sexual and nonsexual mediations. While the text lends itself to a host of interpretations and readings, it is undeniably focused on the figure of Lozana who "heals" both sexually as a prostitute, and nonsexually with her remedies. Because the author deals with the ironic relationship between coitus and syphilis, and between erotic desire and disease, his good intention in relation to the syphilitic *medianera* bifurcates and leads in two directions. The work has a splitting effect in which interpretation can be directed toward the erotic or the therapeutic. Sometimes they are differentiated in the text and sometimes not. For instance, is Lozana *meritoria* (meretorious) in the sense of a diseased *meretrix*, or does she *merit* attention as someone who should be exalted for providing sexual / healing remedies? Delicado uses this word to invoke that splitting in the "Prólogo":

> y si, por tiempo, alguno se maravillare que me puse a escribir semejante materia, respondo por entonces que *epistola enim non erubescit*, y asimismo que es pasado el tiempo que estimaban los que trabajaban en cosas meritorias. (169)

> [Later on, should anyone be amazed that I spent my time writing about such things, I shall only reply that "words feel no shame at what they record." Moreover, the time has passed when those who labored on such worthwhile matters won praise.] (2)

Even though the material in the book is embarrassing, it matters little since prostitutes are so poorly esteemed. The phrase *cosas meritorias* is unstable in meaning and can be interpreted either as things related to prostitution or as things that have merit. Delicado further elaborates on Lozana's and her friends's *merit* or *meretriciousness* in part 3, when Lozana herself discusses the *taberna meritoria* (praiseworthy or meretricious tavern) (44.390).[61]

Along with Delicado's declared intention in writing to relieve his ambiguous pain (as caused either by syphilis or unfulfilled sexual desire), he claims that he is also writing to bring into the memory current events taking place in the world despite the pain they cause: "y también por traer a la memoria munchas cosas que en nuestros tiempos pasan" (170) [I am also bringing to light many unsavory things that are taking place] (2). Narrative writing lifts the burden and pressure of pain despite the fact that the narrated events may be painful. But, Delicado also states that his intention is to "mezclar natura con bemol" (170) [to enliven the truth with entertainment] (2) because readers like to read fanciful books to learn more and to relax. *Bemol* has several meanings, including difficulty, and male and female genitalia. It can also mean "pintar la naturaleza suavizándola" [painting nature while sharpening it], all of which make logical sense in this context, according to aesthetic, erotic, and other hermeneutic readings of the text.[62] Hence, Delicado's attempts to illuminate the text's meaning only further obscure it.

Finally, Delicado invites the authoritative reader, to whom he refers with such titles as *Ilustre Señor* (Most honorable lord), *vuestra señoría* (Your lordship), and *letor* (reader), to actively participate with the text, and tells him to give the book a little varnish (*barniz*) so that reading *La Lozana* may cause two possible effects: pleasure and enjoyment (*gasajo*) (170). Along with Allaigre's erotic reading of the passage, Delicado asks the reader to set the meaning of the portrait himself with a varnish, in order to take advantage of its two possible effects. He suggests that both the text and the main character have to be interpreted, that is, coated and fixed in varnish by the reader in order to achieve their desired effects.[63] But just when Delicado has bestowed the onus of interpretation on his readers, he promptly denies it in the "Argumento" (A Discussion of the Topics Treated in the Present Work) following the "Prólogo": "Protesta el autor que ninguno quite ni añada palabra, ni razón, ni lenguaje" (171) [I, the author, insist that no one add or take away any word, thought, or turn of expression] (4). In the "Cómo se escusa el autor" (How the author apologizes), Delicado does not seem to allude to interpretation at all, but is more interested in showing that he wrote the book for his own recreation or therapy, probably while in the hospital: "Y si dijeren que por qué perdí el tiempo retrayendo a la Lozana y a sus secaces, respondo que, siendo atormentado de una grande y prolija enfermedad, parecía que me espaciaba con estas vanidades" (485) [And if they were to ask why I wasted time portraying Lozana and her followers, I would respond that since I am tormented by a great and enduring illness, it seems that I could cheer myself up with such vanities] (280). Reading and writing both constitute recreation and therapy.

But, what kind of therapeutic mediation can Lozana / *Lozana* possibly supply the reader, given the fact that the text and character constitute in part an intensified version of the abjectified woman healer, Celestina? Lozana is cast as monstrous and undesirable but ironically provides pleasure to her clients. Critics have largely considered the text to be an aggrandizement of "women's" sexuality, which Luis Beltrán most recently has attributed to the fact that the other characters incessantly compliment her on her beauty and good looks:

> This happens so often [flattery of Lozana] that we the readers tend to overlook that, besides minor blemishes (something like a scar in the form of a cross upon her forehead, for instance, or her possible alopecia), she has a hole where her nose used to be before syphilis took it away. . . . the by-now considerable bibliography on *La Lozana andaluza*, while frankly favorable to its protagonist and the way she goes about life and men, shows, for the most part, remarkable discretion concerning her noselessness.[64]

Lozana is the antithesis of her name. She is not beautiful nor does she represent beauty itself as Delicado proclaims in the "Explicit" (explication) near the end of the book: "y Lozana [demuestra] generalmente lozanía, hermosura, lindeza, fresqueza y belleza" (487) [and "Lozana" generally means "exuberance, grace, elegance, freshness, and beauty"] (282). She also wears the signs of disease all over her body. Her noselessness is mentioned three times in the text, once in the first part ("¡Si tuviese asiento para los antojos!" (7.195) [If only the pox hadn't eaten away part of her nose. She couldn't wear glasses if she wanted to!] [7.23]), once in the second ("pues no tiene chimenea, ni tiene do poner antojos" (24.295) [since that chimney piece of hers has no mantel to rest her eyeglasses on] [24.110]), and again finally in the third section ("¿Qué señas daré d'él salvo que a él le sobra en la cara lo que a mí me falta?" (51.416) [What unique feature can I tell about him except that he has on his face what I'm missing on mine?] [51.216]). She also manifests *estrellas* or signs of syphilis that disfigure her, make her into a kind of monster, and are nonetheless frequently ignored by the other characters.

Allusions to her status as a convert also appear throughout the work, and signs (*señales*) in the text refer as much to the signs of syphilis as they do to signs of Jewish ethnicity. In *mamotreto* 9, for instance, Beatriz refers to those men who "llevan aquella señal colorada" (9.202) [you see wearing a red badge] (9.29), thus alluding to the outer sign that Jews were required to wear during this period. These signs of alterity and disease would normally produce disruptions within a text of this time, but ironically they do not in *La Lozana*. Instead of causing other characters to avoid Lozana, they serve as magnets to link the characters together and attract them to her. These signs are like the networks created by Celestina's occupations since they identify Lozana as a prostitute with syphilis. They also connect her to all the other characters in the book who either bear the signs in the present, such as the many courtesans who appear throughout the text, or who will reveal them later. What is surprising about the way in which all of these signs are dealt with is their apparently smooth assimilation into the work.

In an effort to rectify the paradox between Lozana's dubious looks and her nominal "beauty" (not to mention Rampín's awkwardness and further undesirability as her lover and boyfriend, and his ostensible sexual prowess) Beltrán suggests that the intensity of the sexual scenes in the book cause the reader simply to forget about her lack of physical beauty. The pure lust of "the creative act" compels the reader to the extent that she or he is distracted from the characters' objectionable physical features.[65]

Beltrán's argument explains the selective vision of modern critics; but Delicado may offer his own reasoning for the discrepancy. Along with the pleasure that the reading of Lozana produces, Delicado delegates a *gasajo* to the reader (170). Literally, the word evokes a similar meaning to that of *placer* (pleasure), that is, social pleasure or pleasure in the company of others, and has led to the contemporary Castilian verb, *agasajar* (to entertain lavishly).[66] Corominas also gives two interesting derivations in Galician: *agasallo* is connected to *putear* (to pander), and in old Galician *gasallado* is sexual pleasure, or what Corominas claims is a euphemism for copulation.[67] The extent to which the Castilian *gasajo* carried a sexual connotation or one related to prostitution remains unexplored. It is not far-fetched, however, to suggest that in a text as ironic and inconsistent as *La Lozana andaluza*, the author deliberately uses such a word in order to evoke several different meanings, one of which is the erotic, sexual, or prostituted pleasure (*gasajo*) that is also generated by the text.

Another provocative way in which *gasajo* could have signified to an early- to mid-sixteenth-century reader is in relation to its likeness to the Arabic-rooted *gasa* (from the Arabic *qazz*), a fine, silky cloth or thread. Despite the fact that their etymologies are seemingly different, it is possible that their palpable similarities are significant for understanding *La Lozana*. *Gasa* probably came into Castilian by way of commercial trade. Its etymology is somewhat unformed, to the extent that Corominas calls Covarrubias's etymology of the word a false one (Latin *cassis*; Castilian *red*; English *net* or *network*).[68] Yet the *red* / network is precisely what characterizes the work of *medianeras*, that is the making of cloths and objects out of cloth. The extraordinary connection between the nets, networks, and trade routes of the word and those of *La Lozana* suggests that reading *La Lozana* enmeshes the reader in the transactions of something like a commercial relationship. Reading the book is tantamount to buying Lozana's services, and transactions of this kind—or so the book suggests—are never stable.

Delicado evinces the connection between commercial trade, transactions, and syphilis in a simile from the treatise *El modo de adoperare*. The relationship therein between Italian coins and syphilitic symptoms illuminates this important connection:

> quando che comenzó la guerra in Italia, un soldato de quelli, li quali havendo sacchegiato Rapalo et l'hospitale de San Lorenzo, e amazatoui alquanti infermi e toltovi li lor letti e vendutoli, pigliando il precio che fu uno ducato de oro in oro, in quel'instante le nacque una broza, in la forma del ducato, al ditto soldato temerario, nel mezo de la mano. Et fra pochi giorni, miraculosamente e in breve spatio, fu tutto coperto de broze e doglie.[69]

> [when the war started in Italy, a [French] soldier who, having plundered Rapallo and San Lorenzo Hospital, and killed a fair number of patients and removed their beds in order to sell them, learned the value of a gold ducat "firsthand" in gold. For all of a sudden there appeared a pustule in the form of a ducat in the middle of the fearful soldier's hand, and miraculously, in just a few short days, his whole body was covered with pustules and he was in great pain.]

When explaining the origins of syphilis, Delicado says that the French soldier develops pustules (first, he develops one pustule) in the form of the gold ducat, thereby solidifying the relationship between prostitution, syphilis, and monetary transactions. Money is invoked here as another kind of intercessor.

Delicado's interest in mediation, commercial trade, and transactions suggests a further meaning for *gasajo*. In the same way that the Arabic-rooted *gasa* was appropriated into Castilian by way of commercial trade, it is possible that the reading transaction between text and reader generates the *gasajo*. Hence, perhaps reading about Lozana produces the cloth implicit in the *gasa*. In other words, one can take pleasure in this text by employing the light cover of the large cloth (*gasa-jo*) to cover or conceal those aspects that the reader chooses to ignore. It is easy to escape within the "lust" of Lozana's erotic and sexual escapades if one obscures her face and scars. Reading accomplishes that because it impels the reader to focus on the most immediate signs in front of him or her, especially if he or she searches for hygienic information. Previous unpleasant information simply may be forgotten in the face of a new piece of agreeable information on a fresh page. Delicado emphasizes reading throughout the book in order to indicate not only a sure way to avoid the dangerous contagion of the *medianera*, but to posit literacy as a superior form of healing.

Instead of laying a steady claim about the *medianera*'s virtue or lack thereof—which is what Roig and Rojas do—Delicado employs the seemingly innocuous yet ironic ideal of *pleasure* (sexual) to reestablish the syphilitic Lozana as an unattractive healer. But, like in Pulgar's *Letras*, which Delicado evidently invokes in *La Lozana*'s dedication as a kind of guiding model, woman's body and her association with eroto-sexual desire are not without signification or value. In the first of Pulgar's letters, probably written to the medical doctor Francisco Núñez de la Yerba at the University of Salamanca and entitled "Letra de Fernando del Pulgar contra los males de la vejez" [Letter from Fernando del Pulgar against the evils of old age], Pulgar articulates that which Delicado alludes to in *La Lozana andaluza*, that health can only be understood and recognized in contrast to sickness, and that moderation can only be idealized if one knows immoderation:

> Dígolo, señor físico, porque a vos y a otros ommes honrados viejos he oydo loar esta tenplança, y loar y deleitarse tanto en la destenplança de su mocedad pasada, que paresce faltar la obra porque falta el poder,

que está ya tan seco cuanto está verde el deseo para la obra si podiese; así que no sé yo cómo loemos de tenplado al que no puede ser destenplado.[70]

[I am telling you this, most venerable physician, because I have heard you and other honorable, older men praise the moderation of old age, and likewise praise and delight in the immoderation of your past youth so much that it seems that the act never takes place now because of a lack of strength. Even though the desire is there, the act comes up empty and dry. But I do not know how we can praise someone for his moderation when he cannot be immoderate.]

Pulgar argues for the fulfillment of sexual desires even in old age, since in order to make the ideal of moderation possible, the individual must experience immoderation at times.

In a similar way as Delicado, in another letter to a sick friend, Pulgar apparently proposes that sex with diseased women is worth the pain it causes ("Para un caballero, un amigo, de Toledo" [For a gentleman, a friend from Toledo]).[71] Like the two sacks representing satisfaction and contrition that he and his friend gather up at the end of the text, women's disease can be remedied:

Esto considerado, parésceme, señor, que será bueno que comencemos ya a enfardelar para partir; y porque no vayamos penados con la carga mal cargada, verés, si os paresce, que vaya fecha en dos fardelejos, uno de la satisfación, e otro de la contrición.[72]

[Considering this, sir, it seems to me that it would be advantageous to start packing up to leave. And so that we do not leave burdened by poorly bundled cargo, you will see that it is better to travel with two large sacks, one filled with satisfaction, and the other with contrition.]

Sex seems to constitute the bag of satisfaction, and contrition the penitential healing that one pursues after coitus. Pulgar's apparent mistrust of medical professionals is another parallel to Delicado's work, since Pulgar laments the fact that his friend the gentleman is in Toledo where the capable physicians (*buenos físicos naturales*) have been overrun by rowdy drunks (*odreros alborotadores*).[73]

In a similar way as Delicado, Pulgar's writing confirms women's pathological nature instead of plainly opposing itself to the antifeminist discourse against women healers at the time. Unlike Delicado, however, Pulgar is not ironic. In the letter to the gentleman, Pulgar claims that he and his woman companion / enemy had the following exchange:

[Pulgar tells his friend the gentleman] Cuando moço, me atormentó [his companion / enemy] con sus tentaciones; agora me atribula con sus dolencias.

[Then Pulgar asks the woman] ¿Por qué agora te place con tus enfermedades darme tanto pesar en pago de tanto placer? ¿Por qué? dice ella: Porque yo soy enferma de mi natura, y lo enfermo no puedo facer sano. E ese complimiento de apetitos que me feciste pasados, eran principio de las dolencias que vees presentes. Si touieras, dice ella, seso estonces para resistir mis tentaciones, touieras agora fuerça para sofrir mis enfermedades; pero ni sopiste repugnar las tentaciones que se vencen peleando, ni la luxuria que se vence huyendo.[74]

[(Pulgar tells his friend the gentleman) When I was young, she (his companion / enemy) tormented me with her temptations. Now she afflicts me with her pains. (Then Pulgar asks the woman) "Why does it please you so to burden me now in return for all that pleasure?" "Why?" she said. "Because I am sick by my very nature, and the sick can never become well. The fulfillment of past appetites that you gave me was the beginning of these current ailments. If you had had," she said, "the good sense then to resist my temptations, you would now have the strength to tolerate my illnesses. But you did not know how to deflect temptations that are conquered by struggling, nor lust that is conquered by fleeing."]

After placing the etiology of his and the gentleman's disease with women—the conventional Evian source of temptation—he then employs the analogy of the market and its transactions to explain why the two sacks of satisfaction and contrition are useful: "porque esta mercadería es muy buena para aquella feria do vamos, y tanto demandada allá cuanto poco usada acá" [because these bundles will be very useful at the market where we are headed. And what is put to little use here will be very much in demand there].[75] In other words, despite women's disease and inability to heal, and men's incapacity to resist them, the coital transaction is worthwhile because relief can eventually be had. Pulgar invokes that relief through contrition, and Delicado invites it through writing, storytelling, and the reading of his other treatises.

Despite their differences, both Pulgar and Delicado help to stabilize and corroborate the portraits of ordinary *medianeras* such as those found in the *Spill* and *La Celestina*, albeit in a different way than those works. In Delicado's case, Lozana's ironic portrayal allows him and the reader to recreate, entertain himself, and thus relieve pain. Reading the text also facilitates pain relief because the work conveniently produces a sexually related cover in order to hide the disagreeable parts. One of the most provocative yet alarming contentions about reading that Delicado indicates in his three works about disease and healing is that texts and reading can replace mundane healers altogether. The reader can, for instance, avoid the disfigured, earthly healer and prostitute Lozana simply by reading the book and making her beautiful. Yet, Delicado's tripartite constellation of disease remedies goes farther than that and suggests that the text constitutes the mediating agent to be employed when the material functions that it represents have dangerous or life-threatening consequences. The sixteenth-century reader who recognized Lozana as the quintessential discursive *medianera* would have been discouraged from seeking the healing services of women such as her in daily life. He might have been seduced into seeking a prostitute for sex, but may have realized that a *gasajo* or large cloth is applied with more difficulty in daily life than it is in books.

Celestina's Legacy

From the opening illustration of *La Lozana andaluza*, in which Lozana leads a ship of fools to their apparent deaths, the work establishes itself as ironic and parodic (165–66). Its parodic possibilities are numerous, and include not only Costa Fontes's parody of the Holy Trinity, but also a parody of *La Celestina*. The emblematic title page that illustrates the ship of fools also requires the reader's immediate recognition of the genealogical relationship between Celestina / *La Celestina* and Lozana / *La Lozana*, and of their intended difference: "El qual Retrato demuestra lo que en Roma passava y contiene munchas mas cosas que la Celestina" (165) [showing what happened there and containing a great deal more than *La Celestina*] (1). Lozana also practices the same trade as Celestina, which Delicado mentions in the "Prólogo": "ha administrado ella [Lozana] y un su pretérito criado, como abajo diremos, el arte de aquella mujer que fue en Salamanca en tiempo de Celestino segundo" (169) [who with her former servant (as we shall later recount) practiced far and near . . . , the wiles of that woman who lived in Salamanca while Celestine II reigned] (2).[76] According to this second reference in the book, Celestina and Lozana constitute the same kind of intercessor.

Despite the similarity between the two *medianeras*, the works are parodic mostly through their dramatic structure. At the level of characterization, Celestina and Lozana are more ironic than parodic. For, at the same time that their likeness is invoked, Lozana is also ironically distanced from her "genealogical mother." It is this effort at separation that distinguishes *La Lozana andaluza* from *La Celestina*'s parody of the Virgin. The parodic palimpsest in *La Celestina* depends upon the Virgin's image erased by Celestina's imitations of her activities. In contrast, *La Lozana andaluza* is constituted by the ironic parts that make up Lozana. As opposed to the way in which Celestina tries to imitate the Virgin to no avail, *La Lozana* often tries to prove Lozana different from Celestina, which is ironic since Lozana is not unlike her predecessor. In the move from parody in *La Celestina* to irony in *La Lozana andaluza*, Delicado creates an ironic consort of contrasting Lozanas that is more akin to Roig's horizontal distance between the Virgin and ordinary women in the *Spill* than it is to Rojas's parodic palimpsest. The Virgin's absence permits Lozana an ironic distance from Celestina and from undesirable parts of herself.

Celestina is "present" differently in *La Lozana andaluza* than the Virgin is in *La Celestina*. The affiliation between Celestina and Lozana is one of an inheritance of genealogy and disease that Lozana eventually and supposedly surpasses. Lozana is figured as Celestina's daughter, but an ungrateful one at best, for at times Lozana clearly owes what she has inherited to her "mother" Celestina. References to the disease of the *mal de la madre* (suffocation of the womb) in *La Lozana* evoke Celestina's relationship to *madre* (mother), with all of its religious, reproductive, and prostitutive overtones. In a humorous exchange between a courtesan supposedly afflicted with the disease and Lozana who has been called to cure it, the courtesan's servant (Eslava) tells the courtesan that Lozana bears news about her mother, who had ironically died while giving birth to her:

Cortesana: . . . Decíme, señora, ¿conocistes vos a mi madre?
Lozana: Mi señora, no; conocerla he yo para servir a honrar.
Cortesana: Pues, ¿qué me enviastes a decir que me queríades dar nuevas de mi madre?
Lozana: ¿Yo, señora? Corruta estaría la letra, no sería yo. (23.285)

[Courtesan: (*to Lozana*) Tell me, madam, did you know my mother?
Lozana: No, my lady, but I should like to have known her to serve and honor you better.
Courtesan: Then why did you send word to me that you had news of her?

Lozana: I, your ladyship? The message you received was false. I said no such thing.] (23.101)

Lozana's final comment is taken from act 9 of *La Celestina*, when Pármeno counters Celestina's assertion that wine should be drunk twelve times at each meal. He claims that according to writers, the best number of swallows is three, to which Celestina responds: "Hijo, estará corrupta la letra; por treze, tres" (9.225) [That so? That's a corrupt text. It ought to read *thirteen*] (9.143). In other words, Lozana makes the same claim as Celestina, that the mediating instrument, language, is that which deceives, in contrast to the intercessor herself who speaks the truth. Lozana thereby likens herself to the "mother *medianera*" as they both try to distance themselves from the instability of language. But, Celestina's supposed truth serves her drunkenness, and Lozana's serves her efforts to distance herself nobly from the unattractive Celestina. She acccomplishes this goal through her remedy of the problematic suffocation of the womb.

The *mal de la madre* in *La Celestina* was equivalent to the *mal de Celestina* (Celestina's disease), since she was figured as a "mother" throughout the text. In *mamotreto* 23 cited above, Lozana diverges from this kind of matrilineal inheritance by suggesting a remedy for the courtesan's uterine pain, different from that of the standard remedy of childbirth prescribed by both Celestina and medical practitioners. The courtesan claims in contrast that childbirth caused her pain, which leads Lozana to suggest remedies to expel the excess air inside her. Lozana also ironically suggests that she avoid the remedy of doctors and men who encourage coital therapies in order to set the uterus in its proper place (286). Hence, Lozana rejects the conventional medical therapy and thereby tries to separate herself from her mother Celestina. She also suggests that the courtesan avoid sex with the father of her child, the canon, and so encourages her to avoid men on two fronts, as sexual partners and as medical practitioners. But, at the same time that she attempts to discard Celestina and her healing tradition, Lozana ironically invokes her by pointing out the deception of language.

This strategy of simultaneous invocation and rejection corresponds to the ironic way in which Lozana herself is presented. This is evident in the area of witchcraft, since the text sometimes exposes the falsehood of the supposed evil connections of *medianeras* to the devil, and at other times presents Lozana's activities as diabolical. Although Celestina's characterization as a witch was intended to vilify and disparage her, it also indicated that she was a powerful albeit "dangerous" force. *La Lozana* largely tries to prove the *medianera's* mortality not for her beneficent vindication, but for three other reasons: to emphasize instead her services as a prostitute, to demonstrate her ignorance in regard to medicine, and to illustrate the contradiction implicit in those who seek her healing services because of her supposed preternatural power (ironically, perhaps, like Delicado himself). The character who appears with the name of *Autor* (author) and *Auctor* (author) corroborates such an argument in *mamotreto* 42, when he first asks Lozana how she spends her time, and then systematically chastises each task that she describes.[77]

First, Lozana alludes to the way in which she earns money: "que quien veza a los papagayos a hablar, me vezará a mí a ganar" (42.381) [anyone who can teach parrots to talk can teach me my way of earning money too] (42.187). She earns money the way parrots talk, in comprehensible phrases that make no sense in their context, or that show no signs of intelligence or knowledge of any kind. Next, she lists the methods that she uses when someone has been afflicted by an *aojador* (the doer of the "evil eye"). She says that she learned these remedies from an old woman (like Celestina) who was a "healer," and "good" like Lozana:

Yo sé ensalmar y encomendar y santiguar cuando alguno está aojado, que una vieja me vezó, que era saludadera y buena como yo. (42.381)

[I know how to cure by spells and by making the sign of the cross over someone who has been bewitched by the evil eye, for an old crone who was as good a practitioner as I am now taught me.] (42.187)

She basically carries out the kinds of therapies for which many mundane healers were chastised during this period, especially by many medical professionals. Lozana also declares that she learned it all from the medicine woman (*santiguadera*) in *mamotreto* 18 who had cast a spell on her, passing down to her like Celestina did, the knowledge, tasks, and activities that Lozana inevitably exercises in her life. Allaigre further argues that *saludadera* (healer) and *buena* (able) also mean that the old woman was a witch and a prostitute like Lozana herself.[78]

Just as the Autor contradicts himself in this episode in *mamotreto* 42, when he seems almost sympathetic to Lozana and then suddenly criticizes her, the *mamotreto* is also deceptive or ironic in its attempt to debunk superstition. It first alludes to the connection between Lozana's menstruation ("A mí me ha venido mi camisa" 42.380 [I've just started my monthly flow] 42.186) and *aojar* (to give the evil eye), only to argue the ludicrousness of the belief that the giving of the evil eye truly existed. Yet, the ability to give the evil eye was widely thought to be linked to menstruating women during the ancient, medieval, and early modern periods:

> Santo Tomás creía que los aojadores inficionaban el aire hasta determinado espacio; del mismo modo lo hacían, según el Marqués de Villena, las mujeres menstruosas cuando se miran en el espejo y con la vista "facen en él máculas."[79]

> [St. Thomas believed that evil eye givers infected the air in a certain space. The Marquis of Villena also thought that menstruating women did the same thing when they looked in the mirror, and that with their sense of sight they "carried out spells in it."]

It was believed that menstruating women could better emit malevolent signals into the air which would then enter their victim's body through the eyes. At the same time, though, sixteenth-century doctors sought to denounce the evil eye as pure superstition, like the Autor does in this *mamotreto*.[80] The fact that the evil eye is recognized by Lozana and her clients suggests a continued linkage between women's physiology and an intangible evil that proceeded from their bodies. It hints at the concept of gendered lineage and inheritance and suggests the inevitable pathological and matrilineal linkage between mother Celestina, the mother medicine woman, and Lozana.

The Autor's constant and unyielding voice and message later in the *mamotreto* is meant to prove that the maladies that Lozana claims to heal are pure fantasy. Despite his own supposed potential for contagion by the menstruating Lozana, the Autor's speech is comprehensible and logical:

> También decís que hay aojados; esto quiero que os quitéis de la fantasía, porque no hay ojo malo ... mas mala lengua, y dañada intención y venenosa malicia, como sierpe que trae el veneno en los dientes, que si dijera ¡Dios sea loado que lo crió!, no le pudiera empecer. (42.382)

> [You have also said that there are persons bewitched by the evil eye; I want to rid you of this fantasy, because the evil eye does not exist ... It was rather a spiteful tongue, wicked intent, and poisoned malice, like the venom that the snake carries in his teeth, for if she had said, "God

be praised for having formed him so beautifully," she would have done no damage.] (42.186)

The Autor calls the problem of the evil eye one of bad speech, harmful intention, and poisoned malice, and thinks that evil eye givers do not exist but that people say things to harm others. He goes on to indicate that the superstitious incantations of the lowly woman healer are not related to an evil entity with power such as the devil, but that they are, like what the evil eye givers say, improper because they do not heal. The Autor says that the sign of the cross is the only true safeguard against threats and thus would have the *medianera*'s sign system substituted for the Christian one.

Although the Autor's function in the text is as suspicious as any other character's, since he seeks Lozana's "healing" services along with many others, in *mamotreto* 42 he mostly represents the voice of unquestioned authority. Yet, the discussion about the protective power of the sign of the cross leads him to a theological diatribe about the omnipotence of the creator as opposed to the relative weakness of the created baby (*criatura*), which reveals uncharacteristic irony on his part:

> A esto digo que es suciedad creer que una criatura criada tenga poder de hacer lo que puede hacer su Criador ... tú debes creer en el tu Criador, que es omnipotente, y da la potencia y la virtud, y no a su criatura. Ansí que, señora, la cruz sana con el romero, no el romero sin la cruz, que ninguna criatura os puede empecer tanto cuanto la cruz os puede defender y ayudar. (42.382)

> [And I add that it's vile sin to believe that anything created has the power to do what its Creator can ... You should therefore believe in your omnipotent Creator, through Whom come power and strength, not through His creatures. It is in this way, madam, that the cross in the hands of the pilgrim has healing powers; the pilgrim has none of his own. No creature can harm you so much as the cross can defend and assist you.] (42.189)

The Autor's supposed authority falters here, since the passage reveals a possible attack on Jesus as the son of God. He urges Lozana to believe in the healing power of the cross, not of God's son, and to believe in the sanctity of the creator, not in the created thing. While this interpretation goes against Christian doctrine, the Autor is seemingly ironic and wavering since the cross that he so highly esteems is as created a thing as a child.

The passage lends itself to a plethora of interpretations, including the analogy between the creator / author / Autor of the text and his counterpart of *Criador* (creator) / God, and the parent-child affiliation between the mother *Celestina* and the daughter *Lozana*.[81] The Autor indicates that the original creator is more powerful and virtuous than the thing created, which in Lozana / *La Lozana*'s case is ironically Celestina / *La Celestina*. The Autor alludes, however, to the overriding power of the author / creator, thereby attempting to minimize the independence of the text. Yet, even with the Autor's caveat, the paradigmatic Celestina still clearly generates the *medianera* Lozana. Celestina's representation as a reproductive, textual machine is highly ironic, since she is dressed as a nun in the illustration that represents her in *mamotreto* 37, a most biologically ungenerative role (350). Celestina dressed in a nun's habit is meant to be humorous because unlike that representation, she is clearly a prototype who has generated a whole line of textual daughters resembling herself.

The *medianera* legacy between *La Lozana* and *La Celestina* is further characterized by the concern with another aspect of the *medianera*-sex miasma, the legacy of *amor cortés* (courtly love). In the first part of the "Prólogo," Delicado tells the reader that he knows that the reader takes pleasure in hearing speak of things about love:

> Ilustre señor:
> Sabiendo yo que vuestra señoría toma placer cuando oye hablar en cosas de amor, que deleitan a todo hombre, y máxime cuando siente decir de personas que mejor se supieron dar la manera para administrar las cosas a él pertenecientes. (167)
>
> [Most honorable Lord:
> I am well aware that your lordship delights in tales of love, an art that all men enjoy, especially when they concern expert practitioners of it.] (2)

The "Prólogo" is accompanied by an illustration of people in a tall building and a man leading a donkey (168). Allaigre believes that it best refers to Robusto the donkey in *mamotreto* 65, but Damiani also points out its resemblance to Diego de San Pedro's *Cárcel de amor*. One interpretation only enriches the other, as the illustration's main significance is that it solidifies from the beginning *La Lozana*'s supposed relationship to a discursive courtly love tradition. Courtly love in *La Lozana*, however, simply does not exist, even in the formally idyllic and stylized way that it had between Calisto and

4: EVA AND NOT EVA

Melibea in *La Celestina*. One vestige of a courtly love past lies in the courtesans whom Lozana meets in *mamotretos* 23 and 48, and who have nothing to do with the royal court nor with courtly love poetry, but instead who work as prostitutes.

Discursive courtly love and the pairing of Celestina and Lozana are explicitly recalled by the Embajador (Ambassador) and the Caballero (Gentleman) at the end of *mamotreto* 36, when upon proclaiming Lozana's beauty, the gentleman sets Lozana apart from the other *medianerc*:

> Caballero: ¡Mírela vuestra señoría a la ventana; no hay tal Lozana en el mundo! Ya abre, veamos qué dice. Cabecea que entremos donde ni fierro ni fuego a la virtud empece.
> Embajador: ¡Qua'più bella la matre que la filla!
> Caballero: Monseñor, ésta es Cárcel de Amor; aquí idolatró Calisto, aquí no se estima Melibea, aquí poco vale Celestina. (36.349)

> [Gentleman: There she is in the window, your lordship! There's no one like Lozana in the whole world! Now she's opened it; let's see what she has to say. Good! She is beckoning us to enter where neither fetters nor flames impede the triumph of virtue.
> Ambassador: Why, the mother is much more beautiful than the daughter!
> Gentleman: My lord, welcome to Love's Prison: here Calisto is idolized; here Melibea is shown no respect; here Celestina is worth very little.]
> (36.161–62)

The gentleman articulates the primary contradiction and irony in the text: that the *beautiful* prostitute Lozana simply does not exist. Lozana is nevertheless still textually desirable to the two men. The ambassador ironically believes that the bearded and old Celestina is more beautiful than Lozana, who again defies the meaning of her name. The gentleman realizes that they are all situated in love's prison where Calisto gave himself over completely to Melibea, where Melibea is considered unworthy, and where Celestina has little value. The gentleman indicates that they are either jailed by love in the same way as Leriano in *Cárcel de amor*, or that they are trapped by their urges in spite of the fact that Lozana does not strike them as desirable. For them, she represents the "caballero assí feroz de presencia como espantoso de vista" [a knight fierce of bearing and frightful to behold] who calls himself *Deseo* (Desire), and who leads unsuspecting men to their imprisonment.[82] According to the woodcut of desire as a hairy giant in the Spanish edition,

Lozana resembles his monstrousness as a sort of noseless monster herself.[83] She does not lead her victim to a tower like desire does with Leriano, but to an arduous and inevitable hospitalization (imprisonment) caused by syphilis. Ironically more beautiful than Lozana, Celestina can do nothing here because Lozana has superseded her.

Unlike in Celestina's meretricious text, Lozana appears in this scene as both her own intercessor and as the desired and transacted sex-object. She is both Melibea and Celestina, to whom the gentleman and the ambassador have effortlessly surrendered themselves. Celestina can do nothing to remedy this situation in any way, in order to dismantle the men's imprisonment. The depiction of Celestina as a nun that follows *mamotreto* 36 suggests that Celestina's ironic habit is due to her dethroning by the even uglier yet desired Lozana. Celestina carries a rosary and hangs something from the top of the threshold of a doorway, perhaps blessing not only those who enter the building, but also sanctifying the passage between these two texts. For Celestina is only pious and holy compared to Lozana.

Lozana never stops working as a prostitute altogether, but the focus of her activities changes as she ages, especially in part 3. Lozana's physical resemblance to Celestina only gets stronger the older she gets, and like Celestina she is bearded later in life. According to *mamotreto* 28, Lozana lives or works where "la de los Ríos" (28.314) [the prostitutes (sic) de los Rios] (28.129) used to be, reminiscent of Celestina's house near the river.[84] Her healing functions become more accentuated from *mamotreto* 17 on, as she grows older and according to Rampín only earns half the money she had earned before (17.252). Lozana's role as a healer was alluded to early on in the text, but according to a strong desire to separate her kind of healing from that of learned medicine. For instance, after the prose narrator describes the women who live and work in Pozo Blanco, the neighborhood in which Lozana is first placed, he ironically parallels Lozana to the Arabic physician and theorist Avicenna:

> Rosa, Cufa, Cintia y Alfarutía, y otra que se decía la judía del vulgo, que era más plática y tinié más conversación.[85] Y habéis de notar que pasó a todas éstas en este oficio, y supo más que todas, y diole mejor la manera, de tal modo que en nuestros tiempos podemos decir que no hay quien use el oficio mejor ni gane más que la señora Lozana,

como abajo diremos, que fue entre las otras como Avicena entre los médicos. (5.189–90)

[Rosa, Cufa, Cintia, and Alfarutia. There was also a lady called the Jew from Borgo who plied her trade well and talked a blue streak. But it should be said that Lozana knew the business better than any of them and practiced it with more skill, and we can honestly report that no one in our time has ever done better at this profession, nor earned a better return than Lozana did, as we shall disclose later on. Among them she was like Avicenna among the physicians.] (5.18)

The women's trade referred to by the narrator remains unclear, although it could be connected to the earlier mention of shaving or applying makeup (*afeitar*), the making of mercury (*hacer solimán*), and others. It is more likely that it indicates the latter *conversación* (conversation) in the quote above, which during this period often meant sexual intercourse.[86] Hence, in the same way that Avicenna represents the most exceptional physician of all, so does Lozana constitute the prostitute superior to all the women in Pozo Blanco. The parallel attests to Lozana's prowess as a practitioner of *conversación*, but not as a respected medical authority.[87]

Some of the final *mamotretos* paint Lozana's activities in a different, more advantageous light, even in contrast to Celestina's. Moreover, the ironic parallel to Avicenna the medical expert must be contrasted to a scene in the later *mamotreto* 59, in which Lozana's healing methods are complimented and even sought out by a *médico* (doctor), a *físico* (physician), and a *cirúcico* [sic] (surgeon). This episode starts out in a comical and ironic way because it opens with three learned medical practitioners who turn to Lozana's supposed lack of training to inform themselves of the most recent healing treatments. While looking at the pharmaceuticals that Lozana is carrying, they ask her: "¿Qué especiería es ésa que debajo lleváis? ¿Hay curas? ¿Hay curas? ¡Danos parte!" (59.451) [What are all of those drugs you're carrying under your arm? Cures? Remedies? Let us in on it] (59.250). They want to participate in the healing that she apparently commands. Then they proceed to blame her success in healing for their lack of patients:

Cirucigo: Digo que me habéis llevado de las manos más de seis personas que yo curaba que, como no les duelen las plagas con lo que vos les habéis dicho, no vienen a nosotros, y nosotros, si no duelen las heridas, metemos con que duelan y escuezgan, porque vean que sabemos algo cuando les quitamos aquel dolor. Ansimismo, a otros ponemos ungüento egipciaco, que tiene vinagre.

....

Medico: y mandáislos [the patients] lavar con agua fría, que no hay mejor cosa para ellos [their teeth], y para la cara y manos lavar con fría y no caliente. Mas si lo dicimos nosotros, no tornarán los pacientes, y así es menester que huyamos de vos porque no concuerda vuestra medicación con nuestra cupida intención. (59.453–54)

[Surgeon: I said this because you've taken from my care more than six people that I was healing because, since they aren't suffering from plagues, they don't come to us because of what you've told them; and, if their wounds aren't hurting them, we apply something that does make them hurt. That way, they are impressed when we make the pain stop. Likewise, we put Egyptian ointment on others because it contains vinegar.

....

Physician: you order them [the patients] . . . to clean them [their teeth] with cold water because there's nothing better for them, and to wash their face and hands with cold instead of hot water. But, if we tell this to them, the patients won't return; therefore, it's necessary for us to avoid you because your medical treatment doesn't agree with our greedy intention.] (59.251)

The main difficulty in interpreting this episode is its ambiguity when considered within the text as a whole. It could be read as solely ironic, intended to deprecate the supposed unlearnedness of the woman healer. But it also depicts the medical professionals as inept, greedy, and interested in augmenting the diseases of others for their own gain. Allaigre believes that Delicado vilifies and criticizes the physicians and other medical professionals (whom an author such as Roig had so decidedly praised) because he esteemed medicine as a discipline, but reviled the physicians of his time (59.453 n. 7). Allaigre's assessment certainly seems plausible given the incessant attacks on medical doctors and the profession as a whole by syphilis patients who often obtained little if any relief from them.[88] Allaigre's assertion also seems reasonable in the face of Delicado's decades-long battle with syphilis, the pain associated with the disease, and the lack of a real cure.[89]

But the episode in *mamotreto* 59 is further complicated and doubtful because of the ironic fact that Lozana is still a syphilitic prostitute. She is only regarded as knowledgeable in contrast to the medical professionals who are so inept. Insofar as this episode and the entire text contextualize distinct ways of healing and match the appropriate healers to the suitable occasions, Lozana evidently heals certain ailments in this episode while indicating that no one can capably heal syphilis: "Señores, concluí que el médico y la medicina los sabios se sirven d'él y d'ella, mas no hay tan asno médico como el que quiere sanar el griñimón" (59.454) [Gentlemen, I concluded that learned people make use of the physician and his medical treatment, but there's no physician as asinine as the one who wants to cure the pox] (59.251–52). This episode suggests the ironic contradiction between what has been established as Lozana's lack of knowledge and her evident desirabililty from the standpoint of everyday people.

Lozana's "attractiveness" as a healer is acknowledged in this *mamotreto*, but it is founded on her ironic, monstrous physical appearance. Most importantly, her desirability as a healer is ironic because her healing mediations are often guises for prostitution activities, the métier from which she earns the most money. In the same *mamotreto* 59, her methodology about healing is dubious at best:

Señores míos, y veo que me queréis motejar. Mis melecinas son: si pega, pega, y míroles a las manos como hace algo sabe. (59.454)

[My dear gentlemen, I see now that you want to ridicule me. My art of healing includes: if it works, it's right, and I look at their hands like someone who knows what he's doing.] (59.251)

The passage can be considered complementary to Lozana's practical skills. But the sexual allusions are evident in the scatological meaning of *pegar* (to stick or paste) as *ligar* (to flirt with the intent to have sex), and of "mirar a las manos" (looking at hands) as the scatological reference to Lozana's habit of looking at men's hands to "apreciar las dotes viriles" (59.454 n. 10) [take into account their virile endowments] like she did with Diomedes and Rampín. The sexual level of meaning destabilizes and makes uncertain the veracity of Lozana's nominal healing capabilities.

In fact, it is as if her pretensions to heal and the belief in her abilities on the part of the townspeople who request her remedies were mere pretexts for an opportunity to make more money engaging in prostitution. This is evident in *mamotreto* 43, where a number of people visit Lozana and bring her presents to thank her for her remedies. The Autor remains outside Lozana's house and talks with her former and current clients. Their discussions consist of a curious mix of talk about medicine, prostitution, and law. The Autor says:

> Pues aquéllas, ocultas allá van, que por ella demandan, y no me partiré de aquí sin ver el trato que esta mujer tiene. Allá entra la una, y otra mujer con dos ánades. Aquélla no es puta, sino mal de madre; yo lo sabré al salir. (43.385)
>
> [Just look at those women in their disguises approaching her door to ask if she is in. I'll not budge until I see how she treats them. There, one is going in, followed by that other lady with her two ducks. That woman isn't a whore, but she is laid up with female complaints. I'll ask her about it when she leaves.] (43.191–92)

The Autor indicates that the first woman is not a prostitute, but sick with the *mal de madre*. Upon leaving, he calls her *madre* (mother), which equates her with prostitution and disease, and contradicts what he had said before. At the end of the *mamotreto*, he further negates his previous separation of Lozana's clients from prostitution by remarking on the vast number of prostitutes and notaries leaving her house. This comment stands in stark contrast to the earlier representation of her clients as grateful and "healed" (43.386).

Instead of calling into question the validity of the connection between prostitution, disease, and healing—which had constituted Celestina's characterization—*mamotretos* and episodes such as this one only serve to reinforce that prejudicial linkage. In the text, the populace believes that Lozana actually heals. The loyalty of her clientele only aligns her more closely to Celestina's "successes" in healing; that is, Celestina's ability to deceive men, or so it is suggested in *La Celestina*. In fact, Silvano says at the end of *mamotreto* 43 that he is unaware of how Lozana heals nowadays, but that in the past, she deceived people with her words ("embaucaba las gentes con sus palabras" (43.386) [she would deceive her clients with twisted words] [43.193]). He then claims that she healed one man by providing him the (sexual) means for pleasure so that he would not seek pills nor purgatives to remedy himself (386). Lozana and her author both try to provide such curative pleasure in order that their reader / clients will frequent them again.

Evidently, this is the ironic way in which pleasure operates in *La Lozana*: in order that the client / reader return to the prostitute / book. Lozana controls her client's cure, according to Silvano, in the same way that the book directs the reader's attention to Lozana's monstrous incongruities and contradictions, and toward Delicado's own remedies after that. Book and prostitute deceive the client / reader because their confabulations cause dis-ease at the same time that they supposedly provide pleasure. *La Lozana* is a useful instrument or tool for the male reader secluded in a hospital because it makes him laugh and sometimes serves him sexually. Unlike the author who may manipulate his text so that certain blemishes and stains are invisible at particular moments in the book, the so-called *dominating medianera* in daily life may not have been so adept at manipulating herself so as to have caused clients to view her as pleasurable or desirable, like so many contemporary critics have done with the discursive Lozana.

How was this text read in the sixteenth century? Would Lozana's decided rejection of any connection to Celestina in one of the last *mamotretos* have caused the reader to view her favorably or desirably? For in *mamotreto* 54, Lozana refuses to engage in one of the most troubling tasks carried out by Celestina, that of the restoration of virgins. Another *medianera*, Doméstica, attempts to enlist Lozana's help in marrying off a young "virgin" to a wealthy Spanish gentleman (*hombre de bien*). When Lozana protests that no Spanish man would want the responsibility of "deflowering" a virgin, Doméstica says that the young woman is not much of a virgin. However, because her vagina is so narrow, Doméstica continues, she appears to be a virgin (54.429–30). Hence, the young woman may be considered both a virgin and not a virgin, depending on the desires of the go-between and of the man to marry her. In other words, like Celestina to whom Lozana later equates her, Doméstica seeks Lozana's help in a plan of deception. But unlike her predecessor and mother Celestina, Lozana assumes a sincere, moral position, refuses to collaborate with Doméstica, and throws her out of the house. Divicia tells Lozana that Doméstica went to Celidonia's house to enlist her help, to which Lozana replies:

¿Qué más Celidonia o Celestina qu'ella? Si todas las Celidonias o Celestinas que hay en Roma me diesen dos carlines al mes, como los médicos de Ferrara al Gonela, yo sería más rica que cuantas mujeres hay en esta tierra. (54.430)

[Who's a better Celidonia or Celestina than she is? If all of the Celidonias or Celestinas in Rome gave me two *carlines* (coins) a month, as the physicians of Ferrara gave to Gonnella, I'd be richer than all the women living in this country.] (54.230)

Lozana asserts, then, that she is different, that she is not one of those Celidonias or Celestinas who should pay tribute in order to practice.

Lozana's encounter with Doméstica leads her to tell an engaging story to Divicia about how the duke of Ferrara discovered that virtually everyone in the kingdom could be called a doctor because when asked, everybody possessed his or her own remedy for ailments (54.430). Lozana claims that Gonnella told the duke one day that he wanted to charge every doctor in the land two *carlines*.[90] Since the duke believed that there existed no more than ten doctors in the land, he agreed. Gonnella then wrapped his foot and arm in a bandage and traveled around the countryside telling everyone he met that he had a swollen arm and ankle:

> Tengo hinchado esto. Y luego le decían: Va, toma la tal hierba, y tal cosa, y póntela y sanarás. Después, escrebía el nombre de cuantos le decían el remedio, y fuese al duque, y mostróle cuántos médicos había hallado en su tierra. Y el duque decía: ¿Has tú dicho la tal medicina a Gonela? El otro respondía: Señor, sí.—Pues pagá dos carlines, porque sois médico nuevo en Ferrara. Así querría yo hacer por saber cuántas Celidonias hay en esta tierra. (54.430)
>
> ["This is swollen." And then they told him: "Go and get such-and-such an herb thing and put it on it and you'll be cured." Then, he wrote down the names of all the people who told him the remedy and went to the Duke and showed him how many physicians he had found in his country. And the Duke asked each of them in turn: "Have you told Gonnella about such-and-such medicine?" And each one answered: "Yes, sir." "Well, pay him two *carlines* because you're a new physician in Ferrara." I'd like to use this method to find out how many Celidonians there are in this country.] (54.231)

This passage attests to the ease with which anyone could be considered or consider her or himself a doctor at this time, despite the severe and exclusionary measures adopted throughout Europe to exclude nonprofessionals from the field of medicine. The episode also suggests that there is no distinction between doctors (the ten healers whom the duke imagines initially) and unauthorized healers. They are one and the same as long as they provide remedies for the ailments of others.

The great irony in this story is that Lozana apparently thinks that the healers who give money to the duke are actual doctors or physicians, since the point of the story is that they are not. And Lozana is clearly not a medical doctor either. She distances herself from women healers and places herself in the position of either the duke or Gonnella, one of those who charged the fee.

But, Lozana is not the duke of Ferrara, nor is she a medical doctor, nor is she even simply a woman healer. She is a noseless, syphilitic prostitute, characteristics that must be ignored in order to believe her attempts to separate herself from the other Celidonias and Celestinas in this episode. For, as the scene with the physicians and surgeon demonstrates in *mamotreto* 59, despite her occasional success in healing, the medical healers consider her different from them. Although they clearly seek her practical knowledge in healing, she is evidently not one of them. Both episodes may be read as completely ironic since Lozana is a syphilitic prostitute to whom physicians turn for cures, and although she tries to separate herself from Doméstica and Celestina, none of them is that different from the others.

Are these episodes really ambiguous at all, given the fact of Lozana's disease and her other "monstrous" qualities? Coming from the mouth of the unstable Lozana, an ironic parallel to Avicenna, her self-congratulatory separation from the Celestinas and Celidonias of the text is meant to be paradoxical. In order to be read with appreciation, Lozana's negative attributes must be covered or hidden with the large cloth of the *gasa-jo*, which is not impossible while reading. But women's licit marginalization during this period from their traditional jobs in Iberian society, such as healing tasks or controlling prostitution, suggests that the perceived undesirable attributes of women were not so readily overlooked in daily life.

Lozana's lament in *mamotreto* 44 about the displacement of women from the "court" of prostitution and their subsequent lesser earnings only serves to place and fix them in some of the "lowly," disparaging occupations that characterize the paradigmatic *medianera* Celestina:

> ¿Acordáisos de aquellos tiempos, pasados cómo triunfábamos, y había otros modos de vivir, y eran las putas más francas? ... No sé, por mí lo digo, que me maravillo cómo pueden vivir munchas pobres mujeres que han servido esta corte con sus haciendas y honras, y puesto su vida al tablero por honrar la corte y pelear y batallar, que no las bastaban puertas de hierro, ... Y agora ¿qué mérito [also, *meretriz* or meretrix] les dan?, salvo que unas, rotos brazos, otras, gastadas sus personas y bienes, otras, señaladas y con dolores, otras, paridas y desmamparadas, otras que siendo señoras son agora siervas, otras, estacioneras, otras, lavanderas, otras, estableras, otras, cabestro de símiles, otras, alcahuetas,

otras, parteras, otras, cámara locanda, otras que hilan y no son pagadas. (44.387–90)

[Just think how well we lived in the old days, though we could have made our way differently, when whores were whores.... I know I'm speaking only for myself, but I wonder how many unfortunate women can even make a living now; those same women who have served this court with their feats of service and their very honor and have risked their lives in the court's behalf, while they worked and slaved with no iron doors to offer them protection.... And now, how are they rewarded? For some, broken arms; for others, bodies wasted and worldly goods dispersed; for others, scars and pains; for others, bearing children and then abandoned. Some who were ladies are now maids; others ply their trade on the streetcorners; some are washerwomen, or stable women, or whores in the service of other whores; still others are bawds, midwives, or women for rent; others weave and are not paid.] (44.194–95)

As she ironically laments the loss of *courtly* prostitution as she knew it, she also alludes to the host of jobs to which women were forced to turn. Equally ironic is the fact that some of these jobs were either successfully overtaken by men in the fifteenth and sixteenth centuries or were in the process of suffering that fate. Her nostalgia for prostitution as she knew it, when prostitutes were more generous (*francas*), can be interpreted in two ways, either in reference to syphilis (*mal francés*), or with regard to a time when prostitutes did not have to pay tribute.[91] But Lozana does not only lament the loss of one desirable occupation, prostitution, which was replaced by ill-favored ones or all the rest. Instead, the long speech also mocks her as the supposed member of a court. At the same time that she is indignant about some of the abuses against women, such as their broken arms, she bemoans the loss of prostitution as if it had been an idyllic form of labor. While this section indicates compassion toward the loss of women's self-determination in that occupation, the way in which the text reinforces the characterization of prostitutes as diseased and threatening suggests that this passage is likely meant as ironic and funny.

In contrast to Lozana's contention in the episode that women have left prostitution for other kinds of jobs, one of the consequences of women's exclusion from the licit practice of a variety of occupations in the sixteenth and seventeenth centuries was an increase in illicit prostitution. Historians such as Bartolomé Bennassar have pointed out that the seventeenth-century enactment of laws regarding the houses of penitents (*maisons de "Repenties"*), and the establishment of correction facilities such as Madre Magdalena de San Gerónimo's *Galera* (women's jail) in Valladolid represent the exacerbation of clandestine prostitution.[92] In general, many historians have demonstrated the progressive attempts during this period to governmentally control the agents of prostitution, that is, prostitutes and procurers, and the conditions of their practice.[93] The extent to which the establishment of licit prostitution in locally controlled brothels generated more sanitary and safer working conditions for such women (a common argument even today among the proponents of legalized prostitution) remains thus far undetermined. What did accompany the legalization and male control of prostitution in the sixteenth and seventeenth centuries was the establishment or augmentation of conversion and correctional measures against illicit prostitutes:

> Whether people of this period viewed the brothel as a breeding ground for disease or as a defense against it, they agreed that prostitutes who left the brothel had to be placed in another form of enclosure.[94]

While efforts to aid prostitutes can be documented in some Iberian municipalities from as early as the fourteenth century, enclosures for women such as the Magdalen House, the house of penitents, the prison, and the convent were firmly situated throughout the peninsula in the sixteenth and seventeenth centuries. Perry calls women who refused to stay in the brothel or convent Jezebels. She argues that they continued to pose a social problem during this period, and were routinely punished "through public humiliation, whippings, having their noses slit, and exile."[95]

Hence, it is difficult to tacitly agree with the bulk of the criticism about *La Lozana andaluza*, which argues that the syphilitic, disfigured Lozana represents a desirable individual. It is even more challenging to agree that the text exalts women's sexuality. For Lozana, prostitution represents a means of survival. For her clients, the transactions serve their erotic desires. The power of irony in this text equals the power of representation, which is concomitant with domination and control. Instead of the clear-cut representation of the Virgin or even of Celestina, Lozana's representation is ironic and ever-changing. In light of the more stringent conditions within which many women lived in early modern society, this ironic characterization is confounding in many ways. One of the ways in which it appears to vindicate prostitutes and women's agency is by showing that they work independently, despite societal restrictions against them. But the text's mockery and irony always serve to undermine such an affirming contention. This constant displacement of an absolute interpretive stance is paralleled by the text's ambiguous ending.

Lozana's displacement in the last *mamotreto* to the island of Lipari is less a self-determined act of escape in order to spend the rest of her life with her lover than it is an effort on the author's part to resituate her in a place where she will play a "viable" role. Having been edged out of prostitution because of her age and social prejudice against her, she is the monstrous form of Galen's and Huarte's *inventor occasionis*, the "physician" who knows the appropriate places and uses of people and things. Hence, she exiles herself and her lover because they can be of use to one another there. She effectively carries out what Perry and others have observed as the ultimate solution for the problem of Iberian prostitutes in this period, that is, to enclose them.

Lozana's self-imposed exile to Lipari also would have been read by a premodern reader as a definitive attempt at self-healing, since the southern part of the Mediterranean island has been famous for its thermal springs and therapeutic baths, especially at San Cologno. Thus, the trip to Lipari signifies the conclusion of Lozana's worth as a mediator of her clients' health, and it underlines her ironic value throughout the text as a capable healer who also needs to be healed.

The text's significance is analogous to that of its main protagonist. For, when *La Lozana*'s former "use value" as an instrument of pain relief comes to an end, the author / physician's theoretical and practical aptitude takes over. The male reader is encouraged to keep reading Delicado's other two treatises in order to relieve the pain ironically caused by Lozana and her text.

But, perhaps the most disturbing way in which irony functions by the end of this book is that it allows Lozana to be *recreated* with in a way that the Virgin and *La Celestina* do not even invite. Delicado points this out in the "Cómo se escusa el autor," when he admits that he took a great deal of pleasure in writing the book. Play, recreation, and men's pleasure within and from the work are at the expense of women both in the text and ultimately, in the reader's society. Jovial play with women characters is problematic, especially when carried out in the form of irony, mockery, and sarcasm, and when promoted by a male author. The brutal disfigurement of Lozana's body takes on recreational qualities and values at the expense of Lozana, and by extension to the detriment of women in society.

While *La Lozana andaluza* is not a clear condemnation of women on Delicado's part, it is not a "defense" of their worth either. Aside from the case of women's work as prostitutes, the book confounds the value of women workers as healers and, like *La Celestina*, makes the transactions of prostitution virtually indistinguishable from the mercantile mediation and trade that characterizes the business of healing. Rather than clearly exposing the gendered biases of the strictures against prostitutes and women healers, *La Lozana andaluza* ironically demonstrates their appropriateness.

Arguably, *La Lozana andaluza* must connect the woman healer with prostitution and disease because the text is *La Celestina*'s daughter. The former textual models of women such as the Virgin that had supported women healers in the past are replaced by the ironic Lozana who is as desirable as she is monstrous. While at the same time playing out the often ineffectual, institutional mechanisms designed to exclude women healers from their traditional practice in Iberian society, *La Lozana andaluza* connects the desirability of those women with an inevitable, predetermined propensity for sexual activity and disease. The proposal that *La Lozana* makes about women healers' continued popular regard does not disrupt the pejorative models set out in the *Spill* and *La Celestina*; rather, it reinforces their pejorative depiction, and fortifies the maligning of traditional women healers in the readers' society.

Conclusion

In their efforts to discourage male readers from seeking the services of women healers, Roig, Rojas, and Delicado transformed positive medieval models of these healers with misogynist textual strategies. Misogynist rhetorical conventions such as women's excessive speech or their Evian power to disease men provided the authors with an array of strategies to fall back on in trying to mitigate the well-being of the male reader, and in their effort to transform medieval textual models that supported women healers. Perhaps these antifeminist conventions made it easier for Roig, Rojas, and Delicado to malign women in their "entertaining," fictional works, in contrast to the comparative lack of literature directed at traditional Muslim and Jewish male healers. Because Jews and Arabs had constituted for centuries the primary textual transmitters of scientific and medical knowledge in medieval Iberia and to the rest of Europe, maybe there were fewer written traditions of denigration against them than there were against women. Perhaps the severe conversion and expulsion taken against Jews in 1492, and the expulsion of converted Muslims in 1609, made it unnecessary to disparage male healers through literary means.

The historical events in late medieval and early modern Iberia, such as the professionalization of medicine and the rise of medicine as a homosocial domain, also forced these writers to invent their own methods of vilifying women. Roig created a division between Eve and Mary that could not be bridged, Rojas depicted Celestina as a parodic imitator of the Virgin, and Delicado demonstrated the monstrous irony of Lozana's widespread appeal. Textual images of maligned women healers such as these became the increasing norm from the late Middle Ages on, marking a change in the influential depictions of women healers that had authorized their work in the medieval period.

It is not coincidental that these late medieval and early modern misogynist representations coincided with women's progressive invisibility or denigration in early modern medical treatises. Damián Carbón's treatise on midwives is a notable exception, since a majority of these works never presented women in a healing capacity, if they mentioned them at all. For instance, in his sixteenth-century treatise on men's sexual health, *Tractado del uso de las mugeres*, the Castilian doctor Francisco Núñez de Coria discusses women with regard to their value for men's sexual well-being. He immediately discusses their insatiable sexual appetite in the first chapter:

> naturalmente son de apetito insaciable, pues como dize Salamon en el treynta y nueue de sus prouerbios, tres cosas son que nunca se hartan, la boca del infierno, la vulva, el fuego.[1]
>
> [they are naturally of an insatiable appetite, for as Solomon says in proverb 39, there are three things that are never satisfied, the mouth of hell, the vulva, and fire.]

Núñez de Coria goes on to qualify this misogynist statement on women's "natural" insatiability with a physiologically based explanation. He reasons that young women tend to desire coitus more than older women because their vulvas are narrower, making it difficult for seed to be expelled. Thus young women seek coitus more than other women because of a presumably biological need to expel seed. Gone from this manual on men's sexual well-being is the description of the woman healer who intervened on behalf of clients soliciting women's attentions in chapter 8 of the *Speculum al foderi*. Women no longer mediate men's sexual relations in the early modern period. Rather, they serve as tools to employ for men's pleasure and well-being. Hence the *Tractado*'s title, which is on the *use* of women.

In another early modern example of how medical writers describe women in their works, the medical theorist Juan Huarte de San Juan mentions them in his discussion of gender difference, focusing on how their physiology is the reverse of men's. Huarte provides this information on gender difference within a larger discussion of human generation in chapter 15 of the influential, sixteenth-century *Examen de ingenios para las ciencias*.[2] It is notable that women play no more extensive a role than as procreators in Huarte's elaborate ideas on biology and the social order, where biology conditions one's social role, and by extension, the well-being of the republic.

Women's exclusion from healing roles in medical treatises such as these, the literary images that colluded with their ostracizing from traditional healing practice, and the early social restrictions against women healers all culminated in women's eighteenth- and nineteenth-century demotion to what Greilsammer calls "ignorant 'matrons.'"³ Women healers were targets of the early modern change that occurred in the treatment of mental disease in England, whereby medicine and male physicians finally triumphed in their long effort to debunk spiritual explanations for insanity, and to deprecate empirics and all nonmedical healers, such as women. In his study, *Mystical Bedlam: Madness, Anxiety, and Healing in Seventeenth-Century England,* Michael MacDonald argues that restrictive medical practice had deleterious social effects because it meant the destruction of former beliefs in the validity of nonmedical healers and of healing practice based on superstition, astrology, or magic. MacDonald believes that the eighteenth century "was a disaster for the insane," who were restrained in places such as asylums or prisons.⁴ It was not until more than one hundred years later that physicians would improve their curative strategies and thus the living conditions of the mentally ill.

From the later Middle Ages on, medicine increasingly became a homosocial domain that dissociated itself from traditional, popular healing practices, and from its women practitioners. Yet the change in the legal and ideological status of women healers from the medieval to the modern periods does not imply that medieval women experienced a veritable "golden age" of enlightened opportunity in their lives and work. Indeed, a plethora of medieval historians have brought to light the harsh and prejudicial conditions that many medieval women endured.⁵ Scholars such as Judith M. Bennett have even balked at the idea that there occurred a definite change in women's status between the medieval and early modern periods. She views as faulty the master narrative that assumes "a great and negative transition for women," or "a dramatic change in women's lives between 1300 and 1700."⁶ Bennett believes that historical documents reveal continuity in women's work from the late medieval to the early modern periods more than they indicate a massive change. Her approach interprets women's history as a series of "small shifts, short-term changes, and enduring continuities."⁷ Yet in the case of medieval Iberia, it is clear that women who worked as healers without relative restriction in the medieval period before the second half of the fourteenth century were increasingly maligned after that time. Women's exclusion from licit medical practice was gradual, but it was also intensive, especially in the sixteenth century.

Just as it would be naive and misguided to present the medieval period in a totalizing fashion as a tolerant era for women, it also would be erroneous to dismiss what historians have demonstrated was a concerted effort to marginalize women from licit medical practice. This book has attempted to show the progressive nature of the legal devices set forth because of the professionalization of medicine in Iberia from the second half of the fourteenth century on. In so doing, it has further suggested that such mechanisms mark a change in the previous, medieval status of women healers, which is borne out by the transformation of textual models in their favor, and by the particular conditions of medieval healing. Medicine was not dominant in the medieval period, and it seems that all types of healers practiced in a manner relatively free from restraints against them. Medieval Iberia was especially susceptible to a fluid social organization because its political, linguistic, and religious borders were continually shifting. The new controls and increased limitations placed on women with the professionalization of medicine were crucial to their eventual limitations in healing practice. The aggregate of conditions that characterize late medieval and early modern healing were simply nonexistent in their entirety before the second half of the fourteenth century, and perhaps, even as late as the second half of the fifteenth.

The rise of medicine as a judicial discipline had pejorative consequences for traditional women healers, and on a wider scale, for the direction of the Iberian social order, especially from the late fifteenth century on. It authorized itself, its own body of knowledge, as a superior judge of everyday corporeality and morality:

> Medicine is a judicial discipline, a normative science of social conduct, which distinguishes normal and abnormal or pathological, acceptable and unacceptable, permissible and forbidden, good and bad.[8]

The progressively authoritative male physician became a social judge who made corporeal distinctions through his medical theory and practice. He was the conduit for the connection of individual bodies and the social body, as his judgments concerning sickness and health implicitly pronounced him an arbiter of the Iberian moral order. Early modern Iberian authorities relied on medicine and the male physician not only to distinguish between healthy and ill bodies, but to draw moral judgments of character based on an individual's corporeal composition. The physician's declarations resulted in value judgments about individual rectitude, as people were deemed good or bad, just or unjust, clean or unclean, female or male, and noble or plebeian.⁹ Early modern authorities ultimately looked to medicine and the male physician to justify their inquisitorial practice.¹⁰

The interest in the "medicalizing" of numerous facets of Iberian society is evident in the three literary works studied in this book. For instance, the belief that medical sovereignty, and hence biological arguments against women, will produce social and political organization motivates Solomon's dream-speech in book 3 of the *Spill*. *La Lozana andaluza*, on the other hand, demonstrates the problems inherent in this facile equation, and depicts the *medianera* as contentious and ironic. Delicado shows that the powerful metaphors proposed by sixteenth-century physicians such as Enrique Jorge Enríquez, including medicine as king, or the analogy of the king and the physician, both of whom enjoy "great power" and have "subjects," were ironic in the face of sexual disease.¹¹ The fact that Enríquez found it necessary to underscore in 1595 the connection between medical and royal sovereignty, some seventy years after the appearance of *La Lozana andaluza*, only attests to its importance as an organizing device among social authorities. Huarte de San Juan even devotes chapter 14 of his *Examen de ingenios* (1575) to the abilities that make a king, and to the detectable signs of those qualities in men. Hence, Huarte appoints himself the irrefutable medical doctor who dictates the capabilities commensurate with certain vocations, and who provides readers with the necessary information to determine those qualities in others.

Metaphors and ideological relations that physicians such as Huarte and Enríquez shaped as purveyors of the social order were influential in their time. Their long-term effects are palpable in the authoritarian position that medicine continues to occupy in the modern West, and in the obstructed access to medical practice that has characterized much of modern Western history. This book has attempted to elucidate in part the potential force of such writings in the fashioning of society. But it has also inherently stressed the potency of literature or books in their roles as intercessors that negotiate value and meaning between the reader and her or his world. Roig, Rojas, and Delicado all recognized literature's potential strength as a *medianera* in its own right that persuades and dissuades, reinforces and tears down. Their works preceded and participated in tremendous sixteenth- and seventeenth-century cultural apprehension about textual interpretation and meaning, as evidenced by inquisitorial efforts to forbid heretical and otherwise offensive works by placing them on the index of prohibited books, promulgated three times in the sixteenth century. The limitations on the traditional work of ordinary *medianeras* / women healers coincided with the reducing of ways in which the *medianera* / book could potentially negotiate meaning for the reader and her or his society.

Notes

INTRODUCTION

1. This is the contention of a number of medical anthropologists and theorists, including Jean Comaroff, "Medicine: Symbol and Ideology," in *The Problem of Medical Knowledge: Examining the Social Construction of Medicine*, ed. Peter Wright and Andrew Treacher (Edinburgh: Edinburgh University Press, 1982), 49–68; Claudine Herzlich and Janine Pierret, *Illness and Self in Society* (Baltimore: Johns Hopkins University Press, 1987); Kaja Finkler, "Sacred Healing and Biomedicine Compared," *Medical Anthropology Quarterly* 8, no. 2 (1994): 178–97; David B. Morris, *The Culture of Pain* (Berkeley: University of California Press, 1991); Michael T. Taussig, "Reification and the Consciousness of the Patient," *Social Science and Medicine* 14B (1980): 3–13; Peter Wright and Andrew Treacher, introduction to *The Problem of Medical Knowledge: Examining the Social Construction of Medicine*, ed. Peter Wright and Andrew Treacher (Edinburgh: Edinburgh University Press, 1982), 1–22.

2. Comaroff, "Medicine," 51.

3. Michael Solomon, *The Literature of Misogyny in Medieval Spain* (New York: Cambridge University Press, 1997), 11.

4. Ibid., 2–4.

5. For explicit, juridical measures against non-Christian men healers, see Luis García-Ballester, Michael McVaugh, and Agustín Rubio Vela, *Medical Licensing and Learning in Fourteenth-Century Valencia* (Philadelphia: American Philosophical Society, 1989). For instance, see 25–29.

6. The term "homosocial" derives from the social sciences where it is used to describe "social bonds between persons of the same sex," in Eve Kosofsky Sedgwick, *Between Men: English Literature and Male Homosocial Desire* (New York: Columbia University Press, 1985), 1. For further discussion of this term, see Kosofsky Sedgwick, *Between Men*, 1–5, and Eve Kosofsky Sedgwick, *Epistemology of the Closet* (Berkeley: University of California Press, 1990), 87–88.

7. See Diego Gracia Guillén's, "Judaism, Medicine, and the Inquisitorial Mind in Sixteenth-Century Spain," where he examines how three *converso* (converted) physicians successfully defended and justified the capabilities of male converted doctors, in *The Spanish Inquisition and the Inquisitorial Mind*, ed. Ángel Alcalá (Boulder, Colo.: Social Science Monographs, 1987), 375–400.

8. R. Howard Bloch discusses these and other misogynistic tropes in *Medieval Misogyny and the Invention of Western Romantic Love* (Chicago: University of Chicago Press, 1991), especially chapter 2.

9. See Solomon, chapter 3, "The Poetics of Infection," in *Literature of Misogyny*.

Chapter 1

1. Alfonso X, el Sabio, *Cantigas de Santa María*, ed. Walter Mettmann (Madrid: Castalia, 1988), 2:312–16.

2. Juan Manuel, *Libro del cavallero et del escudero, Obras completas*, ed. José Manuel Blecua (Madrid: Gredos, 1982), 1:35.

For a discussion of Juan Manuel's hygienic practice, see Ian Macpherson, "Don Juan Manuel: The Literary Process," *Studies in Philology* 70 (1973): 6–8, and Glending Olson, *Literature as Recreation in the Later Middle Ages* (Ithaca: Cornell University Press, 1982), 84–85.

3. Olson, *Literature as Recreation*, 84–85.

4. Manuel, *Libro del cavallero*, 1:36.

5. José María Doñate Sebastiá, "Saludadores y médicos en la baja edad media," in *Primer Congreso de Historia del País Valenciano. Celebrado en Valencia del 14 al 18 de Abril de 1971* (Valencia: Universidad de Valencia, 1980), 2:806.

6. Antonio Castillo de Lucas, *Folkmedicina* (Madrid: Dossat, 1958), 71.

7. Josep Perarnau i Espelt, "Activitats i fórmules supersticioses de guarnició a Catalunya en la primera meitat del segle XIV," *Arxiu de textos catalans antics* 1(1982): 52–55.

8. See Antoni Cardoner i Planas, "Seis mujeres hebreas practicando la medicina en el reino de Aragón," *Sefarad* 9 (1949): 441–45. Harry Friedenwald's brief article, "Jewish Doctoresses in the Middle Ages," in *The Jew and Medicine: Essays* (New York: Ktav, 1967), 1:217–20, also describes Jewish women doctors who practiced mostly in Germany and France in the Middle Ages. Luis García-Ballester, Michael McVaugh, and Agustín Rubio Vela further cite an almost one-hundred-year presence of women medical practitioners in the Crown of Aragon. See their *Medical Licensing and Learning in Fourteenth-Century Valencia* (Philadelphia: American Philosophical Society, 1989), 30.

9. García-Ballester, McVaugh, Rubio Vela, *Medical Licensing*, 31.

10. Luis García Ballester, *Historia social de la medicina en la España de los siglos XIII al XVI* (Madrid: Akal, 1976), 44.

11. Antoni Cardoner i Planas, "L'exercici professional de la medicina a la Corona d'Aragó (1162–1479)," in *Congrés internacional d'historia de la medicina catalana* (Barcelona, 1970), 1:199.

12. García-Ballester, McVaugh, and Rubio Vela, *Medical Licensing*, 30.

13. García Ballester, *Historia social*, 44.

14. Monica H. Green, "Documenting Medieval Women's Medical Practice," in *Practical Medicine from Salerno to the Black Death*, ed. Luis García-Ballester et al. (New York: Cambridge University Press, 1994), 328.

15. See Green, "Documenting," 328, where she deals with these issues in more detail, especially 335–41.

16. Green illustrates the veracity of this argument in "Women's Medical Practice and Health Care in Medieval Europe," *Signs* 14, no. 2 (1989): 434–73.

17. Teresa Ortiz, "From Hegemony to Subordination: Midwives in Early Modern Spain," in *The Art of Midwifery: Early Modern Midwives in Europe*, ed. Hilary Marland (New York: Routledge, 1993), 95–114, and Michael R. McVaugh, *Medicine before the Plague: Practitioners and Their Patients in the Crown of Aragon, 1285–1345* (New York: Cambridge University Press, 1993), 104.

18. Renate Blumenfeld-Kosinski, *Not of Woman Born: Representations of Caesarean Birth in Medieval and Renaissance Culture* (Ithaca: Cornell University Press, 1990), 91.

Jean Towler and Joan Bramall also attest to the expectation in medieval Britain that midwives performed Caesarean sections when barber-surgeons were unavailable. See *Midwives in History and Society* (London: Croom Helm, 1986), 29.

19. Myriam Greilsammer, "The Midwife, the Priest, and the Physician: The Subjugation of Midwives in the Low Countries at the End of the Middle Ages," *Journal of Medieval and Renaissance Studies* 21, no. 2 (fall 1991): 291.

20. Green, "Documenting," 331.

21. Ibid., 329.

22. Nancy G. Siraisi, *Medieval and Early Renaissance Medicine* (Chicago: University of Chicago Press, 1990), 26.

23. Green, "Documenting," 333 n. 49.

24. Ibid., 329–33.

25. McVaugh, *Medicine before the Plague*, 104 n. 137.

26. Luis García Ballester, "Academicism versus Empiricism in Practical Medicine in Sixteenth-Century Spain with Regard to Morisco Practitioners," in *The Medical Renaissance of the Sixteenth Century*, ed. A. Wear, R. K. French, and I. M. Lonie (New York: Cambridge University Press, 1985), 264–65.

27. Green, "Documenting," 329–30.

28. Rafael Muñoz Garrido, "Empíricos sanitarios españoles de los siglos XVI y XVII," *Cuadernos de historia de la medicina española* 6 (1967): 111–13.

29. See Cristina Segura Graiño, "Posibilidades jurídicas de las mujeres para acceder al trabajo," in *El trabajo de las mujeres en la edad media hispana*, ed. Ángela Muñoz Fernández and Cristina Segura Graiño (Madrid: Asociación Cultural Al-Mudayna, 1988), 24–25, and Green, "Documenting," 329–30.

30. Toby Gelfand, "The History of the Medical Profession," in *Companion Encyclopedia of the History of Medicine*, ed. W. F. Bynum and Roy Porter (London: Routledge, 1993), 2:1122.

31. Towler and Bramall, *Midwives in History*, 28–29.

32. Katharine Park, *Doctors and Medicine in Early Renaissance Florence* (Princeton: Princeton University Press, 1985), 71–72.

33. Siraisi, *Medieval and Early Renaissance Medicine*, 13.

34. al-Nadim, *The Fihrist of al-Nadim: A Tenth-Century Survey of Muslim Culture*, ed. and trans. Bayard Dodge (New York: Columbia University Press, 1970), 2:708. I have been unable to locate al-Razi's provocative document in any archival collection.

35. Siraisi, *Medieval and Early Renaissance Medicine*, 34.

36. See John F. Benton's article, "Trotula, Women's Problems, and the Professionalization of Medicine in the Middle Ages," *Bulletin of the History of Medicine* 59 (1985): 30–53, for a history and description of these important manuscripts and the problems of authorship. With regard to the appearance of these treatises in Iberia, there is a Catalan translation of one of the Trotula tracts, the Latin *De ornatu*, presently kept at the Biblioteca Nacional (Benton, "Trotula," 35 n. 12).

Monica H. Green identifies the extant Latin and vernacular manuscripts in her recent article, "A Handlist of the Latin and Vernacular Manuscripts of the So-Called *Trotula* Texts," *Scriptorium* 50 (1996): 137–75.

37. Benton, "Trotula," 35.

38. Ibid., 52.

39. Ibid., 44–45.

40. *Mirror of Coitus: A Translation and Edition of the Fifteenth-Century* Speculum al foderi, ed. and trans. Michael Ray Solomon (Madison: Hispanic Seminary of Me-

dieval Studies, 1990). The Catalan text is located on 8.10.76, and the English translation on 8.10.32.

41. This widespread belief stemmed from Galenic medicine, as Galen himself describes in *On the Affected Parts*, ed. and trans. Rudolph Siegel (New York: S. Karger, 1976), 184–85.

42. The anonymous *Liber menor de coitu*, written during the first part of the thirteenth century, is the *Speculum*'s most palpable model (*Speculum*, ed. Solomon, xvi). Other treatises that corroborate the hygienic effects of sexual practice include Bernard of Gordon's *Lilio de medicina*, on *ADMYTE*, CD-ROM, ed. Francisco Marcos Marín et al. (Madrid: Micronet, 1992), fol. 170r, and Francisco Núñez de Coria's *Tractado del uso de las mugeres*, written in sixteenth-century Castile. See *Tractado del uso de las mugeres*, transcr. Jean Dangler, Online, L.E.M.I.R., University of Valencia, Spain. Internet. Available: (http://parnaseo.uv.es/Lemir/Textos/Trat_mugeres/Trat_mugeres.html).

43. *Tratado de patología general (Tratado médico)*, on *Textos y concordancias electrónicos del corpus médico español*, CD-ROM, ed. María Teresa Herrera and María Estela González de Fauve (Madison: Hispanic Seminary of Medieval Studies, 1997), and Gordon, *Lilio de medicina*.

44. Ron Barkai, *A History of Jewish Gynecological Texts in the Middle Ages* (Leiden: E. J. Brill, 1998), 136, 149. Barkai believes that this early Hebrew treatise played a key role in the development of gynecology in medieval Iberia, since it was "a major source of later Arabic and Castilian texts" (95).

45. William F. MacLehose, "Nurturing Danger: High Medieval Medicine and the Problem(s) of the Child," in *Medieval Mothering*, ed. John Carmi Parsons and Bonnie Wheeler (New York: Garland, 1996), 4, 12.

46. Ibid., 13, 15.

47. Francisco López de Villalobos, *Sumario de medicina*, on *ADMYTE*, CD-ROM, ed. Francisco Marcos Marín et al., transcr. María Jesús García Toledano (Madrid: Micronet, 1992), fol. 9r, and *Tratado de patología general*, fols. 59r, 60r, and 112v–114r.

48. *Tratado de patología general*, fol. 113v.

49. María Teresa Herrera and Nieves Sánchez's edition of the *Tratado de patología general*, with medieval and modernized versions, has been helpful in translating this difficult passage. See *Tratado de patología general*, ed. María Teresa Herrera and Nieves Sánchez (Madrid: Arco / Libros, 1997), 728.

50. Damián Carbón, *Libro del arte de las comadres o madrinas y del regimiento de las preñadas y paridas y de los niños*, ed. Alejandra Piñeyrua, on *Textos y concordancias electrónicos del corpus médico español*, CD-ROM, ed. María Teresa Herrera and María Estela González de Fauve (Madison: Hispanic Seminary of Medieval Studies, 1997), fol. 7r.

51. Ibid., fol. 7v.

52. MacLehose, "Nurturing Danger," 15–16.

53. John Coulson, ed., *The Saints* (New York: Hawthorn Books, 1958), 184–85.

54. Edward Lewison, "Saint Agatha: The Patron Saint of Diseases of the Breast in Legend and Art," *Bulletin of the History of Medicine* 24 (1950): 419, and Emil F. Frey, "Saints in Medical History," *Clio Medica* 14 (1979): 45–46.

See Miguel Capdevila's *Iconografía de Santa Lucía* (Masnou [Barcelona]: Laboratorios del Norte de España, 1950) for visual examples of Lucy's representation in medieval iconography.

55. David Charles Schechter and Henry Swan, "Of Saints, Surgical Instruments, and Breast Amputation," *Surgery* 52 (1962): 697.

56. Lewison, "Saint Agatha," 419.

57. Antonio González Bueno, *El entorno sanitario del Camino de Santiago* (Madrid: Cátedra, 1994), 97.

58. Ángel Martín Duque et al., *Camino de Santiago en Navarra* (Pamplona: Caja Municipal de Ahorros de Pamplona, 1991), 91–92.

59. *Cantiga* 61 in *Cantigas*, ed. Jesús Montoya (Madrid: Cátedra, 1988), 141.

60. Marina Warner, *Alone of All Her Sex: The Myth and Cult of the Virgin Mary* (New York: Knopf, 1976), 68, 183.

61. Jaroslav Pelikan believes that biblical accounts of Mary provided medieval women "with some sense of what they might be—and of what, by the election of God, they could be." See *Mary through the Centuries: Her Place in the History of Culture* (New Haven: Yale University Press, 1996), 27.

62. Connie L. Scarborough, *Women in Thirteenth-Century Spain as Portrayed in Alfonso X's* Cantigas de Santa María (Lewiston, N.Y.: Edwin Mellen Press, 1993), vi, 23.

63. Ibid., 19.

64. Laura R. Bass, review of *Women in Thirteenth-Century Spain as Portrayed in Alfonso X's* Cantigas de Santa María, by Connie L. Scarborough, *La corónica* 26, no. 1 (1997): 321–24. Bass indicates that Scarborough's work lacks data to support its claim that "the *Cantigas de Santa María* 'neatly reflected' (vi) a patriarchal order" (322).

65. Pelikan, *Mary through the Centuries*, 83–84.

66. Clearly medieval sanctity did not solely function according to rigid gender binaries such as man / woman, nor is Marian literature such as the *Cantigas* without instances of the blending of categories that are otherwise thought to be separate, such as erotic and sacred companionship. Nevertheless, it is important to recognize the Virgin's vast influence as a paragon of the female gender.

Pelikan treats the twelfth- and thirteenth-century Virgin as intercessor in chapter 9, "The Mater Dolorosa and the Mediatrix."

67. Lynda L. Coon, *Sacred Fictions: Holy Women and Hagiography in Late Antiquity* (Philadelphia: University of Pennsylvania Press, 1997), 145.

68. Carbón, *Libro del arte*, fol. 3r.

69. Other educational institutions were created at this time in some parts of Europe. Colleges of physicians were erected during the fourteenth century in parts of northern Italy, specifically Pisa, Bologna, and Milan (Gelfand, "History of the Medical Profession," 2:1124, and Park, *Doctors and Medicine*, 64). They were different from medical faculties, and seem to have functioned almost in a guild capacity, as an organizational body for doctors. In Bologna, for instance, the members of the doctoral college "monopolized the senior teaching positions on the medical faculty" (Siraisi, *Medieval and Early Renaissance Medicine*, 27). They also played regulatory roles since they had the power to license physicians. By the seventeenth century, there were fourteen such colleges in existence (Gelfand, "History of the Medical Profession," 2:1124).

70. Another development of the professionalization of medicine is the formation of increasingly specialized guilds, organized less as "fraternity" groups than as labor associations to secure the interests of their members. See Siraisi, *Medieval and Early Renaissance Medicine*, 18, Park, *Doctors and Medicine*, chapter 1, and ref-

erences in chapter 3 of this book, under the section entitled "The Biology of Work in *La Celestina.*" This development is more difficult to document than the others, but I believe that the significance of these workers' groups in Castile is that they became homosocial nexuses for the meeting of Castilian men, and for the exclusion of women.

I do not include women's inclusion in confraternities (*cofradías*) because they seem to have operated less as trade groups than as religious associations. Despite the fact that these confraternities represent in part an escape for women from the confines of domestic expectations, they do not constitute a direct manifestation of the professionalization of medicine as far as I can tell. For an analysis of women's participation in fifteenth- and sixteenth-century confraternities, see Ángela Muñoz Fernández's excellent article, "Las mujeres en los ámbitos institucionales de la religiosidad laica: las cofradías devocionales castellanas (ss. XV-XVI)," in *Religiosidad femenina: expectativas y realidades (ss. VIII-XVIII)*, ed. Ángela Muñoz and María de Mar Graña (Madrid: Asociación Cultural Al-Mudayna, 1991), 93–114.

71. John Tate Lanning, *The Royal Protomedicato: The Regulation of the Medical Professions in the Spanish Empire* (Durham: Duke University Press, 1985), 14–15.

72. Ibid., 16.

Miguel Eugenio Muñoz cites the early Visigothic and Alfonsine regulations in Capítulo 13, Artículo 8 of his *Recopilación de las leyes, pragmáticas reales, decretos y acuerdos del Real Protomedicato* (Valencia, 1751). See *Fuero juzgo*, Libro 11, Ley 6; and *Siete Partidas*, Partida 7, Título 15, Ley 9; Part. 2, Tít. 9, Ley 10; Part. 7, Tít. 8, Ley 6.

73. García-Ballester, McVaugh, and Rubio Vela, *Medical Licensing*, 3.

The medieval relationship between Aragon and Montpellier was characterized by a great deal of mutual political and cultural contact. Montpellier was part of the Crown of Aragon from 1066 to 1081 and from 1204 until 1340. For this historicl account, see Antoni Cardoner i Planas, *Història de la medicina* (Barcelona: Scientia, 1973), 9–10.

For more information on the professionalization or regulation of medicine in areas of Europe outside Iberia, see Pearl Kibre, "The Faculty of Medicine at Paris, Charlatanism, and Unlicensed Medical Practices in the Later Middle Ages," *Bulletin of the History of Medicine* 27 (1953): 1–20, William L. Minkowski, "Physician Motives in Banning Medieval Traditional Healers," *Woman and Health* 21, no. 1 (1994): 83–96, and Siraisi, *Medieval and Early Renaissance Medicine*, chapters 1, 3.

74. Also, medicine became increasingly exclusionary during this period. For instance, gone was the ancient professional divide between Dogmatists, Empiricists, and Methodists (Gelfand, "History of the Medical Profession," 2:1120–21). Furthermore, physicians increasingly strove to extricate themselves not only from the primitive practices of "charlatans," but also from the practice of surgeons, barber-surgeons, and others who were perceived to augment the conditions of illness rather than minimize them. See Siraisi, *Medieval and Early Renaissance Medicine*, chapter 6, for a concise history of surgery.

75. In his article, "Medical Science in Thirteenth-Century Castile," Luis García Ballester posits four reasons for the scarcity of scholarship regarding thirteenth-century Castilian medicine: (1) the lack of interest on the part of scholars; (2) the relatively late fifteenth-century installation of a functioning medical faculty at the University of Salamanca (the university was founded in the thirteenth century); (3) seeming "indifference" on the part of the Castilian king Alfonso X (1252–84) with respect to the extensive corpus of medical works translated at Toledo; and

(4) the "intellectual inertia" and "poverty" of Castilian monastic communities and their isolation from the new thirteenth-century scholastic science. See Luis García Ballester, "Medical Science in Thirteenth-Century Castile," *Bulletin of the History of Medicine* 61 (1987): 183, 189, 190, 191.

76. Siraisi, *Medieval and Early Renaissance Medicine*, 13.

77. John M. Riddle, "Theory and Practice in Medieval Medicine," *Viator* 5 (1974): 159.

78. Ibid., 167 n. 42.

79. See Siraisi for a reproduction of one of these portable handbooks from medieval England (*Medieval and Early Renaissance Medicine*, 33, figure 3). A chart on bloodletting is reproduced on 139, figure 27.

80. See Siraisi, *Medieval and Early Renaissance Medicine*, chapter 1, and Joan Cadden, *Meanings of Sex Difference in the Middle Ages: Medicine, Science, and Culture* (New York: Cambridge University Press, 1993), 5.

81. See no. 73 above.

82. McVaugh, *Medicine before the Plague*, 83.

83. See appendix 2 in Park, *Doctors and Medicine*, 245–48, where she lists the medical curriculum at Bologna.

84. Mary Frances Wack, *Lovesickness in the Middle Ages: The* Viaticum *and Its Commentaries* (Philadelphia: University of Pennsylvania Press, 1990), xi-xvi, 3–30.

85. Siraisi, *Medieval and Early Renaissance Medicine*, 11–13.

86. Luis García-Ballester, "A Marginal Learned Medical World: Jewish, Muslim, and Christian Medical Practitioners, and the Use of Arabic Medical Sources in Late Medieval Spain," in *Practical Medicine from Salerno to the Black Death*, ed. Luis García-Ballester et al. (New York: Cambridge University Press, 1994), 356.

87. Ibid., 373.

88. García-Ballester, McVaugh, and Rubio Vela, *Medical Licensing*. The Catalan is located on 2–3 n. 6, and the English on 2.

89. Ibid., 6–7.

90. Ibid. The Catalan is located on 59, and the English on 60.

91. Ibid., 8.

92. García-Ballester, McVaugh, and Rubio Vela list the names of Valencian examiners from 1336 through 1400 in *Medical Licensing*, 56–58, appendix 1.

93. Ibid., 53–55.

94. Lanning, *Royal Protomedicato*, 15.

95. Ibid., 16–17.

96. Ibid., 19.

97. Ibid., 15.

98. Ibid., 18.

In 1563, there were three recognized medical faculties in Castilian regions, at the universities of Salamanca, Valladolid, and Alcalá de Henares (Lanning, *Royal Protomedicato*, 18).

99. Ibid., 61–62.

100. McVaugh, *Medicine before the Plague*, 228–30.

101. Stephen R. Ell, "Leprosy and Social Class in the Middle Ages," *International Journal of Leprosy and Other Mycobacterial Diseases* 54, no. 2 (1986): 302.

102. For a discussion of hospices along the Jacobean route to Santiago, see Jonathan Sumption, *Pilgrimage: An Image of Medieval Religion* (Totowa, N.J.: Rowman and Littlefield, 1975), 198–202.

103. In both works cited, Darrel W. Amundsen and Gary B. Ferngren extensively

outline the relationship between "sacred" healers and medical care. See "The Early Christian Tradition," in *Caring and Curing: Health and Medicine in the Western Tradition,* ed. Ronald L. Numbers and Darrel W. Amundsen (New York: Macmillan, 1986), 40–64, and "Medicine and Religion: Early Christianity through the Middle Ages," in *Health / Medicine and the Faith Traditions,* ed. Martin E. Marty and Kenneth L. Vaux (Philadelphia: Fortress Press, 1982), 93–131. See especially "Medicine and Religion," 116–17.

104. Siraisi, *Medieval and Early Renaissance Medicine,* 39.

105. For a study of these hospitals, see Robert I. Burns, "Los hospitales del reino de Valencia en el siglo XIII," *Anuario de estudios medievales* 2 (1965): 135–54.

106. Ell deals with the relationship between hospitals and *leprosaria* in "Leprosy and Social Class." Rubio Vela mentions the hospital that treated cases of St. Anthony's fire in *Pobreza, enfermedad y asistencia hospitalaria en la Valencia del siglo XIV* (Valencia: Institució Alfons el Magnànim, 1984). Park also mentions the building of specialized hospitals in Florence in 1428 (*Doctors and Medicine,* 103).

107. Solomon, *Literature of Misogyny,* 153.

108. Green, "Women's Medical Practice," 439 n. 9.

109. García-Ballester, McVaugh, and Rubio Vela, *Medical Licensing,* 6.

110. Ibid. The Catalan is located on 60, and the English on 61.

111. Ibid., 30.

112. Ibid., 30–32.

113. McVaugh, *Medicine before the Plague,* 3.

114. Ibid., 4.

115. Ibid., 242.

116. Kibre, "Faculty of Medicine," 8–12.

117. Ibid., 7.

118. Joseph Shatzmiller, *Jews, Medicine, and Medieval Society* (Berkeley: University of California Press, 1994), 20–21.

119. Angelina García, *Médicos judíos en la Valencia del siglo XIV. Estudios dedicados a Juan Peset Aleixandre* (Valencia: Universidad de Valencia, 1982), 2:95.

120. Cardoner i Planas, *Història de la medicina,* 110.

121. Perarnau i Espelt, "Activitats i fórmules," 55.

122. Greilsammer, "Midwife," 289 n. 11.

123. Ibid., 287.

124. Ortiz, "Hegemony," 95–114.

125. García-Ballester, McVaugh, and Rubio Vela, *Medical Licensing,* 19–22.

126. García-Ballester, McVaugh, and Rubio Vela claim that Valencian physicians in 1351 were more interested in the amount of their earnings than with the shortage in health practitioners (*Medical Licensing,* 22).

127. Claude Quétel, *History of Syphilis,* trans. Judith Braddock and Brian Pike (Baltimore: Johns Hopkins University Press, 1990), 16–18.

128. Muñoz Garrido, "Empíricos sanitarios," 111–13.

129. From Cornelius Agrippa, *The Certainty and Vanity of All Sciences and Arts* (1530), as quoted in Alison Klairmont Lingo, "Empirics and Charlatans in Early Modern France: The Genesis of the Classification of the 'Other' in Medical Practice," *Journal of Social History* 19 (1986): 590.

130. From Olivier de Serres, *Le théâtre d'agriculture et mesnage des champs* (Paris, 1600), fols. 885v–887r, as quoted in Klairmont Lingo, "Empirics and Charlatans," 593.

Chapter 2

1. For biographical information about Jaume Roig, see vol. 3 of the *Spill*, 3 vols., ed. Josep Alminaña Vallés (Valencia: Del Cenia al Segura, 1990).

2. The Virgin's literary omnipresence at this time is demonstrated by the poetry contests in honor of the gay science, the art of writing poetry, which were started during the reign of Joan I (1387–96), and continued in the fifteenth century. In them, male poets vied for the right to be called the best praiser of the Virgin. See Roger Boase, *The Troubadour Revival: A Study of Social Change and Traditionalism in Late Medieval Spain* (London and Boston: Routledge and Kegan Paul, 1978), 127–32. Also, see the first printed literary book in Iberia, a collection of poems to the Virgin that includes a poem by Roig, *Les trobes en lahors de la Verge Maria* (Valencia, 1474).

3. See Roig, *Spill*, 1:49, 62, 72.

4. Ibid., 1:49.

5. Ibid., 1:62.

6. Rosanna Cantavella, *Els cards i el llir: una lectura de l'* Espill *de Jaume Roig* (Barcelona: Quaderns Crema, 1992), 138–54.

7. As discussed in the introduction, Michael Solomon convincingly argues that the *Spill*, like the fifteenth-century *Arcipreste de Talavera*, is a manual that contains therapeutic information for the maintenance of the male reader's sexual health. See *The Literature of Misogyny in Medieval Spain* (New York: Cambridge University Press, 1997), 1–4.

8. Ibid., 132.

9. R. Howard Bloch, *Medieval Misogyny and the Invention of Western Romantic Love* (Chicago: University of Chicago Press, 1991), 91.

10. Roig is not alone in his contrastive technique. In order to edify Saint Agatha, the anonymous sixteenth-century Catalan play, *Consueta del misteri de la gloriosa Santa Àgata*, opposes her to the mediatrix Afrodisia, who possesses "lo saber de Celestina" [Celestina's knowledge], in *Teatre medieval i del renaixement*, ed. Josep Marsot i Muntaner (Barcelona: Edicions 62, 1994), 83.

11. In his article "More on the Image of the 'Rose among Thorns' in Medieval Spanish Literature," Donald McGrady examines some of the meanings of this trope, especially as it related to the similar epithet *rosa inter spinas*, in *La corónica* 17, no. 2 (1989): 35–39.

12. For instance, see "filles d'Eva" 2:6474–77 [daughters of Eve], and the multiple figures of Jesus and God 2:11313–63. All quotes from the *Spill* are from vol. 2. Verse numbers are given throughout this chapter. See Jaume Roig, *Spill*.

13. Roig refers to himself and his wife in 15995–99, subtly mentioning Pellicer in "Is, primer mort, / lo peix lliçer" (15998–99) [Is, (plus) the first to die (Abel), the fish *lliçer*]. The second phrase is untranslatable, and can only be understood with regard to Roig's wife's last name, Pellicer. See editor's note in the *Spill*, 2:798.

14. For a discussion of this continuum, see Eve Kosofsky Sedgwick, *Between Men: English Literature and Male Homosocial Desire* (New York: Columbia University Press, 1985), 1–2.

15. Roig follows the rhetorical technique of the *praeteritio*, in which a point is emphasized at the same time that it appears to be passed over. For information on this tactic, see Margaret Brose, "Petrarch's Beloved Body: 'Italia mia,'" in *Feminist Approaches to the Body in Medieval Literature*, ed. Linda Lomperis and Sarah Stanbury (Philadelphia: University of Pennsylvania Press, 1993), 15.

16. Juan Ruiz's *Libro de buen amor* will be abbreviated throughout this book as *Lba*.

17. John Dagenais, *The Ethics of Reading in Manuscript Culture: Glossing the* Libro de buen amor (Princeton: Princeton University Press, 1994), 5, 80–81.

18. Ibid., 4.

19. Citations from the *Lba* are verse numbers, in Arcipreste de Hita [Juan Ruiz], *Libro de buen amor*, ed. G. B. Gybbon Monypenny (Madrid: Cátedra, 1989).

20. Solomon, *Literature of Misogyny*, 116–20.

21. Ibid., 117.

22. Ibid., 111.

23. This is John Dagenais's argument throughout *Ethics of Reading*. For instance, see 61.

24. Ibid., 14–15.

25. Raymond Willis points this out in "Two Trotaconventos," *Romance Philology* 17 (1963): 356, 362. Also, see Margaret Parker's discussion of Trotaconventos and mediation in "The Text as Mediator: Ovid and Juan Ruiz," *Comparative Literature Studies* 28, no. 4 (1991): 351.

26. Parker, "Text as Mediator," 350.

27. Solomon, *Literature of Misogyny*, 69–74.

28. Ibid., 71.

29. See Solomon's discussion of this episode in *Literature of Misogyny*, 158.

30. Heath Dillard, *Daughters of the Reconquest: Women in Castilian Town Society, 1100–1300* (New York: Cambridge University Press, 1984), 24–26, 33–35, 68, 128.

31. Ibid., 73.

32. Ibid., 26.

Dillard claims that women's inheritance rights in towns such as Cuenca were very solid and included the rights of many female relatives, not just those of daughters. The *Fuero juzgo*, or Visigothic legal codes translated into Castilian in about 1240, referred "not only to a daughter but to women in all remote and collateral lines" (26).

33. See Dillard, *Daughters of the Reconquest*, 27–28, 32–33.

34. The *cantigas* about the *Virgen de la Leche* [*The Virgin of Milk*] include 54, 93, and 138.

35. Solomon, *Literature of Misogyny*, 161–65.

36. Myriam Greilsammer, "The Midwife, the Priest, and the Physician: The Subjugation of Midwives in the Low Countries at the End of the Middle Ages," *Journal of Medieval and Renaissance Studies* 21, no. 2 (fall 1991): 287–88.

37. See, for instance, *puntacorrent* (1994), a phrase for lace making used metaphorically in this instance to apply to a sexually aggressive woman. See editor's note on this word in the *Spill*, 2:609.

38. Teresa Ortiz, "From Hegemony to Subordination: Midwives in Early Modern Spain," in *The Art of Midwifery: Early Modern Midwives in Europe*, ed. Hilary Marland (New York: Routledge, 1993), 98.

39. Ibid., 98–99.

40. Nancy Siraisi, *Medieval and Early Renaissance Medicine* (Chicago: University of Chicago Press, 1990), chapter 6.

41. See Robyn Rowland's *Living Laboratories* and Janice G. Raymond's *Women as Wombs* for two modern accounts of technology, medicine, and reproduction. Raymond believes that technological reproduction constitutes a further step in the violation of women's bodies: "Technological reproduction is not only part of the

politics of reproduction, but of sexual politics too, for it is primarily about access to women and abuse of women's bodies—for medical research and experimentation, for financial gain, for clinical experience and adventure, for the manipulation of life" (xxv). Roig is horrified by the gender reversal of these kinds of protagonists. Robyn Rowland, *Living Laboratories: Women and Reproductive Technologies* (Bloomington: Indiana University Press, 1992), and Janice G. Raymond, *Women as Wombs: Reproductive Technologies and the Battle over Women's Freedom* (San Francisco: Harper San Francisco, 1993).

42. Mary Elizabeth Perry, "Magdalens and Jezebels in Counter-Reformation Spain," in *Culture and Control in Counter-Reformation Spain*, ed. Anne J. Cruz and Mary Elizabeth Perry (Minneapolis: University of Minnesota Press, 1992), 125.

43. For the development of municipal prostitution, see María Eugenia Lacarra, *Cómo leer* La Celestina (Madrid: Gijón, 1992), and Pablo Pérez García, *La comparsa de los malhechores* (València: Història Local, 1990).

44. Perry, "Magdalens and Jezebels," 125.

45. C. H. Lawrence treats the Beguine movement in *Medieval Monasticism: Forms of Religious Life in Western Europe in the Middle Ages*, 2nd edition (London: Longman, 1989).

46. Francesc Eiximenis, *Contes i faules* (Barcelona: Els Nostres Clàssics, 1925), 67–68.

47. See chapter 3, "The Rehearsal of Cultures," in Steven Mullaney, *The Place of the Stage: License, Play, and Power in Renaissance England* (Chicago: University of Chicago Press, 1988), where he suggests that one of the central motivations for certain colonial stagings or performances was to create "the other."

48. Sebastián de Covarrubias de Orozco, *Tesoro de la lengua castellana o española*, ed. Felipe C. R. Maldonado (Madrid: Castalia, 1994), 767.

49. Citations from Vicente Ferrer's sermons are located in Pedro M. Cátedra, *Sermón, sociedad y literatura en la edad media: san Vicente Ferrer en Castilla, (1411–1412)* (Salamanca: Junta de Castilla y León, 1994). The "Sermón de Ave María" is on 367–77.

50. Page DuBois, *Sowing the Body: Psychoanalysis and Ancient Representations of Women* (Chicago: University of Chicago Press, 1988), 165.

51. See Cátedra, *Sermón*, 375–76.

52. Dillard, *Daughters of the Reconquest*, 24–26 and passim.

53. She resembles a current-day surrogate mother who never asks for custody of the child, which is the ideal situation for people who hire surrogate mothers and for the medical industry that promotes the procedure. See Raymond, *Women as Wombs*, 31–34 and passim, and Rowland, *Living Laboratories*, 159–61 and passim, for discussions of the highly publicized Baby M case, in which the surrogate mother Mary Beth Whitehead claimed that she was entitled to custody of the child.

CHAPTER 3

1. Earlier works including Juan Ruiz's fourteenth-century *Libro de buen amor* also depicted important go-betweens such as Trotaconventos. But Rojas's work focused more on the earthly intercessor than did previous authors.

2. Some critics have examined Celestina's role as a healer, such as Modesto Laza Palacios's inventory of her laboratory, and Félix Marti-Ibáñez's assessment of her healing "arts." However, they also mistakenly take for granted her derogatory char-

acterization as a sorcerer, witch, or charlatan, and do not interpret those descriptions as methods of denigration. These critics have overlooked the social motivations of such a portrayal. See Modesto Laza Palacios, *El laboratorio de Celestina* (Málaga: Instituto de Cultura de la Diputación Provincial de Málaga, 1958), 87–191, and Félix Marti-Ibáñez, "The Medico-Pharmaceutical Arts of *La Celestina*: A Study of a Fifteenth-Century Spanish Sorceress and 'Dealer in Love,'" in *Centaur: Essays on the History of Medical Ideas* (New York: MD Publications, 1958), 149–56.

3. Spanish citations from *La Celestina* are located in Fernando de Rojas, *La Celestina*, ed. Dorothy Severin (Madrid: Cátedra, 1987). All English citations are from Fernando de Rojas, *Celestina: A Play in Twenty-One Acts, Attributed to Fernando de Rojas*, trans. Mack Hendricks Singleton (Madison: University of Wisconsin Press, 1958). Both versions will be referred to with act and page numbers.

4. Roberto González Echevarría has recently argued that Celestina fails to reproduce human beings, and only generates pleasure, pain, and death (9–10). Whereas González Echevarría regards this as a kind of "impasse" in Celestina's characterization, the significance effectively lies in the fact that what she does produce is an infinite circuit of women like Eve and herself. She imparts knowledge through her teaching, and deception through her healing activities. See Roberto González Echevarría, *Celestina's Brood: Continuities of the Baroque in Spanish and Latin American Literature* (Durham: Duke University Press, 1993).

5. Manuel da Costa Fontes, "Celestina as Antithesis of the Virgin Mary," *Journal of Hispanic Philology* 25, no. 1 (1990): 10.

Costa Fontes's provocative article, "Celestina as Antithesis," deals with this issue at length. He cites Ciriaco Morón Arroyo as one critic who has suggested the uncomfortable equation of Celestina and the Virgin Mary. Costa Fontes breaks with that assessment when asserting (as evident in the article's title) that Celestina constitutes the Virgin's antithesis.

6. Costa Fontes's thesis hinges on the biographical veracity of Rojas as the single author of the *tragicomedia*, and of his identity as a convert, both of which are debatable. Nonetheless, his argument is provocative.

7. Ibid., 30.

8. Linda Hutcheon, *A Theory of Parody: The Teachings of Twentieth-Century Art Forms* (New York: Methuen, 1985), 27.

9. Ibid., 33.

10. Ibid., 43.

11. For two critics who try to paint Celestina in a more or less advantageous light, see Mary S. Gossy, *The Untold Story: Women and Theory in Golden Age Texts* (Ann Arbor: University of Michigan Press, 1989), and Diane Hartunian, La Celestina: *A Feminist Reading of the Carpe Diem* (Maryland: Scripta Humanistica, 1992). These characterizations, however, are unconvincing. For instance, Hartunian concludes that women characters in *La Celestina* break with the patriarchal order, and that Rojas supports their efforts. This is a dubious claim especially in light of societal efforts to prohibit women healers from practicing professional medicine, and to eliminate the woman go-between from official municipal prostitution.

12. Of course, other sex-specific actions and phenomena include the expulsion of the Jews in 1492, and the mid-sixteenth-century trials in Valladolid regarding the legal status of indigenous Americans and Spanish rights to their exploitation.

Also, repressive antisuperstitious Castilian treatises of the sixteenth and seventeenth centuries include the following: Pedro Ciruelo's *Reprobación de las supersticiones y hechizerías* (1529), which became famous for its vast number of editions and their rapid publication (Luis S. Granjel, *Humanismo y medicina* [Salamanca: Universidad de Salamanca, 1968], 126); Antonio de Torquemada's *Jardín de flores curiosas* (1570); and Gaspar Navarro's *Tribunal de Superstición ladina* (1631). Latin treatises of the period included the following: Fray Martín de Arlés y Andosilla's *Tractatus de superstitionibus* (1517; reedited in Frankfurt in 1581); Padre Francisco de Vitoria's *Relectio De Arte Magica* (1557); Benito Perrer's *Adversus fallaces et superstitiosas artes* (1603); and Martín Antonio Delrío's *Disquisitionum Magicarum Libri Sex* (1624).

13. In his article, "Laboratorio de Celestina," Laza Palacios inventories many of the herbs, cosmetics, and other elements that Celestina uses throughout the text. At the entry *HIGUERUELA* (bituminous clover), for instance, Laza Palacios invokes the medical theorist Dioscorides to explain that the substance brought on menstruation, and that Celestina kept it as an emmenagogue (143). In the entry for *RAICES DE FUSTE SANGUINO* (roots of red dogwood tree or bush), Celestina is said to have used them as an hemostatic to avoid hemorrhaging (170). And finally, Laza Palacios indicates that *VIOLETAS* (violets) were used for many reasons, including as relaxants and pain relievers (189).

14. See Michael J. Ruggerio, "The Evolution of the Go-Between in Spanish Literature through the Sixteenth Century," *California University Publications in Modern Philology* (Berkeley: University of California Press, 1966), and Julio Caro Baroja's *Vida mágica e inquisición* (Madrid: Taurus, 1966), and *Las brujas y su mundo* (Madrid: Revista de Occidente, 1961). A further series of critical works about *La Celestina* and witchcraft can be found indexed in Joseph T. Snow's bibliographical compilation, *Celestina by Fernando de Rojas: An Annotated Bibliography of World Interest, 1930–1985* (Madison: Hispanic Seminary of Medieval Studies, 1985). Also, see the introduction to María Eugenia Lacarra's recent edition of *La Celestina*, for a current but unchanged opinion about the theme of witchcraft and sorcery in the work, in Fernando de Rojas, *La Celestina*, ed. María Eugenia Lacarra (Madison: Hispanic Seminary of Medieval Studies, 1995), lxii n. 61.

Olga Lucía Valbuena is a partial exception to the critical rule. In "Sorceresses, Love Magic, and the Inquisition of Linguistic Sorcery in *Celestina*," *PMLA* 109, no. 2 (1994): 211, she argues that Celestina's "magic" is constituted by rhetorical manipulation, and not by an authentic diabolism.

15. Caro Baroja, *Brujas*, 151.

16. Ibid., 151–53.

17. Anne Llewellyn Barstow, *Witchcraze: A New History of the European Witch Hunts* (San Francisco: HarperCollins, 1994), 1, and Brian P. Levack, *The Witch-Hunt in Early Modern Europe* (London: Longman, 1995), 2–3.

18. See Barstow, *Witchcraze*, 20–23, and appendix B, 179–81. Levack, *Witch-Hunt*, treats this topic on 21–26.

19. Barstow, *Witchcraze*, 179–81.

20. Ibid., 112.

Chapter 6 of Barstow, *Witchcraze*, is devoted to the bewitching of women healers.

21. Ibid., 114.

22. Dorothy S. Severin, *Witchcraft in* Celestina (London: Queen Mary and Westfield College, 1995), 12.

Also, see a review of this monograph by Manuel da Costa Fontes, "Female Empowerment and Witchcraft in *Celestina*," rev. of *Witchcraft in* Celestina, by Dorothy S. Severin, *Celestinesca* 19, no. 1–2: 93–104.

23. Barstow, *Witchcraze*, 118–19.

24. In her examination of events that paralleled the reading of *La Celestina* and inquisitorial activity on the peninsula, Irene Silverblatt shows how indigenous Peruvian women (often healers) were also pursued by the Spanish authorities, albeit for similar but different reasons. Spain sought to supplant indigenous religious beliefs with Catholic ones, and it tried to enforce civil order. She further discusses women's resistance to Spanish authority in chapter 10. See Irene Silverblatt, *Moon, Sun, and Witches: Gender Ideologies and Class in Inca and Colonial Peru* (Princeton: Princeton University Press, 1987).

25. For a discussion of the force of traditional antifeminist discourse, see chapter 3 of Michael Solomon, *The Literature of Misogyny in Medieval Spain* (New York: Cambridge University Press, 1997).

26. Maria Kotzmanidou, "The Spanish and Arabic Characterization of the Go-Between in the Light of Popular Performance," *Hispanic Review* 48 (1980): 96.

For a recent study of the medieval go-between in romance and near-eastern literature, see Leyla Rouhi's *Mediation and Love: A Study of the Medieval Go-Between in Key Romance and Near-Eastern Texts* (Leiden: Brill, 1999).

27. Samuel G. Armistead and James T. Monroe, "Celestina's Muslim Sisters," *Celestinesca* 13, no. 2 (1989): 3–27.

28. James F. Burke, "The *Mal de la Madre* and the Failure of Maternal Influence in *Celestina*," *Celestinesca* 17, no. 2 (1993): 111–12.

Burke also shows that *mal de la madre* was alluded to as a disease until as recently as the beginning of the twentieth century, 112.

29. Ibid., 112.

30. See James Burke's useful and keen interpretation of Rojas's use of the *mal de la madre*: "My thesis is that Areúsa's 'wandering womb' serves as a symbol which demonstrates the failure of affirmative maternal functions in *Celestina*. The unhappy endings for all the characters in the work result then from a metaphorical 'mal de la madre,' centered in Celestina, which is the opposite of all that which metaphorical positive motherhood can imply" ("*Mal de la Madre*," 114).

31. In chapter 2, some of the transgressions related to Eve and hence to all mundane women were the exercising of women's agency, their desires of all types, and their speech. All of these transgressions are equally applicable to *La Celestina*, and in fact are misogynist tropes to denigrate women.

32. See A. J. Minnis and A. B. Scott, eds. *Medieval Literary Theory and Criticism c. 1100–c. 1375* (New York: Clarendon, 1988), 165.

33. In my view, the final part of this translation inadequately captures the Spanish *vejez virtuosa* and *virtud envejecida*, which mean, respectively, "virtuous old age" and "aged virtue." In Spanish they are nominalizations that directly refer to Celestina, and are not adjectival forms as indicated in the translation.

34. Mary Frances Wack, *Lovesickness in the Middle Ages: The Viaticum and Its Commentaries* (Philadelphia: University of Pennsylvania Press, 1990), 4–30.

35. Michael Solomon, "Calisto's Ailment: Bitextual Diagnostics and Parody in *Celestina*," *Revista de estudios hispánicos* 23 (1989): 44.

Popular medical treatises that discuss *amor eros* include Bernard of Gordon's *Lilio de medicina*, Francisco López de Villalobos's *Sumario de medicina*, Constantine the African's *Viaticum*, and Peter of Spain's *Questiones super Viaticum*. Wack deals with the topic at length in *Lovesickness in the Middle Ages*.

36. Solomon, "Calisto's Ailment," 53.

37. Ibid., 53, 55.

38. Nancy Siraisi, *Medieval and Early Renaissance Medicine* (Chicago: University of Chicago Press, 1990), 171.

Illustrations in surgeons' manuals and treatises usually represented the patient with if not a smile, at least a placid look on his / her face. For two examples, see Siraisi, *Medieval and Early Renaissance Medicine*, 165.

39. Solomon, "Calisto's Ailment," 43.
40. In Wack, *Lovesickness in the Middle Ages*, 86, 227.
41. Solomon, "Calisto's Ailment," 46–47.
42. Bernard of Gordon, *Lilio de medicina*, *ADMYTE*, CD-ROM, ed. Francisco Marco Marín et al., transcr. John Cull and Cynthia Wasick (Madrid: Micronet, 1992), fol. 58r.
43. Galen, *On the Affected Parts*, ed. and trans. Rudolph E. Siegel (New York: S. Karger, 1976), 184–85.
44. Ibid., 185, and Gordon, *Lilio*, fol. 170r.
45. Eva Carrasco and Ismael Almazán, "Prostitución y criminalidad en Cataluña en la época moderna," in *La prostitution en Espagne: de l'époque des Rois Catholiques à la IIe République*, ed. Raphaël Carrasco (Paris: Centre de recherches sur l'Espagne moderne, 1994), 25.
46. Ibid., 32–33.
47. María Eugenia Lacarra, *Cómo leer* La Celestina (Madrid: Gijón, 1992), 24.
48. Ibid., 26.

Lacarra suggests that municipal control of prostitution would have helped to remedy a concern about male prostitution.

49. Pablo Pérez García, *La comparsa de los malhechores* (València: Història Local, 1990), 136.
50. Ibid., 136.
51. Despite the enormously valuable historical scholarship by Valencian historians such as Pablo Pérez García, this is an area that deserves further attention by historians working in other areas of the medieval peninsula. While several historians have analyzed information about prostitutes and concubines largely from ordinances in Aragon and Castile, the Municipal Archive at Burgos possesses ordinances dating from 1388 that are yet to be considered for this kind of study. Many of the essays in the Autonomous University's conference proceedings (for instance, *Las mujeres en las ciudades medievales*) present information about concubines and prostitutes. In *Daughters of the Reconquest: Women in Castilian Town Society, 1100–1300* (Cambridge: Cambridge University Press, 1984), Heath Dillard discusses concubines (see chapter 5) and prostitutes (see chapter 8), and their status in Castilian legislation.
52. Municipally controlled prostitution can have positive results for prostitutes, such as a regulated and consistent salary, potentially better health care, and less violent treatment by johns and pimps. On the other hand, municipal regulation constitutes in part the local, governmental control of sexual practice and workers' (women's) bodies.
53. See Wack, *Lovesickness in the Middle Ages*, 173, and chapter 8, "Recreating a Context for the Lover's Malady."
54. Ibid., 147–48.
55. This linkage was commonly applied to Jews, attacks against whom were based on biological, medical, and hereditary grounds. See Gracia Guillén's fascinating article, "Judaism, Medicine, and the Inquisitorial Mind in Sixteenth-Century

Spain," in *The Spanish Inquisition and the Inquisitorial Mind*, ed. Ángel Alcalá (Boulder, Colo.: Social Science Monographs, 1987), 375–400.

56. While I do believe that this familiar gender binary was thought of as "normative" by theologians and medical theorists alike, medieval gender is often more fluid and expansive than what some modern critics allow. The ways in which medieval gender was conceived and articulated have only recently been explored. At an early point in her provocative essay, "Gendered Sexuality," Joyce E. Salisbury focuses on the woman / man norm proclaimed by Augustine in the *City of God*, in a chapter called "The origin of recorded monstrosities" (Joyce E. Salisbury, "Gendered Sexuality," *Handbook of Medieval Sexuality*, ed. Vern L. Bullough and James A. Brundage [New York: Garland, 1996], 81–102, and Augustine, *City of God*, trans. Henry Bettenson [1972; reprint, with an introduction by John O'Meara, New York: Penguin, 1984], 16.8.661–62). Salisbury argues that it constitutes the overarching *medieval* belief about a binary gender system (82). Her arguments about Augustine and what is commonly regarded as the Iberian medieval period (tenth through fifteenth centuries), however, do not fully convince me. First, the extent of Augustine's influence on the Iberian peninsula remains undetermined. Second, the existence of a "third" gender, that of hermaphrodites, was recognized throughout the Middle Ages and even by Juan Huarte de San Juan in the late sixteenth century. While Salisbury rightly points out references to hermaphrodites and to other "others," I suspect that medieval gender was more fluid and inclusive than Salisbury allows. One biological support for medieval gender fluidity is the medieval belief that women and men alike possessed the same sexual organs. In women they were inverted and in men they were turned outward, as illustrated in Danielle Jacquart and Claude Thomasset, *Sexuality and Medicine in the Middle Ages* (Princeton: Princeton University Press, 1988), ill. 1.5–6, 28–29.

Furthermore, what Augustine emphasizes in the section about "monstrosities" is the need to include every creature within God's sphere. If woman, man, hermaphrodite, and human forms born with dogs' heads were rational beings created by God, they should all be regarded as part of God's design: "He [God] has the wisdom to weave the beauty of the whole design out of the constituent parts, in their likeness and diversity. The observer who cannot view the whole is offended by what seems the deformity of a part since he does not know how it fits in, or how it is related to the rest ... he whose operations no one has the right to criticize knows what he [any deformed one] is about" (*City of God*, 16.8.662). The emphasis on inclusion was more important for some medieval writers than that of imposing gender norms.

57. Aristotle, *Economics*, in *Complete Works*, vol. 2, ed. J. Barnes, trans. E. S. Forster and G. C. Armstrong (Princeton: Princeton University Press, 1984), 2.3.1343b25–1344a8.

58. Quoted in Joan Cadden, *Meanings of Sex Difference in the Middle Ages: Medicine, Science, and Culture* (Cambridge: Cambridge University Press, 1993), 183.

59. Ibid., 186–88.

60. Many of these treatises are collected and edited in *Scriptores physiognomonici graeci et latini*, ed. Richard Foerster, 2 vols. (Stuttgart: B. G. Teubner, 1994). See Roger A. Pack's article, "Auctoris Incerti de Physiognomonia Libellus," *Archives d'histoire doctrinale et litteraire du moyen age* 41 (1974): 113–38, for an introduction to treatises on physiognomy and an edition of an anonymous treatise. An example of a vernacular treatise on this topic is the Castilian *Tratado de Phisonomía*, which was written in 1494. See *Tratado de Phisonomía*, on *Textos y concordancias electrónicos*

del corpus médico español, CD-ROM, ed. María Teresa Herrera and María Estela González de Fauve (Madison: Hispanic Seminary of Medieval Studies, 1997).

61. *Scriptores physiognomonici graeci et latini*, 2:164.
62. Cadden, *Meanings of Sex Difference*, 188.
63. *Tratado de patología general (Tratado médico)*, on *Textos y concordancias electrónicos del corpus médico español*, CD-ROM, ed. María Teresa Herrera and María Estela González de Fauve (Madison: Hispanic Seminary of Medieval Studies, 1997), fols. 173r and 101v, respectively.
64. The sixteenth- and seventeenth-century influence and popularity of this text in Western Europe was phenomenal. It was translated and printed in French, Italian, English, Latin, Dutch, and German. See the editor's comments in Juan Huarte de San Juan, *Examen de ingenios para las ciencias*, ed. Guillermo Serés (Madrid: Cátedra, 1989), 108–25.
65. Ibid., 266. The English translation, which I have modernized, is located in *The Examination of Men's Wits*, trans. M. Camillo Camilli and Richard Carew (1594; reprint, Amsterdam: Da Capo Press, 1969), 21.
66. Ibid., 466–92.
67. Ibid., 523.
68. This is not to say that all medical doctors during this period believed that work was *biologized*. In the reader's prologue to the *Filosofía antigua poética*, for instance, the medical doctor Alonso López Pinciano believed that individual tasks and occupational positions must change according to circumstance and need: "y como acontece que en la nave, forzado de la necesidad, el calafate reme, el remero calafateé y el piloto, patrón y capitán ayuden a poner la vela, sucede también en la república que el ministro de un oficio, suadido de la necesidad, no sin justicia se entre tal hora en el de otro" [and in the same way that it occurs on a ship, when, forced by necessity, the shipwright rows, the rower secures the deck, and the helmsman, skipper, and captain help to hoist the sails, it also comes to pass in the republic that the practitioner of a trade, persuaded by necessity and not without good reason, takes on the trade of another]. See Alonso López Pinciano, *Filosofía antigua poética* (Valladolid, 1894), 3.
69. For further discussion of this change, see José Antonio Maravall, *Estado moderno y mentalidad social (siglos XV a XVII)* (Madrid: Revista de Occidente, 1972), especially 1.79. See also Gracia Guillén, "Judaism, Medicine," 376–79.
70. Renate Blumenfeld-Kosinski, chapter 3, "The Marginalization of Women in Obstetrics," in *Not of Woman Born: Representations of Caesarean Birth in Medieval and Renaissance Culture* (Ithaca: Cornell University Press, 1990), 91–119, and Myriam Greilsammer, "The Midwife, the Priest, and the Physician: The Subjugation of Midwives in the Low Countries at the End of the Middle Ages," *Journal of Medieval and Renaissance Studies* 21, no. 2 (fall 1991): 286–329. Monica H. Green, "Documenting Medieval Women's Medical Practice," in *Practical Medicine from Salerno to the Black Death*, ed. Luis García-Ballester et al. (New York: Cambridge University Press, 1994), argues that attacks by physicians and literate surgeons against women who practiced "informal medicine," such as midwives, suggest that such practice was widespread among women (336).
71. See no. 56 above for an early Christian example of alterity as "natural," as articulated by Augustine.
72. Women's description as daughters of Eve, the sexual (and in other ways) sinner, is much more obviously presented in the *Spill* than in *La Celestina*, where that connection is a commonplace.

73. Green, "Documenting," 332.

Also, in her study of women in the crafts in sixteenth-century Lyon, Natalie Zemon Davis suggests that women identified themselves with no one trade. See "Women in the Crafts in Sixteenth-Century Lyon," in *Women and Work in Preindustrial Europe*, ed. Barbara A. Hanawalt (Bloomington: Indiana University Press, 1986), 167–97.

74. Celestina is not the only character depicted in the work as a healer. For a discussion of Sempronio as physician, see Solomon, "Calisto's Ailment."

75. For instance, see Zemon Davis, "Women in the Crafts," for a study of women workers in early modern Lyon.

76. Cristina Segura Graiño, "Posibilidades jurídicas para las mujeres para acceder al trabajo," in *El trabajo de las mujeres en la edad media hispana*, ed. Ángela Muñoz Fernández and Cristina Segura Graiño (Madrid: Asociación Cultural Al-Mudayna, 1988), 15–26.

77. María del Carmen Pallares Méndez, *A vida das mulleres na Galicia Medieval, (1100–1500)* (Santiago de Compostela: Universidade, Servicio de Publicacións e Intercambio Científico, 1993), 122.

78. Cristina Segura Graiño, "Las mujeres andaluzas en la baja edad media," in *Las mujeres en las ciudades medievales*, ed. Cristina Segura Graiño (Madrid: Universidad Autónoma de Madrid, 1983), 150.

79. María Dolores Cabañas, "La imagen de la mujer en la baja edad media castellana a través de las ordenanzas municipales de Cuenca," in *Las mujeres en las ciudades medievales*, ed. Cristina Segura Graiño (Madrid: Universidad Autónoma de Madrid, 1983), 104.

In her book, *Los espacios femeninos en el Madrid medieval* (Madrid: horas y Horas la editorial [sic], 1992), Cristina Segura Graiño treats women's work in medieval Madrid.

80. Green, "Documenting," 337 n. 60.

81. Toby Gelfand, "The History of the Medical Profession," *Companion Encyclopedia of the History of Medicine*, ed. W. F. Bynum and Roy Porter (London: Routledge, 1993), 2:1122.

82. Jean Towler and Joan Bramall, *Midwives in History and Society* (London: Croom Helm, 1986), 28–29.

83. Katharine Park, *Doctors and Medicine in Early Renaissance Florence* (Princeton: Princeton University Press, 1985), 71–72.

84. See chapter 1 where I discuss the same chronologically contained appearance of Iberian Castilian and Catalan women physicians during the plague years.

85. Siraisi, *Medieval and Early Renaissance Medicine*, 177.

86. See Peter Brown, *The Body and Society: Men, Women, and Sexual Renunciation in Early Christianity* (New York: Columbia University Press, 1988), for a discussion of virginity's role in antiquity. Also, Jane Tibbetts Schulenburg discusses the heroics of virginity in the early Middle Ages. She shows that self-mutilation was a defense against sexual assault, and a desperate effort to preserve one of the few empowering characteristics that many women were allowed, their own chastity. See "The Heroics of Virginity: Brides of Christ and Sacrificial Mutilation," in *Women in the Middle Ages and the Renaissance: Literary and Historical Perspectives*, ed. Mary Beth Rose (Syracuse: Syracuse University Press, 1986), 29–72. For a more recent discussion of this topic, see Tibbetts Schulenburg's *Forgetful of Their Sex: Female Sanctity and Society, ca. 500–1100* (Chicago: University of Chicago Press, 1998).

87. Dillard, *Daughters of the Reconquest*, 51.

The value and quantity of goods given to the bride depended on the town's requirements. Some towns had fixed endowments designed to make betrothal and marriage accessible to all eligible young men.

88. Helen Rodnite Lemay, "William of Saliceto on Human Sexuality," *Viator* 12 (1981): 175–76.

89. Ibid., 176. Lemay attributes William's newly "sympathetic" stance toward women to the physician's main desire to alleviate illness.

90. Costa Fontes, "Celestina as Antithesis," 28.

91. Sexual behavior and disease had always been linked through leprosy in the medieval period. See Stephen R. Ell, "Blood and Sexuality in Medieval Leprosy," *Janus* 71 (1984): 154–64. In *History of Syphilis*, trans. Judith Braddock and Brian Pike (Baltimore: Johns Hopkins University Press, 1990), 21, Claude Quétel cites one writer from 1502 who believed that syphilis was transmitted by coitus, kissing, breastfeeding, and more rarely, by corrupt air.

92. Siraisi, *Medieval and Early Renaissance Medicine*, chapter 6.

93. Antonio de Nebrija, *Dictionarium latino-hispanicum*, on *ADMYTE*, CD-ROM, ed. Francisco Marcos Marín et al., transcr. Antonio Cortijo (Madrid: Micronet, 1992), fols. 19r, 19v, 62v.

Celestina is also called a teacher or master (*maestra*) of virgin-making. According to Covarrubias's dictionary of 1611, about one hundred years after *La Celestina*'s first appearance, a *maestra* is someone who teaches girls (*niñas*) to *labrar*. See Sebastián de Covarrubias de Orozco, *Tesoro de la lengua castellana o española*, ed. Felipe C. R. Maldonado (Madrid: Castalia, 1994), 727. Covarrubias further defines a seamstress (*labrandera*) as a woman who works with fabric, and whose tasks are carried out with a needle (696). Although somewhat anachronistic, Covarrubias's link between women teachers, textile labor, and women pupils reinforces the possible linking and threat caused by women teaching women.

94. Alfonso de Palencia, *Universal vocabulario en latín y romance*, on *ADMYTE*, CD-ROM, ed. Francisco Marcos Marín et al., transcr. Gracia Lozano López et al. (Madrid: Micronet, 1990), fol. 281r.

95. As quoted in Modesto Laza Palacios, *Laboratorio de Celestina*, 180.

96. According to the *Diccionario español de textos médicos antiguos*, ed. María Teresa Herrera (Madrid: Arco / Libros, 1996), 1:73, *alferecía* is a children's disease that causes convulsions and loss of consciousness. Laguna's *Alfirer* seems to derive from *alferecía*, since it has no meaning in the context as a variant of *alfiler* (pin).

97. The phrase *tienda a vender* also seems to bear a scatological meaning related to prostitution.

98. Rosario Ferré, "Celestina en el tejido de la 'cupiditas,'" *Celestinesca* 7, no. 1 (1983): 7.

99. See the articles related to this topic by Alan Deyermond, "*Hilado, Cordón, Cadena*: Symbolic Equivalence in *La Celestina*," *Celestinesca* 1, no. 1 (1977): 6–12, Ferré, "Celestina en el tejido," Otis Handy, "The Rhetorical and Psychological Defloration of Melibea," *Celestinesca* 7, no. 1 (1983): 17–27, and Manuel da Costa Fontes, "Celestina's *Hilado* and Related Symbols," *Celestinesca* 8, no. 1 (1984): 3–13.

100. Costa Fontes, "Celestina's *Hilado*," 9.

101. Ibid., 9.

102. Lemay calls it specifically "suffocation of the womb" in "William of Saliceto," 177.

103. Lemay discusses this in "William of Saliceto," 177–78.

104. Galen, *Affected Parts*, 185.

105. Lemay, "William of Saliceto," 178.
106. According to Guido Cauliaco in the *Tratado de cirugía*, on *Textos y concordancias electrónicos del corpus médico español*, CD-ROM, ed. María Teresa Herrera and María Estela González de Fauve (Madison: Hispanic Seminary of Medieval Studies, 1997), fol. 187v, *muscelino* balm was a hot ointment made from some kind of rubber, such as the oil from the horseradish tree (*azeyte de been [ben]*). For further information, see the entry for *muscelino* in the *Diccionario español de textos médicos*, 2:1087.
107. The Old Spanish *prefocación* derives from the Latin *praefoco,-praefocare*, meaning to choke or suffocate. Hence its relation to the *mal de la madre*, or suffocation of the womb.
108. Ron Barkai, *A History of Jewish Gynecological Texts in the Middle Ages* (Leiden: E. J. Brill, 1998), 139.
109. Celestina and Pármeno also talk about Claudina in 1.120.
110. Singleton's translation of the last word of this passage clearly fails to reflect the Spanish *varonil* (manly or masculine).
111. The chaotic threat that women posed also undergirds the popular sixteenth- and seventeenth-century conduct manuals (*manuales de conducta*) that circulated throughout Europe. While they were written for the edification of both women and men, men's conduct manuals reveal a gamut of possible, acceptable behaviors, whereas women's acceptable position in society was articulated as that of wife. See Emilia Navarro, "Manual Control: 'Regulatory Fictions' and their Discontents," *Cervantes* 13, no. 2 (1993): especially 17–22, and Ruth Kelso's groundbreaking study of the genre, *Doctrine for the Lady of the Renaissance* (Urbana: University of Illinois Press, 1956).

According to Navarro, probably the two most influential conduct manuals for women in Spain were Fray Luis de León's *La perfecta casada* (Salamanca 1583) and Juan Luis Vives's *Instrucción de la mujer cristiana* (trans. 1528), (20 n. 6).

112. The dialogue between "profeminist" and "antifeminist" men writers includes works such as Diego de Varela's *Defensa de las virtuosas mujeres* (fifteenth century), Juan Rodríguez del Padrón's *Triunfo de las donas* (mid-fifteenth century), and Álvaro de Luna's *Libro de las claras y virtuosas mugeres* (1446). They might also be considered conduct manuals, as Ruth Kelso does with Rodríguez del Padrón's and Luna's texts.

CHAPTER 4

1. For a recent discussion of this conflicting biographical information, see Louis Imperiale, *La Roma clandestina de Francisco Delicado y Pietro Aretino* (New York: Peter Lang, 1997), especially 5.
2. I have not included Delicado's original essay, "Introducción que muestra el Delicado a pronunciar la lengua española," as one of his own writings since it was published in his second edition of the *Tragicomedia de Calisto y Melibea* as cited below.
3. Bruno M. Damiani, *Francisco Delicado* (New York: Twayne, 1974), 143.
4. For a recent discussion of Delicado's publications, see Tatiana Bubnova, *F. Delicado puesto en diálogo: las claves bajtinianas de* La Lozana andaluza (Mexico: Universidad Nacional Autónoma de México, 1987), especially 59–61. Bruno Damiani is also informative in *Francisco Delicado*, particularly 143–44. Louis Imperiale's treatment can be found in *Roma clandestina*, chapter 1.

5. Bubnova, *F. Delicado*, 61.
6. Damiani, *Francisco Delicado*, 107–08.
7. Bruno M. Damiani, "Text: Francisco Delicado. 'El modo de adoperare el legno de India occidentale.' A Critical Transcription," *Revista Hispánica Moderna* 36 (1970–71): 255.
8. Damiani, *Francisco Delicado*, 14, and María Luisa García-Verdugo, La Lozana andaluza *y la literatura del siglo XVI: La sífilis como enfermedad y metáfora* (Madrid: Pliegos, 1994), 82.
9. *Mamotretos* 1, 5, and parts of 4 are exceptions since they are composed in a narrative style, as is the beginning prologue and five of the six final pieces following the main body of the text.
10. Claude Allaigre, introduction to *La Lozana andaluza*, by Francisco Delicado (Madrid: Cátedra, 1985), 26–45.
11. For a discussion of the uncertain "origins" of syphilis, see Claude Quétel, *History of Syphilis*, trans. Judith Braddock and Brian Pike (Baltimore: Johns Hopkins University Press, 1990), 37–38.
12. Ibid., 9–49.
13. Ibid., 16.

In their recent book, *The Great Pox: The French Disease in Renaissance Europe* (New Haven: Yale University Press, 1997), Jon Arrizabalaga et al. challenge Quétel's claims about the variety of early modern names used to designate the modern disease of syphilis, arguing that early modern writers called it the French disease. This may be true for medical writers, but the several names for the disease in the recreational *La Lozana* seem to corroborate Quétel's claims.

14. Ibid., 16–18.
15. Damiani, "Text," 251.
16. Torella and Pintor were physicians to Pope Alexander VI (Rodrigo Borgia), and López de Villalobos served the Catholic kings and then Carlos V in Italy. See Quétel, *History of Syphilis*, 19–22.
17. Ibid., 52–53.
18. Maybe he thought that medical advice and healing did not even have to be written by a trained physician. I have been unable to find any documentation about Delicado's training as a professional physician. It is unknown whether he held university degrees and licenses, although Imperiale believes that he was a doctor, and that he also practiced being a *putañero* (a man who whores around), a *jugador* (a gambler), and a *dueño de prostíbulo* (a brothel owner). See Imperiale, *Roma clandestina*, 5.
19. Again, despite their supposed marginalization from the central areas and groups of people in their societies, both characters are the "centers" of the texts.
20. While lovesickness and suffocation of the womb are both mentioned in *La Lozana*, they are not the main diseases dealt with there.
21. García-Verdugo, *Lozana andaluza*, 121.
22. The confraternity parodies stand in contrast to the religious confraternities organized from the medieval period on, centering on figures such as Jesus, Mary, or saints. In fact, the first document in Navarre-romance is believed to be the "Carta de la 'Cofradía en honor de Jesús y la Virgen, San Andrés, San Bartolomé y Santiago'" that dates from Pamplona sometime before 1180. See Georg Gross, "Carta de la 'Cofradía en honor de Jesús y la Virgen, San Andrés, San Bartolomé y Santiago' establecida en Pamplona," *Boletín de la Real Academia de la Historia* 190, no. 3 (September–December 1993): 355–64.

As confraternities became increasingly associated with workers' groups, the sixteenth- and seventeenth-century confraternity poems evidently parody the piety of the older, religious groups with prostitutes who were thought to be most likely to spread syphilis while they were working.

23. Quétel, *History of Syphilis*, 4.
24. Ibid., 4.
25. Cindy Patton, *Inventing AIDS* (New York: Routledge, 1990).

Besides Patton's work, another fascinating commentary on how such high-risk identification functions within AIDS-construction in contemporary society can be found throughout David Wojnarowicz, *Close to the Knives: A Memoir of Disintegration* (New York: Vintage, 1991).

26. Quétel, *History of Syphilis*, 23–24.
27. Allaigre, introduction to *La Lozana andaluza*, 18–26.

Tatiana Bubnova mostly agrees with Allaigre's position, and bases the arguments in her book on Bakhtin's theory of the dialogic. She concludes that *La Lozana* is not univocal, but ambiguous and ambivalent (213).

Yet, the vast majority of the criticism devoted to *La Lozana* has completely missed the work's contradictions and inconsistencies, or at the least, they have been rendered inconsequential. Many critics have treated the main character as a positive representation, while ignoring massive incoherences between, for instance, her noselessness and her nominal beauty. Luis Beltrán concurs in "The Author's Author, Typography, and Sex: The Fourteenth Mamotreto of *La Lozana andaluza*," in *The Picaresque: Tradition and Displacement*, ed. Giancarlo Maiorino (Minneapolis: University of Minnesota Press, 1996), 103. For instance, Edward H. Friedman views the work as a humanistic, noble granting on Delicado's part, since he could have marginalized Lozana if he had wanted to. Instead of excluding her, Friedman believes that Delicado's portrayal is complete and compassionate. See Edward H. Friedman, "*La Lozana andaluza* como retrato del artista," *Letras femeninas* 14, no. 1–2 (1988): especially the conclusion on 56.

28. Linda Hutcheon, *Irony's Edge: The Theory and Politics of Irony* (London: Routledge, 1994), 16.
29. Ibid., 13.
30. Ibid., 29.
31. Ibid., 34, 10, respectively.
32. Ibid., 48–56.
33. Ibid., 13.
34. Ibid., 18, 89.

Hutcheon defines discursive communities as *dynamic groups* that are bound by common aspects, such as beliefs or gender (120).

35. Ibid., 26.
36. Lori Chamberlain, "Bombs and Other Exciting Devices, or the Problem of Teaching Irony," in *Reclaiming Pedagogy: The Rhetoric of the Classroom*, ed. Patricia Donahue and Ellen Quandahl (Carbondale: Southern Illinois University Press, 1989), 98.
37. Linda Hutcheon, *A Theory of Parody: The Teachings of Twentieth-Century Art Forms* (New York: Methuen, 1985), 33.
38. Hutcheon, *Irony's Edge*, 33.
39. Francisco Delicado, *La Lozana andaluza*, ed. Claude Allaigre (Madrid: Cátedra, 1985), 485. All citations from this work will be taken from Allaigre's edition. English translations are found in *Portrait of Lozana the Lusty Andalusian Woman*, trans. Bruno M. Damiani (Potomac, Md.: Scripta Humanistica, 1987). Page num-

bers will be given when quoting from introductory and final sections, and *mamotreto* and page numbers will indicate quotes from *mamotreto* sections.

40. This is Manuel da Costa Fontes's basic argument in two articles, "Anti-Trinitarianism and the Virgin Birth in *La Lozana andaluza,*" *Hispania* 76, no. 2 (1993): 197–203, and "The Holy Trinity in *La Lozana andaluza,*" *Hispanic Review* 62, no. 2 (1994): 93–104.

41. Costa Fontes, "Holy Trinity," 251.

42. Furthermore, Delicado alludes to some of the same ethnic concerns associated with healing that were also asked by the doctor Juan Huarte de San Juan in *Examen de ingenios para las ciencias*: why were Jewish physicians more desirable than Christian physicians throughout history? Or, why were the methods of nonprofessional healers and uneducated physicians sometimes more effective than those of university-trained physcians? See Juan Huarte de San Juan, *Examen de ingenios para las ciencias*, ed. Guillermo Serés (Madrid: Cátedra, 1989), chapter 12, 504–23. Citations will be taken from this edition, and pointed out with chapter and page numbers.

43. Huarte de San Juan, *Examen de ingenios*, 12:501.

44. Ibid., 12:502. English translations are located in *The Examination of Men's Wits*, trans. M. Camillo Camilli and Richard Carew (1594; reprint, Amsterdam: Da Capo Press, 1969), 12:181–82.

45. Huarte de San Juan, *Examen de ingenios*, 12:502, and *Examination of Men's Wits*, 12:182.

This is the function of language and rhetoric throughout the Middle Ages and into the fifteenth and sixteenth centuries. For the criteria that determined an effective and ingenious orator or writer, see Mary Carruthers, *The Book of Memory: A Study of Memory in Medieval Culture* (New York: Cambridge University Press, 1990). She argues that efficacy in writing and oration was contingent on knowing when to use rhetorical figures and classical writings.

Eugene Vance claims that, in a similar way as Galen and Huarte, medieval topical theory consisted of the emptying out of "places" in order for meaning to be made. See *From Topic to Tale: Logic and Narrativity in the Middle Ages* (Minneapolis: University of Minnesota Press, 1987), 42.

46. V. E. Watts, introduction to *The Consolation of Philosophy*, by Ancius Boethius (1969; reprint, New York: Penguin, 1984), 13.

47. The Spanish version is located in Boecio Severino, *Consolación de la Philosophia*, trans. Fray Alberto de Aguayo (Valencia: Cieza, 1966), trans. in Seville, 1518, 1:1, fol. 6v. The English is located in Ancius Boethius, *The Consolation of Philosophy*, trans. S. J. Tester (1973; reprint, Cambridge: Harvard University Press, 1990), 135.

48. Boecio Severino, *Consolación*, 1:5, fol. 12r, and Boethius, *Consolation*, 163.

49. Boecio Severino, *Consolación*, 1:6, fols. 14v–r, and Boethius, *Consolation*, 171.

50. Quétel, *History of Syphilis*, 30.

This is La Laguna's argument against women healers, which was cited in chapter 3.

51. Quétel, *History of Syphilis*, 29–30.

52. Ibid., 63.

53. Damiani, *Francisco Delicado*, 106.

Damiani describes its full structure in chapter 8 of *Francisco Delicado*, and transcribes the treatise in his article, "Text."

54. Damiani, "Text," 253.

55. Ibid., 265.
56. Ibid., 256 n. 6.
57. Ibid., 255–56, 270–71.
58. For instance, one of the typical poses that he assumes is that of a wounded victim with his hands tied behind his back and his body full of arrow holes. One of these statues is on display at Spain's National Sculpture Museum in Valladolid.
59. As far as I have been able to determine, Fernando del Pulgar never wrote this exact phrase. However, he dealt extensively with disease, old age, and pain in his *Letras*, and articulated a very similar sentiment as that "quoted" in Allaigre's edition. It may be argued, of course, as Bubnova does, that Delicado was influenced by Pulgar's *Claros varones de Castilla* because of the connection between Lozana's parodic portrait (*retrato*) (which is not of an important individual [*persona principal*] as Covarrubias defines the phrase) and the "histories" of illustrious male leaders from several Castilian families. See Sebastián de Covarrubias de Orozco, *Tesoro de la lengua castellana o española*, ed. Felipe C. R. Maldonado (Madrid: Castalia, 1994), 864.
60. Allaigre, introduction to *La Lozana andaluza*, 101.
61. Damiani translates this as "shelter." See *Portrait*, 4:196.
62. Allaigre, introduction to *La Lozana andaluza*, 67.
63. Ibid., 74 n. 82b.
64. Beltrán, "Author's Author," 103.
65. Ibid., 111.
66. According to Corominas, the phrase *plazeres e gasajados* (pleasures and delights) was common through at least the fifteenth century. He cites its use in two other texts, the *Libro de buen amor* and the *Arcipreste de Talavera o Corbacho*. See Joan Corominas and José A. Pascual, *Diccionario crítico etimológico castellano e hispánico* (Madrid: Gredos, 1980), 171.
67. Ibid., 72.
68. Ibid., 120.
69. Damiani, "Text," 257.
70. Fernando del Pulgar, *Letras*, ed. J. Domínquez Bordona (Madrid: Clásicos Castellanos, 1929), 2:7.
71. Ibid., 2:23–25.
72. Ibid., 2:25.
73. Ibid., 2:24.
74. Ibid., 2:25.
75. Ibid., 2:25.
76. Allaigre agrees that the allusion to Celestine II, pope in 1143, is intended to be humorous, and adds that the reference to Salamanca also points to the university there, "para expresar que Celestina era maestra en su arte" [to express that Celestina was a master of her art]. See Allaigre, introduction to *La Lozana andaluza*, 169 n. 5.
77. The *Autor / Auctor* character lends itself to many different interpretations about the motivations for his inclusion. Like the rest of the characters, the *Autor / Auctor* acts and speaks ironically throughout the work. *Autor* and *auctor* possibly refer to the author, an actor, or an authority figure. In *mamotreto* 42, he largely constitutes the irrevocable voice of authority, of any figure of authority of the period. Of course, the contradiction lies in the fact that he visits Lozana at all.

In his study *Ironia: Medieval and Renaissance Ideas on Irony* (Leiden: E. J. Brill, 1989), 110, Dilwyn Knox observes that irony is used as a self-protective device or a defense mechanism. Within this context of irony, the Autor's occasional self-deprecation could be interpreted as feigned, as a way to call attention to his self-aggrandizement.

Also, see Beltrán, "Author's Author," for a discussion of this multifaceted figure.

78. Allaigre, introduction to *La Lozana andaluza*, 381 n. 13.

79. Antonio Castillo de Lucas, *Retablo de tradiciones populares españolas* (Madrid: Cosano, 1968), 224.

80. Ibid., 223.

81. Allaigre claims that the Autor desires to have sex with a *cosa limpia* (something unscathed) in order to have a child, but I have been unable to locate that reference in *La Lozana andaluza*. See Allaigre, introduction to *La Lozana andaluza*, 380 n. 10.

82. Diego de San Pedro, *Cárcel de amor*, ed. Keith Whinnom (Madrid: Castalia, 1985), 81–82. The English translation is located in Diego de San Pedro, *Prison of Love*, trans. Keith Whinnom (Edinburgh: Edinburgh University Press, 1979), 4–5.

83. San Pedro, *Cárcel de amor*, 83.

84. Damiani translates "la" in the plural, even though the Spanish is clear in its reference to one woman (*la*).

85. Allaigre notes that *vulgo* could mean *mancebía* or *burdel*, both of which mean *brothel*. See Allaigre, introduction to *La Lozana andaluza*, 189 n. 18.

86. In his edition of the *Lazarillo de Tormes*, Francisco Rico states that *conversación* was used to mean *trato carnal* (carnal relations) or *amancebamiento* (concubinage) during this period. See *Lazarillo de Tormes*, ed. Francisco Rico (Madrid: Cátedra, 1992), 17 n. 21.

87. A strong indication of why Delicado may have chosen the Arabic physician Avicenna over, say, Galen or Hippocrates, is that Arab medicine frequently prescribed mercurial treatments for dermatoses and leprosy, both of which were thought to closely resemble pox or syphilis. Galen, on the other hand, had denounced the mercurial treatments that, during the late fifteenth and sixteenth centuries, were one of the two potential cures for syphilis. See Quétel, *History of Syphilis*, 30.

88. See for instance Grunpeck's personal account in Quétel, *History of Syphilis*, 16–19.

89. As discussed in chapter 1, John M. Riddle has articulated the late medieval and early modern change in healing as one of a privileging of theory over practice. See Riddle, "Theory and Practice in Medieval Medicine," *Viator* 5 (1974): 157–84. Attacks on physicians and surgeons for their lack of practical experience and rampant greed were not uncommon during the sixteenth century and into the seventeenth, and can be found in such works as Calderón de la Barca's *El médico de su honra*. In *History of Syphilis*, Quétel further cites early treatises on syphilis in which individuals attest to the inability of doctors to treat the disease. Moreover, it would be remiss not to reiterate the fact that the "professionalization of medicine" in Iberia, as a series of efforts intended to assure the superior competency of the male physician, did not achieve immediate nor widespread success. Felipe II found it necessary to make sweeping changes three times to the licensing board of the Royal Protomedicato, in 1563, 1588, and again in 1593. See John Tate Lanning, *The Royal Protomedicato: The Regulation of the Medical Professions in the Spanish Empire* (Durham: Duke University Press, 1985), 72.

90. The *carlín* was a silver coin used during Carlos V's reign (1519–58).

91. Covarrubias underscores the connection alluded to by Lozana between business and prostitution when he explains that a market (*feria*) was called *franca* when the sales did not pay for the seller's tax: "Y cuando no pagan de las mercaderías

alcabala (a type of tribute), se llaman ferias francas" [And when they do not pay tribute on their merchandise, they are called tax-free markets]. See Covarrubias, *Tesoro de la lengua*, 541.

92. Bartolomé Bennassar, "Problématique de la prostitution en Espagne à l'époque moderne," in *La prostitution en Espagne: de l'époque des Rois Catholiques à la IIe République*, ed. Raphaël Carrasco (Paris: Centre de recherches sur l'Espagne moderne, 1994), 19–20.

93. For information about sixteenth-century prostitution in Seville, see Mary Elizabeth Perry, *Gender and Disorder in Early Modern Seville* (Princeton: Princeton University Press, 1990), and for an exposition of her more current research, her article "Magdalens and Jezebels in Counter-Reformation Spain," in *Culture and Control in Counter-Reformation Spain*, ed. Anne J. Cruz and Mary Elizabeth Perry (Minneapolis: University of Minnesota Press, 1992), 124–44. Pablo Pérez García's book, *La comparsa de los malhechores* (València: Història Local, 1990), describes Valencian brothels in the early part of the fifteenth century, and cites men's roles in their management. In her works, *Cómo leer* La Celestina (Madrid: Gijón, 1992), and "La evolución de la prostitución en la Castilla del siglo XV y la mancebía de Salamanca en tiempos de Fernando de Rojas," in *Fernando de Rojas and* Celestina: *Approaching the Fifth Centenary*, ed. Ivy A. Corfis and Joseph T. Snow (Madison: Hispanic Seminary of Medieval Studies, 1993), 33–78, María Eugenia Lacarra outlines her research into the domination of prostitution in Castilian municipalities. Raphaël Carrasco's recently edited *La prostitution en Espagne: de l'époque des Rois Catholiques à la IIe République* (Paris: Centre de recherches sur l'Espagne moderne, 1994) offers many excellent studies in French and Spanish about early modern prostitution in Iberia.

94. Perry, "Magdalens and Jezebels," 131.

95. Ibid., 135.

CONCLUSION

1. Francisco Núñez de Coria, *Tractado del uso de las mugeres*, transc. Jean Dangler, Online, L.E.M.I.R., University of Valencia, Spain, Internet. Available: (http://parnaseo.uv.es/Lemir/Textos/Trat_mugeres/Trat_mugeres.html), fol. 290v.

2. Juan Huarte de San Juan, *Examen de ingenios para las ciencias*, ed. Guillermo Serés (Madrid: Cátedra, 1989).

3. Myriam Greilsammer, "The Midwife, the Priest, and the Physician: The Subjugation of Midwives in the Low Countries at the End of the Middle Ages," *Journal of Medieval and Renaissance Studies* 421, no. 2 (fall 1991): 288.

4. Michael MacDonald, *Mystical Bedlam: Madness, Anxiety, and Healing in Seventeenth-Century England* (New York: Cambridge University Press, 1981), 230.

5. See, for instance, secondary sources cited in the works cited, such as *El trabajo de las mujeres en la edad media hispana*, ed. Ángela Muñoz Fernández and Cristina Segura Graiño (Madrid: Asociación Cultural Al-Mudayna, 1988), and Cristina Segura Graiño, *Los espacios femeninos en el Madrid medieval* (Madrid: horas y Horas la editorial [sic], 1992). The essays in *Women at Work in Spain: From the Middle Ages to Modern Times*, ed. Marilyn Stone and Carmen Benito-Vessels (New York: Peter Lang, 1998) are also informative.

6. Judith M. Bennett, "Medieval Women, Modern Women: Across the Great Divide," in *Culture and History, 1350–1600: Essays on English Communities, Identities, and Writing*, ed. David Aers (London: Harvester Wheatsheaf, 1992), 149.

7. Ibid., 164.

8. Diego Gracia Guillén, "Judaism, Medicine, and the Inquisitorial Mind in Sixteeth-Century Spain," *The Spanish Inquisition and the Inquisitorial Mind*, ed. Ángel Alcalá (Boulder, Colo.: Social Science Monographs, 1987), 367.

9. Ibid., 392.

10. Ibid., 376.

11. See Gracia Guillén, "Judaism, Medicine," 393, for a discussion of these metaphors and their relation to Iberian social control. The link of medicine and king is taken from Enríquez's *Retrato del perfecto médico* (1595), which Gracia Guillén believes is "a clear manifestation of Enríquez's awareness of medicine's political power" (393).

Works Cited

PRIMARY SOURCES

ADMYTE: Archivo Digital de Manuscritos y Textos Españoles. Edited by Francisco Marcos Marín et al. Vol. 1. CD-ROM. Madrid: Micronet, 1992.

Alfonso X, el Sabio. *Cantigas.* Edited by Jesús Montoya. Madrid: Cátedra, 1988.

———. *Cantigas de Santa María.* 3 vols. Edited by Walter Mettmann. Madrid: Castalia, 1988.

al-Nadim. *The Fihrist of al-Nadim: A Tenth-Century Survey of Muslim Culture.* Edited and translated by Bayard Dodge. Vol. 2. Records of Civilization: Sources and Studies, vol. 83. New York: Columbia University Press, 1970.

Arcipreste de Hita. *Libro de buen amor.* Edited by G. B. Gybbon Monypenny. Madrid: Cátedra, 1989.

Aristotle. *Economics.* In *Complete Works.* Edited by J. Barnes. Translated by E. S. Forster and G. C. Armstrong, 2130–51.Vol. 2. Princeton: Princeton University Press, 1984.

Augustine. *City of God.* Translated by Henry Bettenson. 1972. Reprinted, with an introduction by John O'Meara, New York: Penguin, 1984.

Barkai, Ron. *A History of Jewish Gynecological Texts in the Middle Ages.* Leiden: E. J. Brill, 1998.

Berceo, Gonzalo de. *Milagros de Nuestra Señora.* Edited by Michael Gerli. Madrid: Cátedra, 1992.

Boecio Severino. *Consolación de la Philosophia.* Translated by Fray Alberto de Aguayo. Valencia: Cieza, 1966. Translated in Sevilla. 1518.

Boethius, Ancius. *The Consolation of Philosophy.* Edited by G. P. Goold. Translated by S. J. Tester. 1973. Reprint, Cambridge: Harvard University Press, 1990.

Calderón de la Barca, Pedro. *El médico de su honra.* Madrid: Espasa-Calpe, 1979.

Carbón, Damián. *Libro del arte de las comadres o madrinas y del regimiento de las preñadas y paridas y de los niños.* Transcribed by Alejandra Piñeyrua. Mallorca, 1541. On *Textos y concordancias electrónicos del corpus médico español,* edited by María Teresa Herrera and María Estela González de Fauve. CD-ROM. Madison: Hispanic Seminary of Medieval Studies, 1997.

Cauliaco, Guido de. *Tratado de cirugía.* Transcribed by María Teresa Herrera. On *Textos y concordancias electrónicos del corpus médico español,* edited by María Teresa Herrera and María Estela González de Fauve. CD-ROM. Madison: Hispanic Seminary of Medieval Studies, 1997.

Constantine the African. *Viaticum.* In *Lovesickness in the Middle Ages,* by Mary Wack. Philadelphia: University of Pennsylvania Press, 1990.

Consueta del misteri de la gloriosa Santa Àgata. In *Teatre medieval i del renaixement.* 1983. Reprint, edited by Josep Massot i Muntaner, 73–95. Barcelona: Edicions 62, 1994.

Corominas, Joan, and José A. Pascual. *Diccionario crítico etimológico castellano e hispánico.* Madrid: Gredos, 1980.

Covarrubias de Orozco, Sebastián de. *Tesoro de la lengua castellana o española.* Edited by Felipe C. R. Maldonado. Madrid: Castalia, 1994.

Delicado, Francisco. *La Lozana andaluza.* Edited by Claude Allaigre. Madrid: Cátedra, 1985.

———. *Portrait of Lozana the Lusty Andalusian Woman.* Translated by Bruno M. Damiani. Potomac, Md.: Scripta Humanistica, 1987.

Eiximenis, Francesc. *Contes i faules.* Barcelona: Els Nostres Clàssics, 1925.

Galen. *On the Affected Parts.* Edited and translated by Rudolph E. Siegel. New York: S. Karger, 1976.

Gordonio, Bernardus de [Bernard of Gordon]. *Lilium medicinae, Lilio de medicina.* Transcribed by John Cull and Cynthia Wasick. Sevilla: Meinardo Ungut and Estanislao Polono, 1495. Reprint, *ADMYTE: Archivo Digital de Manuscritos y Textos Españoles.* Edited by Francisco Marcos Marín et al. Vol. 1. CD-ROM. Madrid: Micronet, 1992.

Herrera, María Teresa, ed. *Diccionario español de textos médicos antiguos.* 2 vols. Madrid: Arco / Libros, 1996.

Huarte de San Juan, Juan. *Examen de ingenios para las ciencias.* Edited by Guillermo Serés. Madrid: Cátedra, 1989.

———. *The Examination of Men's Wits.* 1594. Reprint, translated by M. Camillo Camilli and Richard Carew, Amsterdam: Da Capo Press, 1969.

Jacobus de Voragine. *The Golden Legend: Readings on the Saints.* Translated by William Granger Ryan. Princeton: Princeton University Press, 1993.

Lazarillo de Tormes. Edited by Francisco Rico. Madrid: Cátedra, 1992.

Liber menor de coitu. Edited by Enrique Montero Cartelle. Valladolid: Universidad de Valladolid, 1987.

El libro de Calila e Digna. Edited by John E. Keller and Robert White Linker. Madrid: Clásicos Hispánicos, 1967.

López Pinciano, Alonso. *Filosofía antigua poética.* Valladolid, 1894.

López de Villalobos, Francisco. *Sumario de medicina.* Transcribed by María Jesús García Toledano. Salamanca, 1498. On *ADMYTE: Archivo Digital de Manuscritos y Textos Españoles,* edited by Francisco Marcos Marín et al. Vol. 1. CD-ROM. Madrid: Micronet, 1992.

Manuel, Juan. *Obras completas.* Edited by José Manuel Blecua. Vol. 1. Madrid: Gredos, 1982.

Martínez de Toledo, Alfonso. *Arcipreste de Talavera o Corbacho.* Edited by Michael Gerli. Madrid: Cátedra, 1992.

Mirror of Coitus: A Translation and Edition of the Fifteenth-Century Speculum al foderi. Edited and translated by Michael Ray Solomon. Madison: Hispanic Seminary of Medieval Studies, 1990.

Muñoz, Miguel Eugenio. *Recopilación de las leyes, pragmáticas reales, decretos y acuerdos del Real Protomedicato.* Valencia, 1751.

Nebrija, Antonio de. *Dictionarium latino-hispanicum*. Transcribed by Antonio Cortijo. Salamanca: Impresor de la Gramática de Nebrija, 1492. Reprint, *ADMYTE: Archivo Digital de Manuscritos y Textos Españoles*. Edited by Francisco Marcos Marín et al. Vol. 1. CD-ROM. Madrid: Micronet, 1992.

Núñez de Coria, Francisco. *Tractado del uso de las mugeres*. Transcribed by Jean Dangler. Madrid: Pierres Cosin, 1572. Online. (L.E.M.I.R.) Literatura Española Medieval y del Renacimiento, University of Valencia, Spain. Internet. Available: (http://parnaseo.uv.es/~lemir/Textos/Trat_mugeres/Trat_mugeres.html).

Palencia, Alfonso de. *Universal vocabulario en latín y romance*. Transcribed by Gracia Lozano López et al. Sevilla: Pablo de Colonia, Juan Pegnitzer de Nuremberga, Magno Herbst de Fils and Tomás Glockner, 1490. Reprint, *ADMYTE: Archivo Digital de Manuscritos y Textos Españoles*. Edited by Francisco Marcos Marín et al. Vol. 1. CD-ROM. Madrid: Micronet, 1992.

Peter of Spain. *Questions super Viaticum*. In *Lovesickness in the Middle Ages*, by Mary Wack, 212–51. Philadelphia: University of Pennsylvania Press, 1990.

Pulgar, Fernando del. *Claros varones de Castilla*. Edited by Robert B. Tate. Oxford: Oxford University Press, 1971.

———. *Letras*. Edited by J. Domínguez Bordona. Vol. 2. Madrid: Clásicos Castellanos, 1929.

Roig, Jacme [Jaume]. *Spill*. Edited by Josep Almiñana Vallés. 3 vols. Valencia: Del Cenia al Segura, 1990.

Rojas, Fernando de. *La Celestina*. Edited by María Eugenia Lacarra. Madison: Hispanic Seminary of Medieval Studies, 1995.

———. *La Celestina*. Edited by Dorothy S. Severin. Madrid: Cátedra, 1987.

———. *Celestina: A Play in Twenty-One Acts Attributed to Fernando de Rojas*. Translated by Mack Hendricks Singleton. Madison: University of Wisconsin Press, 1968.

Ruiz, Juan. See Arcipreste de Hita.

Salas Barbadillo, Alonso J. de. *La hija de Celestina*. In *La novela picaresca española*, edited by Ángel Valbuena y Prat, 887–919. Madrid: Aguilar, 1946.

San Pedro, Diego de. *Cárcel de amor*. Edited by Keith Whinnom. Madrid: Castalia, 1985.

———. *Prison of Love*. Translated by Keith Whinnom. Edinburgh: Edinburgh University Press, 1979.

Scriptores physiognomonici graeci et latini. Edited by Richard Foerster. Bibliotheca scriptorum Graecorum et Romanorum Teubneriana. Stuttgart: B. G. Teubneri, 1994.

Sendebar. Edited by María Jesús Lacarra. Madrid: Cátedra, 1989.

Speculum al foderi. See *Mirror of Coitus*.

Textos y concordancias electrónicos del corpus médico español. Edited by María Teresa Herrera and María Estela González de Fauve. CD-ROM. Madison: Hispanic Seminary of Medieval Studies, 1997.

Tratado de patología general (*Tratado médico*). Edited by María Teresa Herrera. On *Textos y concordancias electrónicos del corpus médico español*, edited by María Teresa Herrera and María Estela González de Fauve. CD-ROM. Madison: Hispanic Seminary of Medieval Studies, 1997.

———. Edited by María Teresa Herrera and Nieves Sánchez. Madrid: Arco / Libros, 1997.

Tratado de Phisonomía. Edited by María Nieves Sánchez. On *Textos y concordancias electrónicos del corpus médico español,* edited by María Teresa Herrera and María Estela González de Fauve. CD-ROM. Madison: Hispanic Seminary of Medieval Studies, 1997.

Les trobes en lahors de la Verge Maria. Valencia, 1474.

Villena, Isabel de. *Vita Christi.* Edited by Josep Almiñana Vallés. 2 vols. Valencia: Ajuntament de Valencia, 1992.

Vives, Juan Luis. *Instrucción de la mujer cristiana.* Translated by Juan Justiano. Madrid: Signo, 1936.

Secondary Sources

Allaigre, Claude. Introduction to *La Lozana andaluza,* by Francisco Delicado, 17–162. Madrid: Cátedra, 1985.

Amundsen, Darrel W., and Gary B. Ferngren. "The Early Christian Tradition." In *Caring and Curing: Health and Medicine in the Western Religious Traditions,* edited by Ronald L. Numbers and Darrel W. Amundsen, 40–64. New York: Macmillan, 1986.

———. "Medicine and Religion: Early Christianity through the Middle Ages." In *Health/Medicine and the Faith Traditions,* edited by Martin E. Marty and Kenneth L. Vaux, 93–131. Philadelphia: Fortress Press, 1982.

Armistead, Samuel G., and James T. Monroe. "Celestina's Muslim Sisters." *Celestinesca* 13, no. 2 (1989): 3–27.

Arrizabalaga, Jon, Roger K. French, and John Henderson. *The Great Pox: The French Disease in Renaissance Europe.* New Haven: Yale University Press, 1997.

Barstow, Anne Llewellyn. *Witchcraze: A New History of the European Witch Hunts.* San Francisco: HarperCollins, 1994.

Bass, Laura R. Review of *Women in Thirteenth-Century Spain as Portrayed in Alfonso X's* Cantigas de Santa María, by Connie L. Scarborough. *La corónica* 26, no. 1 (1997): 321–24.

Beltrán, Luis. "The Author's Author, Typography, and Sex: The Fourteenth Mamotreto of *La Lozana andaluza.*" In *The Picaresque: Tradition and Displacement,* edited by Giancarlo Maiorino, 86–136. Hispanic Issues, vol. 12. Minneapolis: University of Minnesota Press, 1996.

Bennassar, Bartolomé. "Problématique de la prostitution en Espagne à l'époque moderne." In *La prostitution en Espagne: de l'époque des Rois Catholiques à la IIe République,* edited by Raphaël Carrasco, 13–21. Annales Littéraires de l'Université de Besançon, vol. 526. Paris: Centre de recherches sur l'Espagne moderne, 1994.

Bennett, Judith M. "Medieval Women, Modern Women: Across the Great Divide." *Culture and History 1350–1600: Essays on English Communities, Identities, and Writing,* edited by David Aers, 147–75. London: Harvester Wheatsheaf, 1992.

Benton, John F. "Trotula, Women's Problems, and the Professionalization of Medicine in the Middle Ages." *Bulletin of the History of Medicine* 59 (1985): 30–53.

Bloch, R. Howard. *Medieval Misogyny and the Invention of Western Romantic Love.* Chicago: University of Chicago Press, 1991.

Blumenfeld-Kosinski, Renate. *Not of Woman Born: Representations of Caesarean Birth in Medieval and Renaissance Culture.* Ithaca: Cornell University Press, 1990.
Boase, Roger. *The Troubadour Revival: A Study of Social Change and Traditionalism in Late Medieval Spain.* London: Routledge, 1978.
Brose, Margaret. "Petrarch's Beloved Body: 'Italia Mia.'" In *Feminist Approaches to the Body in Medieval Literature,* edited by Linda Lomperis and Sarah Stanbury, 1–20. Philadelphia: University of Pennsylvania Press, 1993.
Brown, Peter. *The Body and Society: Men, Women, and Sexual Renunciation in Early Christianity.* New York: Columbia University Press, 1988.
Bubnova, Tatiana. *F. Delicado puesto en diálogo: las claves bajtinianas de* La Lozana andaluza. México: Universidad Nacional Autónoma de México, 1987.
Burke, James F. "The *Mal de la Madre* and the Failure of Maternal Influence in *Celestina.*" *Celestinesca* 17, no. 2 (1993): 111–28.
Burns, Robert I. "Los hospitales del reino de Valencia en el siglo XIII." *Anuario de estudios medievales* 2 (1965): 135–54.
Cabañas, María Dolores. "La imagen de la mujer en la baja edad media castellana a través de las ordenanzas municipales de Cuenca." In *Las mujeres en las ciudades medievales.* Actas de las III Jornadas de Investigación Interdisciplinaria, Madrid, 1982, edited by Cristina Segura Graiño, 103–08. Madrid: Universidad Autónoma de Madrid, 1983.
Cadden, Joan. *Meanings of Sex Difference in the Middle Ages: Medicine, Science, and Culture.* New York: Cambridge University Press, 1993.
Cantavella, Rosanna. *Els cards i el llir: una lectura de l'*Espill *de Jaume Roig.* Barcelona: Quaderns Crema, 1992.
Capdevila, Miguel. *Iconografía de Santa Lucía.* Masnou (Barcelona): Laboratorios del Norte de España, 1950.
Cardoner i Planas, Antoni. *Història de la medicina a la Corona d'Aragó (1162–1479).* Barcelona: Scientia, 1973.

———. "L'exercici professional de la medicina a la Corona d'Aragó (1162–1479)." In *Congrés internacional d'història de la medicina catalana,* 185–203. Vol. 1. Barcelona, 1970.

———. "Seis mujeres hebreas practicando la medicina en el reino de Aragón." *Sefarad* 9 (1949): 441–45.
Caro Baroja, Julio. *Las brujas y su mundo.* Madrid: Revista de Occidente, 1961.

———. *Vida mágica e inquisición.* Madrid: Taurus, 1967.
Carrasco, Eva, and Ismael Almazán. "Prostitución y criminalidad en Cataluña en la época moderna." In *La prostitution en Espagne: de l'époque des Rois Catholiques à la IIe République,* edited by Raphaël Carrasco, 23–65. Annales Littéraires de l'Université de Besançon, vol. 526. Paris: Centre de recherches sur l'Espagne moderne, 1994.
Carruthers, Mary. *The Book of Memory: A Study of Memory in Medieval Culture.* New York: Cambridge University Press, 1990.
Castillo de Lucas, Antonio. *Folkmedicina.* Madrid: Dossat, 1958.

———. *Retablo de tradiciones populares españolas.* Madrid: Cosano, 1968.
Cátedra, Pedro M. *Sermón, sociedad y literatura en la edad media: san Vicente Ferrer en Castilla (1411–1412).* Salamanca: Junta de Castilla y León, 1994.

Chamberlain, Lori. "Bombs and Other Exciting Devices, or the Problem of Teaching Irony." In *Reclaiming Pedagogy: The Rhetoric of the Classroom*, edited by Patricia Donahue and Ellen Quandahl, 97–112. Carbondale: Southern Illinois University Press, 1989.

Comaroff, Jean. "Medicine: Symbol and Ideology." In *The Problem of Medical Knowledge: Examining the Social Construction of Medicine*, edited by Peter Wright and Andrew Treacher, 49–68. Edinburgh: Edinburgh University Press, 1982.

Coon, Lynda L. *Sacred Fictions: Holy Women and Hagiography in Late Antiquity*. Philadelphia: University of Pennsylvania Press, 1997.

Costa Fontes, Manuel da. "Anti-Trinitarianism and the Virgin Birth in *La Lozana andaluza*." *Hispania* 76, no. 2 (1993): 197–203.

———. "Celestina as Antithesis of the Virgin Mary." *Journal of Hispanic Philology* 25, no. 1 (1990): 7–41.

———. "Celestina's *Hilado* and Related Symbols." *Celestinesca* 8, no. 1 (1984): 3–13.

———. "Female Empowerment and Witchcraft in *Celestina*." Review of *Witchcraft in* Celestina, by Dorothy S. Severin, *Celestinesca* 19, no. 1–2 (1995): 93–104.

———. "The Holy Trinity in *La Lozana andaluza*." *Hispanic Review* 62, no. 2 (1994): 249–66.

Coulson, John, ed. *The Saints*. New York: Hawthorn Books, 1958.

Dagenais, John. *The Ethics of Reading in Manuscript Culture: Glossing the* Libro de buen amor. Princeton: Princeton University Press, 1994.

Damiani, Bruno M. *Francisco Delicado*. New York: Twayne, 1974.

———. "Text: Francisco Delicado. 'El modo de adoperare el legno de India occidentale.' A Critical Transcription." *Revista Hispánica Moderna* 36 (1970–71): 251–71.

Damiani, Bruno M., and Louis Imperiale. La Lozana andaluza: *a través de los siglos*. San Francisco: International Scholars Publications, 1998.

Deyermond, Alan. "*Hilado-Cordón-Cadena*: Symbolic Equivalence in *La Celestina*." *Celestinesca* 1, no. 1 (1977): 6–12.

Dillard, Heath. *Daughters of the Reconquest: Women in Castilian Town Society, 1100–1300*. Cambridge: Cambridge University Press, 1984.

Doñate Sebastiá, José María. "Saludadores y médicos en la baja edad media." In *Primer Congreso de Historia del País Valenciano. Celebrado en Valencia del 14 al 18 de Abril de 1971*, 803–10. Vol. 2. Valencia: Universidad de Valencia, 1980.

DuBois, Page. *Sowing the Body: Psychoanalysis and Ancient Representations of Women*. Chicago: University of Chicago Press, 1988.

Ell, Stephen R. "Blood and Sexuality in Medieval Leprosy." *Janus* 71 (1984): 153–64.

———. "Leprosy and Social Class in the Middle Ages." *International Journal of Leprosy and Other Mycobacterial Diseases* 54, no. 2 (1986): 300–05.

Ferré, Rosario. "Celestina en el tejido de la 'cupiditas.' " *Celestinesca* 7, no. 1 (1983): 3–16.

Finkler, Kaja. "Sacred Healing and Biomedicine Compared." *Medical Anthropology Quarterly* 8, no. 2 (1994): 178–97.

Frey, Emil F. "Saints in Medical History." *Clio Medica* 14 (1979): 35–70.

Friedenwald, Harry. "Jewish Doctoresses in the Middle Ages." In *The Jew and Medicine: Essays*, 217–20. Vol. 1. New York: Ktav, 1967.

Friedman, Edward H. "*La Lozana andaluza* como retrato del artista." *Letras femeninas* 14, no. 1–2 (1988): 52–56.

García, Angelina. *Médicos judíos en la Valencia del siglo XIV: estudios dedicados a Juan Peset Aleixandre*. Vol. 2. Valencia: Universidad de Valencia, 1982.

García Ballester, Luis. "Academicism versus Empiricism in Practical Medicine in Sixteenth-Century Spain with Regard to Morisco Practitioners." In *The Medical Renaissance of the Sixteenth Century*, edited by A. Wear, R. K. French, and I. M. Lonie, 246–70. Cambridge: Cambridge University Press, 1985.

———. *Historia social de la medicina en la España de los siglos XIII al XVI*. Madrid: Akal, 1976.

———. "A Marginal Learned Medical World: Jewish, Muslim and Christian Medical Practitioners, and the Use of Arabic Medical Sources in Late Medieval Spain." In *Practical Medicine from Salerno to the Black Death*, edited by Luis García-Ballester, Roger French, Jon Arrizabalaga, and Andrew Cunningham, 353–94. Cambridge: Cambridge University Press, 1994.

———. "Medical Science in Thirteenth-Century Castile: Problems and Prospects." *Bulletin of the History of Medicine* 61 (1987): 183–202.

García-Ballester, Luis, Michael R. McVaugh, and Agustín Rubio Vela. *Medical Licensing and Learning in Fourteenth-Century Valencia: Transactions of the American Philosophical Society*. Philadelphia: American Philosphical Society, 1989.

García-Verdugo, María Luisa. *La Lozana andaluza y la literatura del siglo XVI: la sífilis como enfermedad y metáfora*. Madrid: Pliegos, 1994.

Gelfand, Toby. "The History of the Medical Profession." In *Companion Encyclopedia of the History of Medicine*, edited by W. F. Bynum and Roy Porter, vol. 2, 1119–50. London: Routledge, 1993.

González Bueno, Antonio. *El entorno sanitario del Camino de Santiago*. Madrid: Cátedra, 1994.

González Echevarría, Roberto. *Celestina's Brood: Continuities of the Baroque in Spanish and Latin American Literature*. Durham: Duke University Press, 1993.

Gossy, Mary S. *The Untold Story: Women and Theory in Golden Age Texts*. Ann Arbor: University of Michigan Press, 1989.

Gracia Guillén, Diego. "Judaism, Medicine, and the Inquisitorial Mind in Sixteenth-Century Spain." In *The Spanish Inquisition and the Inquisitorial Mind*, edited by Ángel Alcalá, 375–400. Boulder, Colo.: Social Science Monographs, 1987.

Granjel, Luis S. *Humanismo y medicina*. Salamanca: Universidad de Salamanca, 1968.

Green, Monica H. "Documenting Medieval Women's Medical Practice." In *Practical Medicine from Salerno to the Black Death*, edited by Luis García-Ballester, Roger French, Jon Arrizabalaga, and Andrew Cunningham, 322–52. Cambridge: Cambridge University Press, 1994.

———. "A Handlist of the Latin and Vernacular Manuscripts of the So-Called 'Trotula' Texts." *Scriptorium* 50 (1996): 137–75.

———. "Women's Medical Practice and Health Care in Medieval Europe." *Signs* 14, no. 2 (1989): 434–73.

Greilsammer, Myriam. "The Midwife, the Priest, and the Physician: The Subjugation of Midwives in the Low Countries at the End of the Middle Ages." *Journal of Medieval and Renaissance Studies* 21, no. 2 (fall 1991): 285–329.

Gross, Georg. "Carta de la 'Cofradía en honor de Jesús y la Virgen, San Andrés, San Bartolomé y Santiago' establecida en Pamplona." *Boletín de la Real Academia de la Historia* 190, no. 3 (September–December 1993): 355–64.

Handy, Otis. "The Rhetorical and Psychological Defloration of Melibea." *Celestinesca* 7, no. 1 (1983): 17–27.

Hartunian, Diane. *La Celestina: A Feminist Reading of the Carpe Diem.* Potomac, Md.: Scripta Humanistica, 1992.

Herzlich, Claudine, and Janine Pierret. *Illness and Self in Society.* Baltimore: Johns Hopkins University Press, 1987.

Hutcheon, Linda. *Irony's Edge: The Theory and Politics of Irony.* New York: Routledge, 1994.

———. *A Theory of Parody: The Teachings of Twentieth-Century Art Forms.* New York: Methuen, 1985.

Imperiale, Louis. *La Roma clandestina de Francisco Delicado y Pietro Aretino.* New York: Peter Lang, 1997.

Jacquart, Danielle, and Claude Thomasset. *Sexuality and Medicine in the Middle Ages.* Princeton: Princeton University Press, 1988.

Keller, John E., and Richard P. Kinkade. "Iconography and Literature: Alfonso Himself in Cantiga 209." *Hispania* 66 (1983): 348–52.

Kelso, Ruth. *Doctrine for the Lady of the Renaissance.* Urbana: University of Illinois Press, 1956.

Kibre, Pearl. "The Faculty of Medicine at Paris, Charlatanism, and Unlicensed Medical Practices in the Later Middle Ages." *Bulletin of the History of Medicine* 27 (1953): 1–20.

Klairmont Lingo, Alison. "Empirics and Charlatans in Early Modern France: The Genesis of the Classification of the 'Other' in Medical Practice." *Journal of Social History* 19 (1986): 583–603.

Knox, Dilwyn. *Ironia: Medieval and Renaissance Ideas on Irony.* Leiden: E. J. Brill, 1989.

Kotzmanidou, Maria. "The Spanish and Arabic Characterization of the Go-Between in the Light of Popular Performance." *Hispanic Review* 48 (1980): 91–109.

Lacarra, María Eugenia. *Cómo leer La Celestina.* Madrid: Gijón, 1992.

———. "La evolución de la prostitución en la Castilla del siglo XV y la mancebía de Salamanca en tiempos de Fernando de Rojas." In *Fernando de Rojas and Celestina: Approaching the Fifth Centenary,* edited by Ivy A. Corfis and Joseph T. Snow, 33–78. Madison: Hispanic Seminary of Medieval Studies, 1993.

Lanning, John Tate. *The Royal Protomedicato: The Regulation of the Medical Professions in the Spanish Empire.* Durham: Duke University Press, 1985.

Lawrence, C. H. *Medieval Monasticism: Forms of Religious Life in Western Europe in the Middle Ages.* 2nd ed. London: Longman, 1989.

Laza Palacios, Modesto. *El laboratorio de Celestina.* Málaga: Instituto de Cultura de la Diputación Provincial de Málaga, 1958. 87–191.

Lemay, Helen Rodnite. "William of Saliceto on Human Sexuality." *Viator* 12 (1981): 165–81.

Levack, Brian P. *The Witch-Hunt in Early Modern Europe.* London: Longman, 1995.

Lewison, Edward. "Saint Agatha: The Patron Saint of Diseases of the Breast in Legend and Art." *Bulletin of the History of Medicine* 24 (1950): 409–20.

MacDonald, Michael. *Mystical Bedlam: Madness, Anxiety, and Healing in Seventeenth-Century England.* New York: Cambridge University Press, 1981.

MacLehose, William F. "Nurturing Danger: High Medieval Medicine and the Problem(s) of the Child." In *Medieval Mothering*, edited by John Carmi Parsons and Bonnie Wheeler, 3–24. New York: Garland, 1996.

Maravall, José Antonio. *Estado moderno y mentalidad social (siglos XV a XVII).* Vol. 1. Madrid: Revista de Occidente, 1972.

Marti-Ibáñez, Félix. "The Medico-Pharmaceutical Arts of *La Celestina*: A Study of a Fifteenth-Century Spanish Sorceress and 'Dealer in Love.' " In *Centaur: Essays on the History of Medical Ideas*, 149–66. New York: MD Publications, 1958.

Martín Duque, Ángel J., Carmen Jusué Simonena, Fermín Miranda García, Eloísa Ramírez Vaquero, Juan Ramón Corpas Mauleón, eds. *Camino de Santiago en Navarra.* Pamplona: Caja Municipal de Ahorros de Pamplona, 1991.

McGrady, Donald. "More on the Image of the 'Rose among Thorns' in Medieval Spanish Literature." *La corónica* 17, no. 2 (1989): 35–39.

McPherson, Ian. "Don Juan Manuel: The Literary Process." *Studies in Philology* 70 (1973): 1–18.

McVaugh, Michael R. *Medicine before the Plague: Practitioners and Their Patients in the Crown of Aragon, 1285–1345.* Cambridge: Cambridge University Press, 1993.

Minkowski, William L. "Physician Motives in Banning Medieval Traditional Healers." *Women and Health* 21, no. 1 (1994): 83–96.

Minnis, A. J. and A. B. Scott, eds. *Medieval Literary Theory and Criticism, c. 1100–c. 1375.* New York: Clarendon, 1988.

Morris, David B. *The Culture of Pain.* Berkeley: University of California Press, 1991.

Las mujeres en las ciudades medievales. Actas de las III Jornadas de Investigación Interdisciplinaria, 1982, edited by Cristina Segura Graíño. Madrid: Universidad Autónoma de Madrid, 1983.

Mullaney, Steven. *The Place of the Stage: License, Play, and Power in Renaissance England.* Chicago: University of Chicago Press, 1988.

Muñoz Fernández, Ángela. "Las mujeres en los ambitos institucionales de la religiosidad laica: las cofradías devocionales castellanas (ss. XV-XVI)." In *Religiosidad femenina: expectativas y realidades (ss. VIII-XVIII)*, edited by Ángela Muñoz and María del Mar Graña, 93–114. Madrid: Asociación Cultural Al-Mudayna, 1991.

Muñoz Garrido, Rafael. "Empíricos sanitarios españoles de los siglos XVI y XVII." *Cuadernos de historia de la medicina española* 6 (1967): 101–33.

Navarro, Emilia. "Manual Control: 'Regulatory Fictions' and Their Discontents." *Cervantes* 13, no. 2 (1993): 17–35.

Olson, Glending. *Literature as Recreation in the Later Middle Ages.* Ithaca: Cornell University Press, 1982.

Ortiz, Teresa. "From Hegemony to Subordination: Midwives in Early Modern Spain." In *The Art of Midwifery: Early Modern Midwives in Europe*, edited by Hilary Marland, 95–114. New York: Routledge, 1993.

Pack, Roger A. "Auctoris incerti de physiognomonia libellus." *Archives d'histoire doctrinale et litteraire du moyen age* 41 (1974): 113–38.

Pallares Méndez, María del Carmen. *A vida das mulleres na Galicia Medieval (1100–1500)*. Santiago de Compostela: Universidade, Servicio de Publicacións e Intercambio Científico, 1993.

Park, Katharine. *Doctors and Medicine in Early Renaissance Florence*. Princeton: Princeton University Press, 1985.

Parker, Margaret. "The Text as Mediator: Ovid and Juan Ruiz." *Comparative Literature Studies* 28, no. 4 (1991): 341–55.

Patton, Cindy. *Inventing AIDS*. New York: Routledge, 1990.

Pelikan, Jaroslav. *Mary through the Centuries: Her Place in the History of Culture*. New Haven: Yale University Press, 1996.

Perarnau i Espelt, Josep. "Activitats i fórmules supersticioses de guarició a Catalunya en la primera meitat del segle XIV." *Arxiu de textos catalans antics* 1 (1982): 47–78.

Pérez García, Pablo. *La comparsa de los malhechores*. València: Història Local, 1990.

Perry, Mary Elizabeth. *Gender and Disorder in Early Modern Seville*. Princeton: Princeton University Press, 1990.

———. "Magdalens and Jezebels in Counter-Reformation Spain." In *Culture and Control in Counter-Reformation Spain*, edited by Anne J. Cruz and Mary Elizabeth Perry, 124–44. Hispanic Issues, vol. 7. Minneapolis: University of Minnesota Press, 1992.

La prostitution en Espagne: de l'époque des Rois Catholiques à la IIe République. Edited by Raphaël Carrasco. Annales Littéraires de l'Université de Besançon, vol. 526. Paris: Centre de recherches sur l'Espagne moderne, 1994.

Quétel, Claude. *History of Syphilis*. Translated by Judith Braddock and Brian Pike. Baltimore: Johns Hopkins University Press, 1990.

Raymond, Janice G. *Women as Wombs: Reproductive Technologies and the Battle over Women's Freedom*. San Francisco: HarperSanFrancisco, 1993.

Riddle, John M. "Theory and Practice in Medieval Medicine." *Viator* 5 (1974): 157–84.

Rouhi, Leyla. *Mediation and Love: A Study of the Medieval Go-Between in Key Romance and Near-Eastern Texts*. Leiden: Brill, 1999.

Rowland, Robyn. *Living Laboratories: Women and Reproductive Technologies*. Bloomington: Indiana University Press, 1992.

Rubio Vela, Agustín. *Pobreza, enfermedad y asistencia hospitalaria en la Valencia del siglo XIV*. Valencia: Institució Alfons el Magnànim, 1984.

Ruggerio, Michael J. "The Evolution of the Go-Between in Spanish Literature through the Sixteenth Century." *California University Publications in Modern Philology*. Berkeley: University of California Press, 1966.

Salisbury, Joyce E. "Gendered Sexuality." In *Handbook of Medieval Sexuality*, edited by Vern L. Bullough and James A. Brundage, 81–102. New York: Garland, 1996.

Scarborough, Connie L. *Women in Thirteenth-Century Spain as Portrayed in Alfonso X's Cantigas de Santa María.* Lewiston, N.Y.: Edwin Mellen Press, 1993.

Schechter, David Charles, and Henry Swan. "Of Saints, Surgical Instruments, and Breast Amputation." *Surgery* 52 (1962): 693–98.

Schulenburg, Jane Tibbetts. *Forgetful of Their Sex: Female Sanctity and Society, ca. 500–1100.* Chicago: University of Chicago Press, 1998.

———. "The Heroics of Virginity: Brides of Christ and Sacrificial Mutilation." In *Women in the Middle Ages and the Renaissance: Literary and Historical Perspectives,* edited by Mary Beth Rose, 29–72. Syracuse: Syracuse University Press, 1986.

Sedgwick, Eve Kosofsky. *Between Men: English Literature and Male Homosocial Desire.* New York: Columbia University Press, 1985.

———. *Epistemology of the Closet.* Berkeley: University of California Press, 1990.

Segura Graiño, Cristina. *Los espacios femeninos en el Madrid medieval.* Madrid: horas y Horas la editorial [sic], 1992.

———. "Las mujeres andaluzas en la baja edad media." In *Las mujeres en las ciudades medievales.* Actas de las III Jornadas de Investigación Interdisciplinaria, 1982, edited by Cristina Segura Graiño, 143–52. Madrid: Universidad Autónoma de Madrid, 1983.

———. "Posibilidades jurídicas de las mujeres para acceder al trabajo." In *El trabajo de las mujeres en la edad media hispana,* edited by Ángela Muñoz Fernández and Cristina Segura Graiño, 15–26. Madrid: Asociación Cultural Al-Mudayna, 1988.

Serés, Guillermo. Introduction to *Examen de ingenios para las ciencias,* by Juan Huarte de San Juan, 11–122. Madrid: Cátedra, 1989.

Severin, Dorothy S. "Witchcraft in *Celestina.*" Papers of the Medieval Hispanic Research Seminar, 1. London: Queen Mary and Westfield College, 1995.

Shatzmiller, Joseph. *Jews, Medicine, and Medieval Society.* Berkeley: University of California Press, 1994.

Silverblatt, Irene. *Moon, Sun, and Witches: Gender Ideologies and Class in Inca and Colonial Peru.* Princeton: Princeton University Press, 1987.

Siraisi, Nancy G. *Medieval and Early Renaissance Medicine.* Chicago: University of Chicago Press, 1990.

Snow, Joseph T. *Celestina by Fernando de Rojas: An Annotated Bibliography of World Interest, (1930–1985).* Madison: Hispanic Seminary of Medieval Studies, 1985.

Solomon, Michael. "Calisto's Ailment: Bitextual Diagnostics and Parody in *Celestina.*" *Revista de estudios hispánicos* 23 (1989): 41–64.

———. *The Literature of Misogyny in Medieval Spain.* New York: Cambridge University Press, 1997.

———. Introduction to *Mirror of Coitus,* by Anonymous, vii–xxvii. Madison: Hispanic Seminary of Medieval Studies, 1990.

Sumption, Jonathan. *Pilgrimage: An Image of Medieval Religion.* Totowa, N.J.: Rowman and Littlefield, 1975.

Taussig, Michael T. "Reification and the Consciousness of the Patient." *Social Science and Medicine* 14B (1980): 3–13.

Towler, Jean, and Joan Bramall. *Midwives in History and Society.* London: Croom Helm, 1986.

El trabajo de las mujeres en la edad media hispana. Edited by Ángela Muñoz Fernández and Cristina Segura Graiño. Madrid: Asociación Cultural Al-Mudayna, 1988.

Valbuena, Olga Lucía. "Sorceresses, Love Magic, and the Inquisition of Linguistic Sorcery in *Celestina.*" *PMLA* 109, no. 2 (1994): 207–24.

Vance, Eugene. *From Topic to Tale: Logic and Narrativity in the Middle Ages.* Minneapolis: University of Minnesota Press, 1987.

Wack, Mary Frances. *Lovesickness in the Middle Ages: The* Viaticum *and Its Commentaries.* Philadelphia: University of Pennsylvania Press, 1990.

Warner, Marina. *Alone of All Her Sex: The Myth and Cult of the Virgin Mary.* New York: Knopf, 1976.

Watts, V. E. Introduction to *The Consolation of Philosophy,* by Ancius Boethius, 7–32. 1969. Reprint, New York: Penguin, 1984.

Willis, Raymond S. "Two Trotaconventos." *Romance Philology* 17 (1963): 353–62.

Wright, Peter, and Andrew Treacher, eds. Introduction to *The Problem of Medical Knowledge: Examining the Social Construction of Medicine,* 1–22. Edinburgh: Edinburgh University Press, 1982.

Wojnarowicz, David. *Close to the Knives: A Memoir of Disintegration.* New York: Vintage, 1991.

Women and Work in Spain: From the Middle Ages to Early Modern Times. Edited by Marilyn Stone and Carmen Benito-Vessels. New York: Peter Lang, 1998.

Zemon Davis, Natalie. "Women in the Crafts in Sixteenth-Century Lyon." In *Women and Work in Preindustrial Europe,* edited by Barbara A. Hanawalt, 167–97. Bloomington: Indiana University Press, 1986.

Index

abject: women healers, 101, 106. *See also* Celestina
AIDS, 133
Alfonso X, 35, 87; his illness, 19
al-Razi, 24–25, 28, 37, 108
alterity: medieval, 110; women as other, 12
Aristotle, 107, 109
Augustine, 196 n. 56
Avicenna, 28, 37, 100, 123, 162–63, 169

Bartholomew the Englishman, 107
Berceo, Gonzalo de, 31, 33, 53, 80, 87
Bernard of Gordon, 28, 100–102, 107–9, 123
body: ethnic difference, 203 n. 42; gender difference, 107–10, 175, 196 n. 56; humoral theory, 106–9; organization of, 11, 19; physiognomy, 107–8; professionalization of medicine, 109–10; social order, 127, 175, 177–78; work, 107–11, 126–127, 197 n. 68
Boethius, 129; *consolatio*, 139–42, 144–45; *quadrivium*, 140
book: as mediator, 137, 154, 178–79
Burke, James F., 194 n. 28, 194 n. 30

Cadden, Joan, 108
Cantigas, 19, 31–32, 53, 65, 80
Carbón, Damián, 29, 33, 174–75
Catholic kings (Reyes Católicos), 40, 88, 104
Celestina: abject, 102, 148; access, 96–97, 116, 117–18, 120; *alcahueta*, 85, 91–92, 98–99, 102–4, 106, 112, 117, 125; analogy with *La Celestina*, 154, 160; antithesis of the Virgin, 87, 125; as cause of death, 90; disease, 92, 100, 156; gender, 100, 106, 124–26; go-between, 99, 111, 114, 118; healer, 87, 93, 94–95, 98–102, 105, 112, 114, 118–20, 122–25; imitator of Virgin, 86–87, 91, 106, 125, 126, 155, 174; love-discourses, 97–98, 104–5; *mal de la madre*, 92–94, 122–24, 155, 156, 194 n. 30; mother, 85, 93, 155–56; multivocational, 97–98, 102, 111–12, 118, 120–21, 125; other, 126; popularity, 97, 106, 121; reproductive machine, 160; sexuality, 124–25; speech, 94–95; virgins, 114–17, 120; witch, 88, 112, 119, 156–57
coitus: as a transaction, 153; as therapeutic, 146; well-being, 101–2; women healers, 26–28, 123–24, 175
confabulator, 19, 59, 61, 95
Constantine the African, 37, 100
Costa Fontes, Manuel da: *La Celestina*, 86, 115, 122; *La Lozana andaluza*, 137, 154
courtly love, 105, 160–61
Covarrubias de Orozco, Sebastián de, 79, 150, 199 n. 93, 204 n. 59, 205–6 n. 91
Crown of Aragon: professionalization of medicine, 35–36, 37–39, 44, 47, 186 n. 73; women healers, 20–21, 182 n. 8

Damiani, Bruno, 143, 144, 160
Delicado, Francisco: as healer, 142, 167; biography, 128–29; convert, 128, 137; ethnic concern, 203 n. 42; his illness, 128–29, 131, 136, 142, 143, 145, 147–48, 164; isolation, 142; pleasure, 172; tripartite notion of disease, 128, 136–37, 137–54
disease: social ramifications, 78

Eiximenis, Francesc, 76–77
Eve. *See* Virgin
evil eye, 74, 157–59

Felipe II, 41, 48
Fernández de Oviedo, Gonzalo, 144
Fernando and Isabel. *See* Catholic kings
Ferrer, Vicente, 70, 79–82; healing, 81

Galen, 37, 107, 122–23, 124, 139, 146, 172
García-Ballester, Luis, 23–24, 38–39, 44, 45
gay science, 189 n. 2
Green, Monica, 21, 42–43, 47
Greilsammer, Myriam, 22, 47, 68, 176

homosocial. *See* professionalization of medicine; *Spill;* well-being
hospitals: professionalization of medicine, 35, 41–42; prostitution, 103
Huarte de San Juan, Juan, 109, 138–39, 172, 175, 178, 196 n. 56; ethnicity, 203 n. 42
Hutcheon, Linda: *La Celestina*, 86; *La Lozana andaluza*, 133–36, 202 n. 34

illness: conditions of, 55, 77
Inquisition, 88, 90, 110, 111; index of prohibited books, 178
integumentum, 95–96

Lacarra, María Eugenia, 193 n. 14, 195 n. 48, 206 n. 93
La Celestina: entertaining, 84; go-between, 85, 87, 92, 104, 192 n. 11; parody, 86–88, 98, 126; *Spill*, 86; witchcraft and women healers, 88–91; women healers, 84, 88, 100–101; work, 111, 113, 114
Laguna, Andrés, 119–20
Libro de buen amor: go-between, 61, 191 n. 1; men's well-being, 59; reader, 58–59, 61; Trotaconventos, 58, 60
literacy, 36; as healing, 151
literature: as recreation, 14–15, 131–32, 172; as therapeutic, 136–37; entertaining, 136, 174; illness, 11; reader, 174; social order, 11–12, 15, 62, 88, 92, 178. *See also* women
López de Villalobos, Francisco, 29, 50, 84, 124, 131

lovesickness: *La Celestina*, 95, 97–106, 126; *Spill*, 77. *See also* syphilis
Lozana: analogy with disease, 138; analogy with *La Lozana andaluza*, 148, 154, 160, 167, 172; analogy with syphilis, 130, 133; Celestina, 134, 149, 154–73; convert, 149; desirable, 134, 145, 161, 162, 165, 167, 171, 173; diabolical, 156–57; diseased, 130, 134, 136; gender, 126, 135; go-between, 167; healer, 162–66, 169, 172; inheritance, 155–56, 158; ironic, 127, 133–34, 136, 145, 148–49, 155, 164–65, 169, 171, 174; isolation, 172; monstrous, 127, 136, 148–49, 162, 165, 167, 172–73; pleasure, 166; prostitute, 129–30, 161, 162–63, 165–66, 169–72; sexuality, 126, 171; sick, 137; speech, 166; syphilis, 146; transaction, 162, 205–6 n. 91; virgins, 167–68
Lozana andaluza, La: as therapeutic, 131, 136, 145–46, 148, 153- 54; authority, 159; coitus, 129, 136, 156; entertaining, 138; go-between, 132, 145; healers, 168–69, 173; ironic parody of *La Celestina*, 154–73; irony, 127, 133–36, 137, 155, 159, 161, 166, 168, 172, 178, 204 n. 77; isolation, 167; *La Celestina*, 132, 134–36; *mal de la madre*, 155; *mamotreto*, 129; morality, 133–34; parody, 134–35, 137; pleasure, 147, 149–51, 166; reader, 136, 139, 142, 147, 150, 153, 166–67, 172; recreation, 136, 153, 172; scatalogical, 131, 165; sex, 131; sexuality, 148, 167; sick, 137; social organization, 135–36; *Spill*, 134–36, 155; women healers, 129

mal de la madre, 108, 132; definition, 92–93; remedies, 122–24
Manuel, don Juan, 19
McVaugh, Michael, 22, 38–39, 44, 45
medianera: analogy with books, 60, 154, 179; anxiety about 84; cultural value, 138; definition, 9; importance, 60–61; syphilis, 142; textual strategies against, 88–97

mediation: language, 144, 145, 155; link in women, 83; literature, 58–59, 62; men's, 10, 42, 48, 53–55, 58, 67; women's, 9–12, 25, 34, 53–55, 57–58, 60, 62, 67, 73, 77

medicine: in America, 41; in medieval Iberia, 19; social order 41, 45–46, 177–78

medieval to early modern period, transition from, 45–46, 48, 90, 109–10, 137, 174, 176–77. *See also* alterity

midwife, 21–22, 44, 46–47, 108, 123–24; *Spill*, 58, 67–70; Virgin, 31

misogyny: and literature, 12–14, 52, 53, 60–61, 92, 175; and men's well-being, 14; *Spill*, 56, 79; textual strategies, 174

Nebrija, Antonio de, 117, 199 n. 93
Núñez de Coria, Franciso, 175

Ortiz, Teresa, 22

pain: analogy, 58; condition of illness, 55; isolation, 140; *La Celestina*, 84–85; *La Lozana andaluza*, 139; *Spill*, 58, 59, 77. *See also* Delicado, Francisco, illness; syphilis

Palencia, Alfonso de, 117
palimpsest, 86–88, 106, 125, 127, 135, 155
Pérez García, Pablo, 104, 195 n. 51, 206 n. 93
Perry, Mary Elizabeth, 171–72
Peter of Abano, 108
Peter of Spain, 100–102
physician: *inventor occasionis*, 139, 172
pilgrimage, 56, 60–62, 78–79, 143
professionalization of medicine, 34–50; guilds, 185–86 n. 70; homosocial, 174, 176, 185–86 n. 70; ineffectiveness, 10, 45, 47–49, 88, 127; licensing, 10, 35, 38–41; marginalization of Jews and Muslims, 13, 35, 110, 174; marginalization of women, 34–35, 43–49, 87, 108, 110, 177; social order, 177; witchcraft, 78, 89. *See also* hospitals

prostitution: control of, 103–5, 107–8, 110, 170–72, 195 n. 52; punitive measures, 74–75; relation to syphilis, 116; transaction, 205–6 n. 91

Pseudo-Albertus Magnus, 114–15, 123
Pulgar, Fernando del, 151–53
punishment: social order, 78–79, 82

ramería, 57, 61
reading: therapeutic, 151, 153; transaction, 150–51, 173
Real Protomedicato, 40–41, 43, 48, 70, 110
reproduction, 64–71, 73, 81–82, 175, 190–91 n. 41, 191 n. 53; failure, 192 n. 4; gynelineal, 74; *La Celestina*, 85, 93, 100, 117; textual, 84, 93, 160; woman-to-woman, 127, 155–56, 158
Roig, Jaume: biography, 51; physician and medical examiner, 58, 59; wives, 55–56, 60, 63–65, 67, 69, 78, 189 n. 13
Rojas, Fernando de: convert, 86; medicine, 84
Ruiz, Juan, 58–62

saints: dead, 56, 60; healers, 19, 30–31, 95, 144
San Pedro, Diego de, 160, 161–62
Santiago, 143; effeminate, 145
Santiago de Compostela, 30–31
sewing: *La Celestina*, 85, 120–22, 125; relation to surgery, 117-18; *Spill*, 64, 69, 73, 190 n. 37
Solomon, 51, 54, 59, 71–74, 76–80; parallel to Roig, 62–63, 71; women's sexuality, 66–67
Solomon, Michael, 12–14, 62, 98
Speculum al foderi, 26–28, 102, 105, 126, 175
Spill: as guide to devotion 53, 83; as therapeutic manual, 53, 54, 59, 62, 80; autobiography, 55–58; go-between, 53, 61, 75–76; homosocial, 56, 77; *Libro de buen amor*, 58–62; marriage, 62–65, 71; reader, 52, 55, 58–59, 61; women healers, 54–56, 64, 67–69, 77–78, 82–83

syphilis, 50; construction of, 130–32; gaiac, 129, 142–44; high-risk groups, 132; ironic, 135; isolation, 140, 142, 162; literature, 131; lovesickness, 132–33; *medianeras*, 142; morality, 132; national affiliation, 130; pain, 164; prostitution, 133; sex, 116

translation, medieval, 37–38
Tratado de patología general, 28, 29, 108, 124
Trotula, 25–26, 114–15

Valencia: Roig in, 51; legislation, 38–39, 43–45; plague, 55; social control, 71–74, 80
Vilanova, Arnau de, 37
Villena, Isabel de, 32
Virgin, 10; as city, 79–81; as goal, 56–57, 62; authority, 143–44; contrast to Eve (Eva/Ave), 53–56, 73, 81–82, 85, 174; contrast to women, 52–53, 56–57, 62, 65, 77, 79, 81–83, 114, 144, 155; gender, 185 n. 66; healer, 31–34, 50, 53–54, 70, 136; icon, 53–54; mediator, 60; model for women, 32–34, 49, 54, 88; Philosophy, 140

Wack, Mary Frances, 105
well-being: and the homosocial, 13–14; men's, 12–13, 53–55, 57, 59–60, 62–64, 82, 105, 116–17, 121, 174–75; reader's, 85, 117, 128–29; social order, 175
William of Saliceto, 114–15
women: and literature, 9–11, 14, 25–34, 49, 126; and recreation, 15; as agents, 61, 63–64, 67, 77, 85, 92, 171; as superior, 49; as wives 55–56, 63–65, 72, 78 (*see also* Roig, Jaume); control of, 200 n. 111; debate about, 127, 200 n. 112; diseased, 61–62, 77–78, 106, 111, 121, 152, 173; gender, 13, 54, 68, 70–71, 78, 90, 104, 105–6, 107–8, 158, 173; guilds, 24, 107, 112–13, 125, 185–86 n. 70; harmful, 29–30; healers, 9–12, 20–25, 100–101, 113, 119–20, 124, 157, 173–76; infectious, 14, 54, 67; inheritance, 64–65; sexuality, 171; speech, 76–77; stories about, 61–62, 76–77; work, 69, 107, 109, 111–13, 121, 173. *See also* professionalization of medicine; reproduction; Virgin